Judson D. Purdy

THE
MEDIEVAL MANICHEE

THE
MEDIEVAL MANICHEE

A Study of the
Christian Dualist Heresy
by

STEVEN RUNCIMAN

THE VIKING PRESS · NEW YORK

COMPASS BOOKS EDITION
Issued in 1961 by The Viking Press, Inc.
625 Madison Avenue, New York 22, N.Y.

Distributed in Canada by
The Macmillan Company of Canada Limited

This edition published by arrangement with
Cambridge University Press

Printed in the U.S.A. by the Murray Printing Company

To

MY FATHER

Foreword

IN the following pages I have attempted to trace the history of the Dualist Tradition in Christianity from its Gnostic beginnings to its final florescence in the later Middle Ages. Theologically speaking, the title which I have given to the book is unjustifiable; for Christian Dualism and Manichaeism were two distinct and separate religions. But to the ordinary Medieval churchman, in the East as in the West, all Dualists were Manichaean; and I have used a name that they would have found intelligible and natural. And indeed in many ways this popular misnomer was reasonable, for the Christian Dualists, though they would never have acknowledged Mani's system, were fundamentally nearer to it than ever they were to Medieval or Modern Christianity. I hope therefore that the inaccuracy will be forgiven me, and that no one will open this book hoping to find in it an exhaustive account of those true Manichaeans who lingered on into the Middle Ages in the far-off recesses of Turkestan.

The recent circumstances of the world and certain personal handicaps have prevented me from having access to certain material that I should have liked to consult and from handling more fully one or two points on which I have touched. I must ask for indulgence for such omissions. I do not, however, believe that they affect the main argument. A certain unevenness of treatment in the various chapters has been forced upon me by the nature of the evidence. If, for example, I have dealt scantily with the theology of the Bosnian Patarenes and amply with their political history, it is because we know practically nothing of the former, whereas the latter provides the key to the long existence of the church. On the other hand, it would have been possible, from the plentiful records at our disposal, to give a far fuller account of the French Cathars. But much of the material there is redundant. I have therefore, to keep some proportion in the book, selected from it what I considered to be essential and relevant to the story.

At the end of the volume I give a bibliography of the books that I have consulted. There are hardly any books that treat the history of the Tradition as a whole. But I am indebted to many works on various aspects of it. For my chapter on the Paulicians, I have made great use of F. C. Conybeare's *Key of Truth*. I disagree with almost all of his conclusions, but every student of the Armenian Church must be immeasurably grateful to his memory for the work that he did on the sources for its history. For the Bogomils, I owe much to the studies of the Bulgarian historian, Ivanov, on Bogomil literature. For the Cathars, the volumes of M. Guiraud are invaluable. I much regret that I had written the text of my chapter before the second volume of his *History of the Inquisition* was published. I should like to mention also the personal help and encouragement that I have had from Professor Henri Grégoire. I have also had the advantage of many helpful criticisms and suggestions from Prince D. Obolensky.

My thanks are also due to the Syndics of the Cambridge University Press for their unfailing kindness.

S. R.

Athens

1946

Since this book was first published several important works on medieval Dualism have appeared. I give a list of them on page 199, as a supplement to the Bibliography, and recommend them to the reader who wishes to follow up later research on some of the points covered here.

S. R.

28 December 1954

Contents

x　　　　　　　　　　　　*Contents*

THE MEDIEVAL MANICHEE

CHAPTER I

Introduction

TOLERANCE is a social rather than a religious virtue. A broad-minded view of the private belief of others undoubtedly makes for the happiness of society; but it is an attitude impossible for those whose personal religion is strong. For if we know that we have found the key and guiding principle of Life, we cannot allow our friends to flounder blindly in the darkness. We may recognize that without the key they may yet lead virtuous and admirable lives, but their task is made unnecessarily hard; it is our duty to help them on to the true Path, to show them the light that will illuminate it all. Opinions may vary as to the nature of the help that should be given, whether peaceful persuasion and a shining example, or the sword and the *auto da fé*. But no really religious man can pass the unbeliever by and do nothing.

Still more than the unbeliever it is the wrong believer, the heretic rather than the infidel, whose conversion is the concern of the faithful. For the infidel is often impossible to win. No one can prove that Christianity is better than Buddhism or Islam. Those who believe it to be so, do so not from logical argument but from an instinctive conviction that its fundamental message is the true revelation, whereas those of other creeds are false or unimportant. But the heretic Christian is in a different position. He believes, like the orthodox, in the basic article of the Christian faith, that Jesus of Nazareth died to redeem us. But he gives his faith another interpretation, an interpretation that leads him, in orthodox eyes, into dangerous and avoidable error.

His crime is therefore the more serious. The infidel in his unbelief leaves Christianity alone. The heretic accepts its principles but by perverting them destroys their value, undermining the whole Christian position. Yet heresy is hard to exterminate. "For there must be also heresies among you", said St Paul;[1] and indeed orthodox doctrine is complex and difficult, and it is tempting to make some simplification here or there—tempting, but not to be endured. For the vast superstructure that orthodox theologians have built over the fundamental Christian revelation is not the baroque expression of the whims of a few pedants and eccentrics, but the attempt of the best brains of a great intellectual era to display all the implications of that revelation. Sceptical historians might mock at the passion with which early Christian ecclesiastics would fight over some tiny doctrinal delicacy; but even an iota might clarify or might mar an essential aspect of the Faith. In Islam the tendency to heresy is smaller; for the revelation of Islam is a simpler thing, contained in the word of Mahomet. A logical and historical exegesis of the *Koran* should explain it all. Nevertheless, in Islam divergencies could not be kept down. The Christian revelation is far harder to fit into simple language; the room for error is infinitely great.

The orthodox theologians reached their conclusions by continual arduous efforts of the intellect, rejecting any easy compromise or attractive gnosis that might weaken part of their structure. It was not to be expected that a body whose creed was too subtle for Tertullian and who saw weakness even in Origen, should tolerate without irritation men who sought solutions more childish or more irrelevant. The Church was narrow-minded because the true Path is narrow, and it knew that for Christians no other path led to Salvation.

This irritation led to intolerance and at length to persecution. In the first centuries of the Christian era persecution between Christians could not occur. The whole Christian community was a struggling minority, itself subject to periodical persecution. In self-defence schism was deprecated even by those that disagreed with the official theology. Sects indeed would perpetually be formed, in particular amongst the Gnostics. But they were treated as unimportant in view of the struggles for the existence of Christendom. Moreover, on

[1] I Corinthians xi, 19.

many issues the orthodox doctrine had not yet been pronounced. There would be time for that later.

With the Triumph of the Cross under Constantine, the position was altered. Official recognition did not in itself create an official church; but as soon as the Emperor adopted Christianity its creation was inevitable. With the appearance of an official church, the heterodox were driven into schism. There was no longer room for elasticity. The State preferred its new servant to be united and uniform. And the State gave the Church a weapon with which to enforce uniformity. Official recognition is followed soon by the persecution of the heretic.

Persecution involves the co-operation of the State. The Church by itself has only spiritual arms; and threats of excommunication mean nothing to a wilful schismatic. But the State can bring all its physical force to bear on him. It is the State, not the Church, that persecutes, and the State that should be blamed for the cruelties of persecution. This necessarily limits the scope of persecution. Not every heretic is arraigned. Still more, on certain fundamental doctrines, such as the doctrine of Grace itself, by the wishes of all a final decision is avoided, so as to embrace as many views as possible. When a sect is persecuted it is because the State is convinced that that sect is undesirable. It may be that the sectaries, by attacking the orthodox hierarchy, weaken it as an instrument of State, and so must be punished. But the fiercest and most bloodthirsty persecutions have taken place when the heretics have seemed more seriously dangerous, when their teachings have run counter to the welfare of society, when, were they tolerated, the State itself might collapse.

This alliance of Church and State altered the tone of Christian polemics. In the second century Tertullian, for most of his life the great champion of orthodoxy, presented his opponents' cases fully and fairly, for he knew that he could demolish them by theological argument, and he was writing for a public well trained in theology. But the theologians of the fourth century onwards treat the heretics less honestly. In the great Christological battles of the fourth and fifth centuries it was still the theological issue that was at stake and roused passionate interest; but the State itself was uncertain then

which body to accept as the official Church. The difference of out-
look is shown when the orthodox Church, the officially recognized
hierarchy, is dealing with some definitely schismatic sect. The
Church is out to crush such dissident bodies and it needs the help of
the State. The arguments thus become not so much theological as
social. The theological sins of the sectaries may be presented, but the
State will not be interested in them. Therefore a greater emphasis is
laid on their habits, which are shown to be incompatible with a
well-run government. And so, with the orthodox polemical writer
acting as special pleader before the tribunal of the State and with the
defendants' case no longer fairly stated, it grows harder to discover
what the heretics truly thought. Moreover, the use of catchwords
to attract the attention of the authorities and to alarm them becomes
more frequent. These catchwords were not usually unfounded nor
unfair, but their use was often misleading.

Of these catchwords, the most used in the Middle Ages was the
epithet "Manichaean", flung opprobriously at various sects that
never knew Mani. It is the object of this study to inquire how far
these sects deserved the epithet, how far they were interconnected
and how far they represent an organic dualist tradition.

CHAPTER II

The Gnostic Background

THE Fathers of the Church, usually so careful and so precise, were now and then hesitant on matters of fundamental theology. Indeed, to one most essential question they long gave no clear answer. Concentrating their attention on the Redemption from sin, they ignored the problem of the original cause of sin. Yet sin was a very real thing to the Early Christians. The world that they knew, the cruel, luxurious, uncertain world of the Roman Empire, was undoubtedly a wicked place. How had such wickedness come into creation? If God was the Creator, and God was omnipotent and good, why did he permit such things to be? The Fall might explain why man was enchained in sin, but the Fall could not create sin; rather it was sin that created the Fall.

It is a desire to solve the problem of Evil that lies at the base of Gnosticism. The heretics and philosophers, complained Tertullian, were always asking the same question: "Whence came Evil, and in what does it exist?" and the question that arises out of it: "Whence and how came Man?"[1] Unguided by the Church the heretics and philosophers sought out their own solutions and out of their searching Christian dualism was founded.

The origin of Gnosticism must remain obscure. Partly it is to be sought in the age-long magical tradition. Gnostic writings such as the *Pistis Sophia* seem to be connected with the Hermetic occultism of the Egyptians, and the Gnostic doctrine of the Eons resembles Kabalistic lore with its archangels.

But of the earlier Gnostics and their doctrines little is known. Such heresiarchs as Cerdon or Cerinthus, who disputed with St John the Divine at Ephesus, must remain semi-legendary. According to

---

[1] *Eadem materia apud haereticos et philosophos volutatur; iidem retractatus implicantur: Unde malum et qua in re? Unde homo et quomodo? et quod maxime Valentinus proposuit: Unde Deus?* Tertullian, *De Praescriptionibus*, § 7, *M.P.L.* vol. II, col. 22.

Irenaeus. it was a sect contemporary to them, called the Nicolaïtes after a certain deacon Nicholas, who first promulgated the distinguishing doctrine of Gnosticism, the doctrine that the visible world was created not by God but by the Demiurge.[1] By the middle of the second century Gnostic thought, infinitely varied but fundamentally the same, was widespread throughout the Roman Empire, under such great leaders as Basilides, Valentine and Marcion.

The solution of the Gnostics was to take from God the responsibility of having made the visible world. God the Father, the First Principle, was far removed from it, with many heavens lying in between. Basilides in the early second century counted 365 of them,[2] but the later Gnostics were satisfied with a mere seven or eight.[3] Beneath God were the eons, semi-divine eternal beings ranged in groups, usually of eight, ten and twelve, the ogdoad, the decad and dodecad. To Valentine the eons were abstractions, with such names as Silence, Intellect and Truth, while God Himself was the Abyss;[4] but he grouped them as it were in married couples. The later Gnostics turned the eons into more concrete beings, giving them fantastic names without meaning, and usually leaving them unpaired. God and the eons formed the Pleroma, the perfect group. The visible world was created owing to a Fall within the Pleroma, due usually to the curiosity or desire of one of the eons. This disturbance produced a new emanation, as a result of which the world was ultimately called into being. Here again many stages may have to be gone through before we come down to the Creator of the World, the Demiurge. The exact placing of the Demiurge varied amongst the sects. He might be a fallen eon; he might be Jehovah, God of the Jews, who, we learn from Genesis, made the earth and all things in it. In any case he was either ignorant of or hostile to God the First

[1] Irenaeus, *Adversus Haereticos*, I, 26, 3, M.P.G. vol. VII, col. 687.
[2] Irenaeus, *op. cit.* I, 24, 3, M.P.G. vol. VII, col. 676. Migne's text reads "trecentos septuaginta quinque", but then refers to the number being that of the days in a year.
[3] Valentine chose seven, to fit his Hebdomad: Irenaeus, *op. cit.* I, 5, M.P.G. vol. VII, coll. 493-6. Others preferred the number to coincide with the Ogdoad.
[4] Irenaeus, *op. cit.* I, I, M.P.G. vol. VII, col. 445: Tertullian, *Adversus Valentinianos*, § 7, M.P.L. vol. II, coll. 550-1. The word employed is Βυθός or Βύθιος.

Principle. But somehow into this created world and into the Demiurge's proudest creation, Man, a spark of divinity was inserted, either by accident or by the deliberate work of God or one of the eons. Henceforward it became God's task to give this figment of the Demiurge knowledge of Himself, so that He could rescue the pieces of divinity imprisoned in it. This knowledge He gave by sending Jesus into the world. According to some Gnostics Jesus was merely one of the eons, differentiated even from Christ; to others Jesus was an emanation from God, the eternal God the Son; or again, He might be called into being by God as part of Himself for this particular task. But whichever He might be, He was unquestionably divine. It was impossible for Him to become a man, a creature of the world of the Demiurge. He could only seem to be so. The Gnostics were necessarily Docetist in their Christology. The Virgin Mary became therefore of no great importance. Some Gnostics, like Heracleon and Marcion, declared that Christ only appeared in the fifteenth year of Tiberius Caesar at Capernaum.[1] Most, like Valentine, using a phrase often to be heard later, spoke of Him passing through Mary as through a canal.[2]

How far the Gnostic sects varied in their practices we cannot say. But they all seem to have had some sort of initiation ceremony. The very word Γνῶσις meant the knowledge of the initiate, as opposed to Πίστις, the faith of the mere believer. And most sects divided mankind into three categories, according to the amount of divine sparks that existed in each man. According to Valentine these were: the Spirituals, the Πνευματικοί, who were full of divinity and only needed for their salvation the Gnosis and the words of mystery. Christ only brought them the doctrine of illumination. Next the Psychics, the Ψυχικοί, who had a little spark in their souls but were not assured of salvation. They must do good to earn it. Christ was necessary for them too, by His life-work and His seeming death upon the Cross. Finally, there were the Materials, the Ὑλικοί or Χοϊκοί, men without the spark, who return inevitably to the dust

---

[1] Tertullian, *Adversus Marcionem*, I, 19, IV, 6, *M.P.L.* vol. II, coll. 267–9.
[2] Irenaeus, *op. cit.* III, 11, 3, *M.P.G.* vol. VII, col. 881: "quasi aquam per tubum".

from which they came.¹ Such was the usual Gnostic view at the time. Nor was it confined to the Gnostics. Origen, too, had his initiated Perfects and thought that the salvation of the simple believer differed from that of the elect,² while Clement of Alexandria wanted to have his chosen few initiated.³ But the doctrine faded out of the Orthodox Church. It was one great Gnostic organization that kept it alive.

This organization was the offspring of Marcion. Whereas the other great Gnostic leaders had been essentially philosophers founding short-lived schools of religious thought, Marcion was a religious leader who founded not a school but a church, which lasted for several centuries and was the main conservator of Gnostic ideas. Marcion was less ambitious in his views than the other Gnostic teachers. Though he taught in the midst of the second century, when Gnostic speculation was at its height, he was not interested in discovering families of eons. To him the universe was simple. There was the visible world in which we live, a cruel world governed by the principle of retribution; there was the heaven of the Creator-God, the Demiurge, the stern Jehovah of the Old Testament. Finally, as it were in another dimension, there was the true God, the Kind Stranger, gentle and merciful, Who always existed but only revealed Himself to man by sending His spirit, Jesus Christ, on earth to oppose the bleak teaching of Jehovah with the gospel of Love. Marcion was profoundly struck by the divergency between the messages of the Old and New Testaments. The latter he in no way saw as the complement of the former; even the Messiah prophesied in the Old Testament, the warrior avenger, could have nothing to do with Jesus. The two teachings, he considered, were in utter opposition to one another, and he made this opposition the basis of his creed.⁴

Marcion was thus a thorough-going dualist. But his dualism was

---

¹ Irenaeus, *op. cit.* I, 7, 5, *M.P.G.* vol. VII, coll. 517–20: Tertullian, *Adversus Valentinianos*, § XXIX, *M.P.L.* vol. II, coll. 583–4.
² Origen, *In Johannem*, VI, 36, 37, *M.P.G.* vol. XIV, coll. 293–301.
³ Clement of Alexandria, *Stromata*, VII, *M.P.G.* vol. IX, coll. 416 ff.
⁴ Tertullian, *Adversus Marcionem*, IV, 16, *M.P.L.* vol. II, col. 368 : *Philosophumena*, X, 19, *M.P.G.* vol. XVI, 3, col. 3435.

not of the usual type; he did not oppose evil and good, but justice and mercy, cruelty and love. In practice, however, the difference was slight. The created world might not be wicked but merely just; nevertheless, it was to be avoided and left behind if the Kind Stranger's arms were to be reached. Asceticism was therefore needful. Marcion took over the Gnostic division of mankind into the Pneumatics, the Psychics and the Hylics, the elect, the ordinary believer and the infidel; but he made it one of ecclesiastical organization rather than of predestined fate. To Marcion all indulgence in earthly pleasures was deplorable. Above all, marriage and generation were to be avoided, for that was to help the Creator-God in his work. The baptized Marcionite had therefore to give up any earthly partner; he or she could only be married to Christ. But the baptized Marcionites formed but a small proportion of the Marcionite Church. The average Marcionite believer postponed his baptism till his deathbed, or till the circumstances of his life permitted him to indulge in such asceticism without inconvenience. This strict view of continence and consequent postponement of baptism was not uncommon throughout the Christian Church in Marcion's day and was probably the usual rule in Syria.[1] But Marcion seems to have fitted it into the Gnostic idea of initiation and thus to have given it a stricter and more lasting form.

Marcion's views made him sparing in his acceptance of the Canonical Books. The Old Testament, though he studied it carefully to prove his argument, was rejected as inspired by the wrong God. The only Gospel that he admitted was St Luke's, though he disliked its earlier chapters on the infancy of Jesus, Who, he said, appeared first at Capernaum. He accepted the Pauline epistles more willingly. Indeed, according to Tertullian,[2] it was the Epistle to the Galatians on which he based his ideas. But the Marcionite Church edited its own New Testament, a Testament purged of the Judaisms that the earlier authors had not dared to omit.

The Marcionite Church was the first great dualist Christian

[1] See Burkitt's essay in Mitchell, *St Ephraim's Prose Refutations*, vol. II, pp. cxvii–cxxii.

[2] Tertullian, *Adversus Marcionem*, I, 19, 20, *M.P.L.* vol. II, coll. 267–9.

Church; and later orthodox writers had some justification in hurling the epithet "Marcionite" at dualist Christian heretics. But Marcion's own dualism, even amongst his disciples, soon was changed into a cruder form. By the early third century the opposition in the Marcionite creed was no longer between the good God and the just God; the just God was becoming inevitably the wicked God.[1] The Kind Stranger was now ranged against Satan, and Satan was the creator of the world.

Marcion's theories added to the growing eccentricities of the Gnostics. If Jehovah were in opposition to God, then the villains of the Old Testament must be heroes. Sects arose that paid reverence to Cain, to the Sodomites and the Egyptians. Above all, the Serpent was applauded, as the creature that tried in Eden to give Adam and Eve the knowledge that Jehovah withheld from them. Such sects were grouped by the orthodox under the name of the Ophites, the Serpent-worshippers; and dark stories were told of their practices. Nor, despite Marcion's insistence upon asceticism, were the stories wholly unjustified. Some were doubtless due to the disbelief, held by so many cynics, that perfect asceticism is obtainable; outward asceticism must mean secret vice. But certain of the sects were frankly licentious, such as the Carpocratians, who believed that to achieve freedom from human law one must ignore the distinction between what is good and what is bad.[2] Moreover, the tendency towards magic, fashionable at the time and very noticeable amongst the Neoplatonists, had a strong effect on Gnosticism. Stories of the origin of the world multiplied and became more fantastic. The eons were given bizarre names of no known derivation, till a list of them, such as Irenaeus gives in his account of the Adepts of the Mother, has the same nonsensical sound as a list of the devils in a medieval *Grimoire*—and indeed many medieval devils may have had names of Gnostic origin. The initiation ceremony from being a mere baptism began to acquire a more complex magical form, and the

[1] *Philosophumena, loc. cit.*: "Οἱ δὲ πάντες τὸν μὲν ἀγαθὸν οὐδὲν ὅλως πεποιηκέναι, τὸν δὲ δίκαιον οἱ μὲν τὸν πονηρόν, οἱ δὲ μόνον δίκαιον ὀνομάζουσι."
[2] *Philosophumena*, VII, 31, *M.P.G.* vol. XVI, 3, col. 3338.

initiate became himself to some degree a magician. Marcion seems to have held that the faith through which the elect found his salvation implied some identification of himself with God, while even Clement of Alexandria declared that the perfect Christian initiate became God.[1]

The minor Gnostic sects, such as the Sethians or the Naassenes, the Barbelognostics or the Cainites, were none of them of great importance in Church history. None of them achieved a long existence, nor did their strange theories of the Cosmogony much affect the course of religious thought. But in their short lives they often spread widely; and a memory of their fairy-stories with their oddly named heroes lingered vaguely on in various secluded hills and valleys.

The main current of Christian dualism flowed elsewhere. There is no reason to suppose that Marcion derived his theories from anywhere other than the Syrian Christian background in which he was brought up. But east of Syria across the desert lay the great kingdom of Persia whose State religion was dualistic, the creed of Zoroaster. In Zoroastrianism the opposing forces were, fundamentally, light and darkness, and the world was made up out of a blending of these two elements. It is improbable that early Gnostic dualism had been at all directly affected by Zoroastrian thought, though the Zoroastrians undoubtedly had an influence on later Judaism and so indirectly on Christianity. But in the second half of the second century a Christian teacher arose who showed distinct traces of Zoroastrianism. Bardaisan came from Edessa, a town that might be called either Syrian, Mesopotamian or Armenian, where Christianity had recently been established under the patronage of the Kings of the house of Abgar. He was self-consciously not a Gnostic, often attacking Gnostic doctrines and disapproving in particular of such sects as were ascetic. His theory of the origin of the world was that God and the five uncreated elements lived in happy harmony, Light in the East, Wind in the West, Fire in the South, Water in the North, and Darkness, the enemy, in the Depth below. But owing to some unexplained cataclysm Darkness began

[1] Clement of Alexandria, *Stromata*, IV, xxiii, 149, *M.P.G.* vol. VIII, col. 1360.

to emerge from the Depth and mingle with the other elements; who appealed to God to rescue them. God did so, sending Darkness down again, and out of the mixture caused by the invasion of Darkness into the other elements He made the world and set it in their midst. Jesus was sent by God His father into this world to show the way of Light; and the souls of those that kept His word passed straight on death into the domain of Light. Reproduction and birth were desirable in that they created more souls to escape from the world into the Light.[1]

Bardaisan founded no lasting school. His attitude was that of the scientist rather than of the inspired preacher. But he is important for the influence that his teaching had on a far greater religious leader, Mani. It is fashionable nowadays to regard Mani as lying outside of the pale of Christianity. He was born, he taught and he suffered martyrdom within the realm of the Zoroastrian King of Persia; he must therefore be regarded as a Zoroastrian rather than a Christian heretic. And he himself befogged the issue by declaring that Buddha and Zoroaster, and, elsewhere, Hermes and Plato, as well as Jesus, taught God's message to men. But earlier writers, such as St Ephraim, who wrote within a century of Mani's death, were probably correct when they classed him with Marcion and Bardaisan among the chiefest of heterodox Christians. The main Zoroastrian element in Mani's teaching, the opposition of Light and Darkness, he probably derived from Bardaisan. The elaborate tales of his cosmogony are very similar to those of the more complicated Gnostics; and his church organization was clearly copied from the Marcionites, with whose pronounced asceticism he agreed. But he always carefully called himself Mani, Apostle of Jesus Christ.[2]

It must suffice here to give the briefest account of Manichaean doctrines. From all eternity the two realms of Light and Darkness existed side by side. In the former dwelt the Eternal God, the Lord

[1] For Bardaisan, see Burkitt's account in *Religion of the Manichees*, pp. 75–9 and his appendix in Mitchell, *op. cit.* vol. II, pp. cxxii–cxxxi, and Nau, *Bardesane l'Astrologue*.
[2] This account of Mani's doctrines is based mainly on Burkitt, *Religion of the Manichees*. Consult also Williams Jackson, *Researches in Manichaeism*.

of Greatness with His light, His power and His wisdom, in His five dwellings of Sense, Reason, Thought, Imagination and Intention. In the latter dwelt the Lord of the Dark with his disorderly anarchical restless brood. Evil began when the denizens of the Dark, impelled by curiosity or some vague unregulated desire, began to invade the realm of Light. The realm of Light had no natural defences, so the Lord of Greatness evoked the Mother of All who evoked the Primal Man to ward off the attack. It should be noticed that Mani avoids any word suggesting reproduction. These beings are evoked by each other, not generated by any union. Secondly, Mani believed that God alone existed for all time, unlike the orthodox Christians who believed that the Trinity was eternal, or most of the Gnostics who gave eternity to their Ogdoad.

The Primal Man set out for the fight clothed in the Five Bright Elements, Light, Wind, Fire and Water, and a fifth called variously the Breeze, Aether, Air or Hyle. But in the battle he was defeated and left unconscious on the field, and the Five Bright Elements were swallowed by the princes of Darkness, the Archons. Primal Man on his recovery begged God for further help. God therefore evoked more beings of Light, the Friend of the Luminaries, the Great Ban and the Living Spirit. These, by methods never clearly explained, succeeded in defeating and capturing the Archons of Darkness. But they had already digested the Five Pure Elements, and the Realm of Light was thereby the poorer. A wall had to be built to prevent the Darkness spreading farther; then these mixed elements had to be localized. To do so, the Universe was created, held in place by five spirits evoked by the Living Spirit, of which Atlas is the most familiar.[1] Here the Archons were placed. Enough Light was disgorged at once to make the great luminaries. From dismembered parts of the Archons, the sky and the earth were made, so that more Light could be distilled in dew and rain; and finally, to rescue what remained, God indulged in a third evocation, calling into being the

[1] The whole five are *Splenditenens*, who holds the world like a chandelier: the *King of Honour* whose rays collect stray fragments of Light: *Adamas*, the warrior, to drive off attacks from Darkness: *The King of Glory* who rotates the spheres: and finally *Atlas* who bears the universe on his shoulders.

Messenger, the prototype of the later Messengers that would bring God's word to men. The Messenger appeared in a superlatively attractive form before each of the Archons, so that in a wild access of desire they began to give out the rest of the Light within them, just as amongst the Nicolaite Gnostics the Great Mother Barbelo had rescued sparks of divine power from the wicked Archons of Gnostic lore. With this giving out of light, sin also was given out, which was transformed into the vegetable world. But the King of Darkness was not utterly outwitted. He begot of his infernal spouse a fresh being, made in the image of the Messenger, in which he hid most of the remaining Light. This being was Adam. A little later Eve was similarly born, but she contained less Light. It will be seen that amongst the powers of Darkness, beings are created by generation not evocation.

As Adam lay inert on the ground, God sent one of his heavenly beings, Jesus, to tell him what he was and what Light was, and to make him taste of the tree of Knowledge. Adam realized the truth and cursed his creation and at first abstained from intercourse with Eve. She, a weaker vessel, yielded to the lust of the Archons and bore them Cain and Abel. But at last Adam forgot his self-restraint and Seth was begotten; and so the human race was continued, with particles of Light still imprisoned in it.

To Mani all the great religious leaders were Messengers, but Jesus was above them all. Mani, like the Gnostics, considered Jesus a divine being who only seemed to be mortal and to take the bodily form of the man of Nazareth. But he held also a pantheistic conception of Jesus. Jesus to the Manichaeans was not only revealed Light, but He was everywhere, He signified the Divine Redemption of man, through Divine suffering for man. Suffering Jesus, said the Manichaean Faustus to St Augustine, was not a Divine Man, but the fruit which is man's food, "man's life and man's salvation hanging on every tree". That is why the Manichaeans would pay no special reverence to the Bread and Wine of the Communion.[1]

Man being a compound of Darkness and Light could not wholly be saved. But Jesus had instituted a mechanism by which the souls

[1] Augustine, *Contra Faustum*, XX, 2, *M.P.L.* vol. XLII, col. 369.

of the dead could be caught up and the Light be distilled from them in the moon by the sun (the monthly waning is due to the Light thus purged being taken up into the sun); and finally they are gathered into the Column of Glory. When all the Light held in mankind is rescued, as it will be some day, then the framework of this universe will be burnt in a great fire to endure for 1468 years, while the last fragments of the heavenly material are refined from it: till in the end all Light is restored again to the realm of Light, and Darkness is once again separate and restricted by the walls that the Great Ban built to confine its Powers for ever.

In the organization of his church, Mani copied Marcion. The Manichaeans were divided into two classes, initiates and ordinary believers, monks and laity, or, as Mani called them, Elect and Hearers.[1] The Elect had passed through strict initiation ceremonies and periods of preparation. He—or she, for women were equally eligible—had as a result become full of the Light, and he must therefore do nothing that might mingle the Light back with earthly things or might hurt the Light still imprisoned on earth. He might not marry, he might not hold property. No Manichaean should eat meat but the Elect might not touch wine either. He might not help in agriculture nor even break bread himself. He must lead a wandering life, possessing only food for the day and clothes for the year. With him must go a disciple, one of the Hearers, who being free as yet from the *tabu* could prepare his food for him.

The Elect was the only true Manichaean, so receptive of the Light that the very food that he ate left by a process of metabolism its imprisoned Light in his body. The Hearers, who formed the bulk of the church, were strictly speaking only adherents or catechumens. Nevertheless, they had to live lives according to specified rules. They could marry and hold property, but they must observe certain fasts, for fifty days in the year; they must confess to God and the Elect (apparently on Mondays); there were many forms of blasphemy

[1] The division is very like that between the monks and laity in the Buddhist Church. But there is no reason to suppose that Mani copied it from Buddha. It was a not unusual division at the time, and Mani would find it much nearer at hand amongst the Marcionites. But Buddhism not improbably had an indirect influence.

that they must avoid; they must kill no living animal; they must not commit the social offences of fraud, perjury, sorcery and the like. Above all they must see to every need of the Elect, devoting their alms to him, ensuring that he is properly fed and clothed—the giving of alms to the non-Manichaean was without merit and might indeed even be harmful, hindering the liberation of the Light.

At the head of the Elect there were higher officials, Bishops, apparently, and a supreme Master, who must dwell, as Mani had dwelt, in Mesopotamia. But of the functions of this upper hierarchy we know nothing.

It may seem strange that a religion with so bizarre a theology and so much greater a concern for the welfare of the Light than for that of mankind should have ever won much popularity. But the multiplicity of Gnostic legends shows how large a public there was ready to believe literally in any tale of the cosmogony however fantastic; and in the wicked world of the Roman Empire it seemed to many an insult to morality that salvation should be possible for all men. One could only hope to salvage the good and let the rest go to be tidied away in perdition. Certainly Manichaeanism found a wide and ready acceptance. Mani began his preaching at Ctesiphon in Mesopotamia in A.D. 242. In 276 he was martyred at Gundeshapur in south-west Persia. Within a century of his death there were Manichaean churches established from Turkestan to Carthage, and it seemed not unlikely that Mani's faith would dominate the world. But this was not to be. It was in eastern Turkestan that the Manichaeans had their most permanent triumphs; in the year A.D. 1000 they were still the most powerful sect there.[1] In Africa their career was better known, for there they won their most eminent convert. St Augustine himself from 373 to 382 was a Manichaean, and though he later bitterly attacked his former faith he never entirely rid himself of its doctrines. But in Africa Manichaeanism seems to have faded out with the Vandal invasions and the severance of contact with the East. The heart of the movement was in Western Asia, in Syria and in Mesopotamia. There such anxious orthodox polemists as St

[1] A. von Le Coq, *Manichaica*, vol. III, p. 40: Lindquist, *Manikeismens Religionshistorika Stellning*, pp. 32–44.

Ephraim and Mark the Deacon of Gaza in the fourth and early fifth centuries and a host of later Greek and Syrian and ultimately Arabic writers show it to have flourished up till the tenth century,[1] despite persecution by Orthodox Christian, Zoroastrian and Moslem alike. The history of the Manichaeans is very obscure. It is probable that by the sixth century the force of their impetus was spent. But the Christian and Moslem worlds had been given a fright.

Manichaeanism failed because it was too anti-social. The authorities in that hard bellicose age, with civilization on the defensive against the barbarian invader, could not approve of a faith wherein all killing, even of animals, was forbidden, and whereof a considerable number of believers wandered about, refusing to work, refusing to notice secular regulations, living on the charity of others and exercising a vast influence on the whole community. The rigorous monasticism that grew up in orthodox Christian countries was to worry the governments quite enough. But monks were enjoined, by both Basil's and Benedict's rules, to labour as well as to pray. Moreover, they lived safely secluded in monasteries. The ordinary Christian obeyed a hierarchy easier for the State to control. The Manichaeans inevitably met with persecution; and their church was too passive, too non-resistant to survive severe repression. In the end it was stamped out.

But the alarm that it had caused was proved by the horror with which the word "Manichaean" came to be regarded. In future the average orthodox Christian, when faced with any sign of dualism, would cry out "Manichaean", and everyone would know that here was rank heresy, and the authorities be seriously disquieted and take action. Ideas that were Gnostic or Marcionite or crudely Zoroastrian were swept up into this all-embracing epithet. If the Marcionite Church had been so great and menacing, if Marcion had been refuted by a Father so well known and so revered as St Augustine, then "Marcionite" would have been the usual term of opprobrium. But Marcion's Church had a quieter career and was less noticed by the public. Mani's greater notoriety gave him the dishonour of supplying the accepted adjective. Consequently the historian who meets the

[1] Flügel, *Mani*, pp. 105–6: Browne, *Literary History of Persia*, vol. I, pp. 163–4.

word "Manichaean" in medieval writers cannot at once assume that Mani's teaching in all its complexity is meant. It may be so, but more probably it is not.

With Mani Gnostic dualism reached its height of eminence. New Gnostic sects would still be formed here and there, but they contributed nothing new. Manichaeanism absorbed the bulk of the Gnostically-minded public. But meanwhile other schools of heresy were growing up, to have in their turn an influence that lasted and to supply by their names further epithets of vulgar and uncritical abuse.

The Montanists, most spectacular of the heretics of the later second century, especially after the great Tertullian himself joined their number, contributed little to the development of heretic thought. Montanus and his fellow-prophetesses were religious reactionaries, desiring to go back to the most primitive Christianity that they could imagine. They distrusted the intellect and relied solely on inspiration. Their lives were to be one long Pentecost, the Holy Ghost perpetually guiding them, till the New Jerusalem appeared on the Phrygian plain; and that would be soon. Revivalism always has its devotees; and the Montanist Church lasted for some centuries. In the sixth century congregations of Montanists burnt themselves alive in their churches rather than suffer persecution at the hands of Justinian. In the eighth century the remnants of the sect perished in a similar holocaust.

The Montanists were theologically unproductive; but two facts about them are of interest. First, women played a large role in their services. After Montanus's death the head of the Church was the prophetess Maximilla. The Holy Ghost inspired men and women alike; therefore the Church on earth should make no distinctions of sex. Secondly, the inspiration of the Holy Ghost made the Montanist prophet himself divine, himself a Christ. "I am not an angel nor a messenger. I am the Lord God, the Almighty present to you in man's form", said Montanus, or again, "I am the Father, the Son and the Paraclete". Priscilla was "Christ assuming the outward form of a woman". "I am hunted as a wolf from the fold", cried Maximilla. "I am no wolf. I am the Word and Spirit and Power."[1]

---

[1] Epiphanius, *Adversus Haereses*, II, I, xlviii (ed. Oehler, p. 30): Eusebius of Caesarea, *Historia Ecclesiae*, v, xvi, *M.P.G.* vol. xx, col. 472.

Neither of these characteristics was unusual at the time. Among the Gnostic sects women could belong to the ranks of the Elect. Similarly, many of the Gnostic leaders, such as the strange Pythagorean numerologist Marcus,[1] behaved in ceremonies as though they were Christ; and the Adoptionists were generally led to the same conclusion, while Marcion and even Clement of Alexandria identified the perfect Christian with God.[2] But it is probable that Montanism with its evangelical fervour popularized both ideas.

Adoptionism was a creed more intellectually formidable. Whether or not it was started by the renegade Theodotus of Byzantium who excused his temporary betrayal of Christ on the grounds that he had renounced a man, not God,[3] it also represented a reactionary movement towards a simpler, more Judaistic theology. Adoptionism found its greatest spokesman in the middle of the third century, in Paul of Samosata, Bishop of Antioch—though he never claimed a connection with the earlier Adoptionists. To Paul of Samosata God was essentially One Person, with two simple attitudes, His Word and His Wisdom. He engendered the Word, and therefore it can be called the Son. This Word inspired Moses and the prophets. Above all it inspired Jesus of Nazareth, son of the Virgin by the dispensation of God. Jesus was a mere man, nor did Mary remain a Virgin after His birth; but at His baptism the Holy Word entered Him and dwelt in Him. He thus became a perfect being, attaining an excellence which could never be attained without the help of the Word. As a result of this excellence, He could perform miracles, and He overcame sin not only in Himself but in us, so that His death redeemed and saved us. Therefore He experienced a sort of apotheosis and will judge the quick and the dead; and, as God announced Him through the Prophets, we can say that He pre-existed.[4]

Paul, too, had women to play a prominent part in his services.[5] And Paul, too, was thought to put himself on an equality with Christ. If Jesus of Nazareth could be inspired by the Holy Word, so could Paul of Samosata. "I too, if I wish, shall be Christ", he said,

[1] Irenaeus, *Adversus Haereticos*, I, 13, *M.P.G.* vol. VII, coll. 577 ff.
[2] See above, p. 11, n. 1.
[3] Epiphanius, *Adversus Haereses*, I, 1, liv (ed. Oehler, p. 120).
[4] For Paul's doctrines, see Bardy, *Paul de Samosate*, pp. 361–98.
[5] Eusebius, *Historia Ecclesiae*, VII, 30, 10, *M.P.G.* vol. XX, coll. 709–21.

"since I and Christ are of one and the same nature";[1] and again, according to Theodore of Mopsuestia, "I do not envy Christ because he has been made God. For what he was made, I was made, since it is in my nature."[2] Indeed, his enemies complained that during his episcopate at Antioch psalms were sung there in praise not of God but of Bishop Paul.

Paul of Samosata's influence undoubtedly was great. His condemnation cost the orthodox much work and much worry, and for a long time it was ignored in Antioch. Even after his fall, his ideas were not forgotten. The great fifth-century Antiochene Nestorius was largely affected by his teaching. Numbers of disciples followed him into heresy; and the so-called Paulinian Church was still in existence two centuries later. Above all, Paul had frightened the orthodox. His strong, blatant personality, his uncompromising eloquence, his vast political influence won by his friendship with Zenobia, all gave him a terrible prestige. His name roused alarm and was quoted freely, and not always accurately, as that of a dangerous heretic, a name that made the lay authorities also suspicious, as they remembered his Palmyrene connection and the nationalism of Syria.

But none of these early heresies founded a strong lasting Church. Paul's Adoptionism only succeeded while its founder was alive to preach it. Similarly, Montanism with its inspired evangelical anarchy declined into provincial obscurity once its first great prophets and prophetesses were dead. The Gnostic Churches faded out from an opposite cause. Their fantastic speculations on the origin of evil, important though the question seemed to their intellects, did not respond to an emotional need of the ordinary man. Marcion's bold contrast between kindliness and justice was too subtle to be generally

---

[1] Quoted by Simeon of Beit Arsam (*Epist. de Bar Sauma*, in J. S. Assemani, *Bibliotheca Orientalis*, vol. i, p. 347).

[2] "Non invideo, inquit, Christo cum factus est Deus. Quod enim factus est, ego factus sum, quia meae naturae est." Marius Mercator, *Excerpta Theodori Mopsuestiae*, v, 12 (*M.P.L.* vol. XLVIII, coll. 1063–4). Ibas of Edessa used the same words: "Οὐ φθονῶ τῷ χριστῷ γενομένῳ θεῷ· ἐφ' ὅσον γὰρ αὐτὸς ἐγένετο, κἀγὼ ἐγενόμην." Ibas passed as orthodox at the Council of Tyre (449) and was confirmed as such at Chalcedon (451), after repudiating these words (Mansi, *Concilia*, vol. VII, p 229). They must have been Paul's.

accepted. Even Mani's well-organized Church could not survive the complication of its cosmology and creed. Dislike of Matter found an easier outlet in the growth of Monasticism. Moreover, from the early fourth century onwards theological thought was occupied so intensely over the Arian controversy and then the Nestorian and Monophysite controversies that small notice was given to the heresies that had gone before. Little but their names was remembered to enrich the vocabulary of theological abuse.

The early heretical tradition was preserved only by two things. First, there was the literature of the Gnostics. The Gnostics had always had a taste for fairy-stories. Their familiar method of exegesis had been to publish a book of the visions of some famous Biblical character, Enoch or Isaiah or Baruch or an Apostle, in which the seer described the heavens as being planned according to a Gnostic model. Or they would adopt some traditional fable and give it a Gnostic moral. Some of these stories were adopted from the Jews, others seem to have travelled from the East, from the Buddhists who sought to find much the same moral as the Gnostics. These stories were very much to the taste of the general public, and remained in circulation. Their heretical tendencies were unnoticed or ignored. Many of them are to be found abridged in the popular Byzantine histories of the world. Some even, like the story of Barlaam and Josaphat, a Buddhist story with Buddhist-Gnostic moral, was accepted as almost holy writ and was attributed to that unimpeachable figure of orthodoxy, St John Damascene.[1]

The second agent in preserving heretical tradition was a sect known as the Messalians or Massalians, sometimes called by the Greeks the Euchites or Praying People—"Messalian" is a Graecized form of the Syriac word for "praying"—and sometimes the Enthusiasts or the Choreutes or Dancers. The Messalians were Gnostic in origin but they were less interested in intellectual speculation. As their various names imply, they were decidedly evangelical and emotional in their religious habits, in which they probably inherited

[1] Indeed St John Damascene may well have been the author of the present Greek version (see preface to the Loeb edition). For a further discussion of Gnostic books, see below pp. 82–6.

Montanist traditions. They laid great stress on Initiation, on creating a class of Adepts. They called themselves Pneumatics, like the grade of the Elect amongst the Gnostics. Like most Gnostics they utterly rejected the Old Testament. Their Christology is hard to discover. They were not apparently Docetist like the Gnostics; their attitude was more Nestorian, for they believed that the Holy Spirit entered the mortal body of Jesus with the mortal seed, but Jesus and the Holy Spirit never became one. Like Nestorius, they would not pay reverence to the Virgin Mary, who was only the mother of the man Jesus. They regarded the Cross as an object to be loathed rather than to be worshipped. Their theory of the Creation was one of the Gnostics'. Satan to them was the elder son of God the First Principle, and Christ the younger son. Satan rebelled from pride against his Father and fell; and the material world was his creation after his fall, and as such was a wicked place.[1] Every man was bound to this wicked material world, for in his soul there was a demon. It was in the methods used to eject these demons that the Messalians showed their strange evangelical ardour. If the demon was to be expelled and the Holy Ghost let in, not baptism but prayer was necessary. If one prayed hard enough then the demon emerged down the nose in mucus or out of the mouth in saliva, for prayer clearly involved snivelling and slobbering. But frequent and fervent though prayer had to be, the only prayer that must be said was the Pater Noster. Once the demon was gone it was necessary to cultivate an attitude of impassivity, in the course of which one could enter into union with the Holy Ghost and even behold God. This was only achieved by a three years' novitiate involving the strictest abstinence. But once the union with the Holy Ghost was complete, nothing else mattered; sin was no longer possible. The initiate could return to the world and lead a life of luxury and debauchery without any danger to his salvation, for he was now part of God.[2] Indeed, according to

[1] Psellus (*De Operatione Daemonum*, M.P.G. vol. cxxii, coll. 824–5) says that the Manichaeans believed in two First Principles but the Euchites in Three, the Father and two Sons. This is probably a slight error. The Euchite doctrine was more properly Monarchian, the Father being the only Principle.

[2] Epiphanius, *Adversus Haereses*, iii, 2, lxxx (ed. Oehler, 462 ff.): Maximus Confessor in *M.P.G.* vol. xci, col. 548: Timotheus Constantinopolitanus. in *M.P.G.* vol. lxxxvi, col. 28.

Epiphanius, if you asked a Messalian adept: "Are you Patriarch? Prophet? Angel? Jesus Christ?" he always answered "Yes".[1] Women could belong to the initiated class just as well as men. Indeed, Timothy of Constantinople declares that they revered their women doctors even more than their priests.[2] They had a considerable secret literature.[3]

The history of the Messalians is not easy to trace. Coming at a time when Gnostic extravagances were no longer in fashion, they were universally loathed and despised. Even the Nestorians and Monophysites were as shocked by them as the orthodox and were as eager to persecute them. Their reputation also suffered by their popular identification with a very primitive and licentious sect called by Epiphanius the Pagan Messalians, who revered as gods their own previous martyrs and indulged in some form of devil-worship.[4] In the mid-fourth century, in Constantius's reign, the Messalians appear as a troop of vagabond preachers, coming from the land of Osrhoene whose capital is Edessa.[5] By 390 they were formidable enough to be condemned under the name of the Adelphians, after their leader at the time, a certain Adelphius, at the Synod of Side in Pamphylia. The neighbouring bishops thereupon took action. Flavian of Antioch discovered their tenets from Adelphius by the old trick of feigning a desire for conversion. Horrified by his discoveries, he began to persecute with the full force of the newly Christianized State. Letoïus of Melitene followed his example and burnt down the Messalian meeting-houses in his diocese. But on Flavian's death in 404 they were more numerous than before.[6] The Bishops of Iconium and Side presented one of their heretical books, . *The Asceticon*, for condemnation to the Third Œcumenical Council. Other heretical

---

[1] Epiphanius, *op. cit.* p. 466.

[2] Timotheus Constantinopolitanus, *M.P.G.* vol. LXXXVI, col. 52. Epiphanius, *op. cit.* p. 466.

[3] See below, pp. 90–2.

[4] Epiphanius, *op. cit.* pp. 464, 466. These Pagan Messalians had no Christian tenets. They were, according to Epiphanius, also called Martyrians because they worshipped their martyrs put to death by the general Lupician, and were the ancestors of the Satanians.

[5] Epiphanius, *op. cit.* p. 466.

[6] Theodoretus, *Haereticarum Fabularum Compendium*, IV, 2, *M.P.G.* vol. LXXXIII, col. 432: Photius, *Bibliotheca*, *M.P.G.* vol. CIII, coll. 88 ff.

books of theirs, whose contents are not specified, were in circulation a few years later.[1] They were active in Armenia in the fifth century[2] and were numerous round Edessa in the sixth century, where they were sometimes called Eustathians or Marcianites after two of their leaders, Eustathius of Edessa and a banker, Marcian.[3] They still flourished in the seventh century when Maximus the Confessor told with distress of their activities and described their bishops,[4] a description echoed by a monkish theologian later in the century.[5] Probably the Arab conquests drove them westwards about now. Thenceforward they retire into a long period of obscurity. When next they appear in history, in the eleventh century, they are a vigorous community living in the hinterland of Thrace. There we shall meet them later, proselytizing their neighbours.[6]

The importance of the Messalians lies in their combination of Dualist Gnostic doctrine with popular evangelical fervour. But they buttressed their teaching with books and so preserved for the heretics of the future a vast bulk of Gnostic literature. There are reasons for supposing that the *Asceticon* condemned at Ephesus was none other than the Homilies of Macarius, that curious vaguely Gnostic work which certainly was not by Macarius.[7] The names of their other books are not given by contemporary authorities except for a certain Diatheke or Testament, in which it is permissible to see an amended New Testament similar or perhaps identical with the Marcionites'.[8] The rest must have been Gnostic stories of too doubtful an orthodoxy to be accepted by the general public. The Messalians were the agents that were to keep alive the rich Gnostic tradition in Byzantium.

[1] Photius, *loc. cit.*
[2] Ter Mkrttschian, *Die Paulikianer*, p. 39.
[3] Timotheus Constantinopolitanus, *op. cit.* coll. 45–52.
[4] Maximus Confessor, *M.P.G.* vol. xci, col. 548.
[5] The Monk Georgius, whose account is published and edited by Diekamp in the *Byzantinische Zeitschrift*, vol. ix, pp. 20–3.
[6] See below, p. 91.
[7] For this complicated question, see Stiglmayr's article in *Zeitschrift für Katholische Theologie*, vol. xlix, pp. 244–60, and Amann's article (under "Messaliens") in Vacant, *Dictionnaire de Théologie Catholique*, vol. x, coll. 792–5.
[8] See above, p. 9.

Meanwhile "Messalian" joined the other epithets of religious abuse. But it was a word that was used on the whole with accuracy; for writers that mentioned the Messalians were dealing with a church that was extant in their day, however disreputable and subterraneous it might be. When an educated orthodox theologian spoke of sects or doctrines being "Manichaean", he had no intention of evoking all the complicated tenets that were Mani's. He merely wished to imply Dualism, and Dualism in its strictest form. When he spoke of the Messalians he intended to be more precise.

CHAPTER III

The Paulicians

I

WHEN the waters of the Flood subsided. God brought the Ark to rest upon the slopes of Ararat; and Armenia, thus chosen to be the cradle of Mankind, remained for numberless centuries the centre of the Ancient World. From its mountains rivers flowed into Persia on the East, into Asia Minor on the West, and into Syria and Mesopotamia on the South, and up their courses came the thought of the Ancient World, Persian, Greek and Aramaic. In the Armenian market-towns these ideas might quarrel and clash, just as the Roman and Persian monarchs fought to secure the allegiance of their princes. In the more distant valleys where feudal lords reigned over a simple peasantry, they would develop undisturbed, to emerge upon the world again when the people of the valleys grew too many for their narrowness and overflowed abroad.

Christianity soon reached the Armenian highlands. The saints to whom the conversion of the country is officially due, Gregory the Illuminator and the martyred princess Rhipsime, lived in the latter half of the third century. Gregory was born at Ashtishat, in the south of Armenia, and probably learnt his faith from Antiochene teachers, that is to say, from a school that was still vague in its Christology and still unwilling to accept fully the Logos-Christianity of Alexandria. But Gregory had no wish to found a schismatic church.[1] The great family to which he belonged, its power and wealth enhanced by his prestige, used its influence to spread the orthodox doctrine; and his disciples of the next century, the Catholicus

---

[1] Conybeare (*Key of Truth*, pp. cx–cxii) tries to prove that Gregory was himself an Adoptionist. The evidence is not sufficient. Indeed the first sentence of Gregory's that he quotes (" As the Son of God became Son of Man") would, as Conybeare naïvely remarks, prove his case better had it run the other way round.

Nerses and Mesrob, the founder of the Armenian alphabet, worked in with St Basil and the orthodox school of Caesarea. The centre of the Armenian church was moved northward, away from the dangerous confines of Syria, the home of so much heresy, into the valley of the Araxes, beyond Ararat to Valarshapat.

The orthodox saints had a hard task, for heresy had reached the country already. Adoptionism, the creed of Paul of Samosata, was contemporaneous there with orthodoxy, whether or no St Gregory had Adoptionist tendencies. Archelaus, Bishop of Karkhar, the one great Adoptionist whose belief we know from the account of his disputation with Mani, was a bishop of Pers-Armenia,[1] and presumably was not an isolated phenomenon. The existence of Armenian Gnostics is several times attested. According to Moses of Chorene Bardaisan the heresiarch, who visited Ani, disputed with the Marcionites of the Upper Euphrates.[2] The Armenian bishop Esnik talks of Armenian Marcionites.[3] The Archontics, a fourth-century Gnostic sect, founded by Peter of Capharbarucha and akin to the Adepts of the Mother, spread quickly to Armenia Minor where Eutaches of Satala made their teachings fashionable in smart society, and later attracted large congregations in Armenia proper. The Archontics, despite their Palestinian origin, were strongly anti-Judaistic. The demon, the author of evil, was, they considered, the son of Sabaoth, God of the Jews, who lived in the Seventh Heaven. To reach the Mother of Light in the Eighth Heaven it was necessary to avoid both the Baptism of the Church and Sabaoth.[4] Mani, too, had his Armenian followers to whom he addressed an epistle;[5] and Manichaean books were still being translated into Armenian in the sixth century.[6]

[1] I follow Conybeare's argument (*Key of Truth*, pp. ci–ciii) as to the location of Karkhar.
[2] Moses Chorensis, II, 66, ed. Le Vaillant de Florival, vol. I, pp. 306–8.
[3] See Harnack, *Beiträge zur Geschichte der markionitischen Kirchen*, p. 92.
[4] Epiphanius, *Adversus Haereses*, I, 3, xi, ed. Oehler, vol. I, pp. 534–48. St Augustine in the *De Haeresibus* merely copies his account.
[5] Eznik of Kolb (ed. Venice), pp. 116–17.
[6] Samuel of Ani, *ad ann.* 588: Kirakos (writing in the thirteenth century), *Opera Armenice* (ed. Venice, p. 29), mentions Nestorian and Manichaean books indiscriminately as having been introduced into Armenia in 588.

But the two sects that seem most to have worried orthodox preachers were the Messalians and a more mysterious body called the Borborites.

In 447 a great synod of the Armenian church was held at Shahapivan, largely to deal with the problem of the Messalians. In the Nineteenth Canon of the Synod it was laid down that any priest, deacon or monk found to have lapsed into Messalianism[1] was to be unfrocked, to have a fox branded on his forehead and to be segregated to a hermitage till he repented. If he relapsed he was to be ham-strung. If he were married, he and his wife and those of his children that were of an age of discretion were all to receive the brand of the fox and to be relegated to a hospital till they repented. Children too young to realize their shame were to be removed and dedicated to the service of God. The Twentieth Canon went on to provide that Messalianism was duly reported to the Church authorities. The priest that failed to report a case of the heresy in his parish to the bishop was to undergo similar punishments and could never serve as priest again all his life. Similarly the bishop that failed to take action when a case was reported to him with reliable witnesses was to be removed from his see. Lay authorities that tried to protect the heretics from the bishop were to be excommunicated till they handed them over. If a case of heresy was found in a lay magnate's family, the magnate was to be cut off entirely from human intercourse till he handed the culprit over to the Church for correction, or, were he himself the culprit, till he made repentance. These regulations were slightly modified according to the particular rank of the lay authority. Another canon[2] strictly forbade any ecclesiastic to employ a Messalian housekeeper.[3]

These anxious provisions show that Messalianism was a definite

---

[1] The Armenian word Ირծղս. Ს.Ֆ. Ֆ, used in this context, is translated in Armenian dictionaries (e.g. Aucher or Miskgian) as Immunditia or filthiness, but it clearly is the word Messalianism and is to be interpreted here in that theological sense. See Ter Mkrttschian, *Die Paulikianer*, pp. 41 ff.

[2] The Fourteenth.

[3] I quote from Ter Mkrttschian, who transcribes and translates from an Armenian MS. (Peterman 34) in the Royal Library at Berlin (Ter Mkrttschian, *op. cit.* pp. 42–5).

menace to the Armenian Church. Nor need we suppose that the Armenian clergy were ignorant of what they denounced. These Messalians belonged to the same flourishing sect whose writings, reported by the Pamphylian bishops, had shocked the holy fathers gathered at Ephesus a few years previously, in 431.[1]

The Borborites raise greater problems. About this same time the Patriarch Atticus of Constantinople wrote to the Armenian Catholicus Sahak to urge him in the name of the Emperor Theodosius II to do something about the sect of the Borborites;[2] and Sahak himself on another occasion came across the Borborites and enquired into the problem. He found neither mildness nor sternness of any avail and had to resort to the use of the death-penalty.[3]

It has been suggested that these Borborites were the Messalians under a more abusive name.[4] "Borborites" means "muddy ones"[5] and may have been used as a general term of disapprobation for any nasty-mannered heretic. But the leading heresiologues, Epiphanius and Theodoret, treat the Borborites as a definite body of Gnostics. Neither, however, tells us much about them. Epiphanius calls them Borborites because, he says, they were dirty as mud. He adds that they were also called Coddians from the Syriac word Codda, a platter, because their lives were so revolting that they had to eat apart. In Egypt he says they were called Stratiotics and Phibionites while others call them Zachaeans and Barbelites.[6] Theodoret is no more helpful. They were composed, he says, of the Naasseans, Stratiotes and Phemionites, who were all given the name of Borborites because their ceremonies surpassed in horror one's wildest imagining.[7]

These names clearly indicate a Gnostic body. Barbelites indeed

---

[1] See above, p. 23. Conybeare maintains that these so-called Messalians were really early Paulicians and Adoptionist (*Key of Truth*, pp. cvii, cviii). He is not convincing.

[2] Moses Chorensis, pp. 154–6.

[3] *Ibid., loc. cit.*

[4] Ter Mkrttschian inclines towards this identification (pp. 39–42).

[5] From the Greek βόρβορος, mud.

[6] Epiphanius, *Adversus Haereses*, I, 2, xxvi, ed. Oehler, vol. I, p. 174.

[7] Theodoretus, *Haereticarum Fabularum Compendium*, I, 13, *M.P.G.* vol. LXXXIII, col. 364.

only means worshipper of Barbelo, the Great Mother of the later Gnostics. *Phibionite* and *Phemionite* may just be corruptions of the Coptic *Ebionite*, the name of a Gnostic church. The other names are almost certainly those of the grades of initiation within the sect. The word Borborian may have been used by the sectaries themselves to describe the lowest uninitiated Hylic class. The Coddians, who eat apart, have presumably passed some degree of initiation, unless perhaps the name signifies those who have tasted the first fruits of learning. The Mithraists, whom the Gnostics sometimes copied, called their third grade Soldiers; hence come the names Stratiotic or Stratiotes. The Zachaeans were a high rank of initiates, who, like Zachaeus, had climbed the Tree to see the Lord.[1]

The Borborites were flourishing in the fifth century. Aëtius the Arian was out-argued by a Borborite;[2] and the Borborites are mentioned in the Code of Theodosius II amongst the heretics whose assemblies were unlawful.[3] It is unlikely therefore that Moses of Chorene would use their name to describe a well-known and very different non-Gnostic sect such as the Messalians. He might perhaps intend it to include their fellow-Gnostics the Archontics; for they both were adepts of the Great Mother. But one must assume from his words that there were strong and distinct Gnostic influences at work in fifth-century Armenia.

Thus there were many brands of heretics to battle with the Orthodox and each other amongst the early Armenian Christians; and medieval Armenia was fit ground for heresy. The Church was a hereditary affair. The Catholicate and the bishoprics passed regularly from uncle to nephew. Dynastic interests outweighed spiritual interests in the minds of most of the hierarchy. The feudal nobility usually did its utmost to secure the favour of the Church. The poor peasant might well feel resentful to find no ecclesiastical help against his often oppressive lay over-lord; he would yearn for some less

---

[1] See Bareille's discussion under the heading *Borboriens* in *Dictionnaire de Théologie Catholique*, vol. II. Conybeare tries to prove the Ebionites Adoptionist (*Key of Truth*, p. xcii).

[2] Philostorgius, *Epitome Historiarum*, III, 15, M.P.G. vol. LXV, coll. 501-5.

[3] *Codex Theodosianus*, XVI, tit. v, 65.

proud and splendid church to give him comfort and answer his depression. The heretic sects thus attracted a large congregation. Unfortunately in the darkness of the following centuries we cannot tell precisely which of them was to fall and which to persist. After the Fourth Œcumenical Council, at Chalcedon in 451, the whole Armenian Church, from injured pride and petty patriotism rather than from deep theological sentiment, lapsed into the Monophysite heresy. Henceforward the Greek orthodox writers in view of this major problem could not take any interest in the minor heterodoxies of Armenia. Nor do the Armenian historians give us any help. Only Lazar of Pharb, who wrote about the year 480, mentions the question of heresy; and he, perhaps because he was himself suspected of heretical tendencies, is singularly unhelpful. "The heresy of our Armenian land", he says, "is not named after any teacher, nor is it written down in words. Its adherents are ignorant in their faith and in their teaching; in their actions they are slow and infirm." After a little vague abuse he then declares that one can apply to them the proverb: "For the bride of the swine, a bath of drain-water."[1]

In so far as Lazar's words mean anything, they imply that there was now one dominant heresy in Armenia, that it was to be found among ignorant illiterate people, that its habits were unpleasant and perhaps that it rejected the baptism of the Church. The description would fit almost any heretical sect except the more sophisticated type of Gnostic.[2] It is unlikely that Lazar had any specific creed but was referring merely to the ignorance of the poorer Armenian Christians and to the pagan practices that lingered on amongst them.

II

Suddenly, with the coming of the eighth century, a heresy with a new name appears and concentrates upon itself the attention of right-thinking Christians. The situation in Eastern Christendom by now was utterly changed. The many flourishing little sects and

[1] Lazar of Pharb, *Letter to Vahan Mamikonian*, ed. Emin (in Armenian).
[2] The passage is taken by Conybeare (*Key of Truth*, p. cviii) to refer to the Paulicians. But his whole argument is that the Key of Truth is an ancient Paulician manual. It is therefore strange of him to annex for his Paulicians a description that clearly states the heretics in question to have no books.

congregations that had ornamented the East were no more. The Arab Conquest, itself largely the outcome of the Monophysite schism, had simplified everything and swept them away. In the Arab Empire the Orthodox Church held proudly on, weakened, but conscious of being the Church of the Orthodox Emperors, the champions of Christendom; but only the richer of the heretical churches could survive, the Copts in Egypt, the Jacobites and Nestorians in Syria. Even in the still Christian lands of Asia the Arab advance had its religious effect. Many people felt that the Church had been inadequate and was in need of reform. The taste of the time for Puritanism, the taste which had made the spread of Islam so rapid, was reflected in Christian Church politics. The Orthodox under Arab rule ignored it, realizing that their role was to emphasize their rich ritual, their saints and their images; the Puritans would inevitably prefer Islam. But in Asia Minor and in Armenia good Christians yearned to simplify their faith.

This yearning encouraged a heretical revival. Within the Empire it was to show in the great Iconoclastic movement, which for a time controlled the Imperial government. In Armenia it was less spectacular but no less persistent.

In the year 717[1] John of Otzun in Tascir became Catholicus of Armenia, and in 719 he held a great Synod at Dovin. The Synod dealt with various problems of Church government and discipline; but the thirty-second and last canon runs as follows:

No one ought to be found in the places of that most wicked sect of obscene men who are called Paulicians, nor to adhere to them nor speak to them nor exchange visits with them; but one ought to retreat from them in every way, to curse them and pursue them with hatred. For they are the sons of Satan, fuel for the eternal fires and alienated from the love of the Creator's will. And if anyone joins them and makes friends with them, he is to be in every way punished and visited with severe penalties until he repents and is confirmed in the Faith. If, however, he is caught as a relapsed heretic, we order him to be forthwith excommunicated and cast out as a pest from the Church of Christ, lest "the root of bitterness spread and germinate and through it many be lost".[2]

[1] This is the date given by Laurent (*L'Arménie entre Byzance et l'Islam*, p. 250, n. 3). Conybeare (*Key of Truth*, p. 152) gives 718.
[2] John of Otzun, *Opera*, ed. Venice, pp. 1 ff.

In his Synodal address John had apparently already referred to the heresy, but the passage has not survived.[1] But so anxious was he that shortly afterwards he published a tract on the subject of these sectaries.

The tract is not, however, informative. John regarded the heresy as an extreme outcome of Iconoclasm, regretting the progression of its devotees from "denying Images into denying the Cross and showing hatred to Christ and thence into atheism and worship of the Devil". It was, indeed, their attack on the Cross that offended him, and he was particularly indignant with them for "calling us idolaters because of the worship that we pay towards the Lord's symbol of the Cross". But apart from that one point, he knew little about them. He denounced their iconoclasm in terms usual for an image-worshipper to use; he accused them of consorting with sun-worshippers and heathens, of adoring the devil, and of mixing the blood of children with the communion-food. Next he declared that they exposed their dead on the roofs of their buildings, that they invoked the sun and the demons of the air and that they would swear oaths clasping the hand of a first-born male infant and saying "I swear by the only-begotten son".[2]

Clearly John did not understand the doctrines of his Paulicians in detail. The exposure of the dead on roofs was a Zoroastrian habit, unpractised as far as we know by any Christian sect. The strange oaths and unpleasant communion must represent a libellous travesty of practices that we cannot now identify. Demon-worship was an accusation that could plausibly be brought against any Gnostic. On their history, however, he was more sure.

The Paulicians, he declared, had been persecuted by the Catholicus Nerses and had fled into hiding. There they had been joined by Iconoclasts expelled from Aghovania, the Albania of the Caucasus, by the local Catholicus. Already they had sought the help of infidel powers (the Moslems). They thought, he added, that they had found something great and new, whereas it was really old and out-of-date.

[1] Chapter XII was headed "Steps against those who forbid the worship of the Cross and the use of the oil called Myrrh". *Ibid.* p. 4.
[2] John of Otzun, *op. cit.: Contra Paulicianos, ibid.* pp. 78–106.

Finally he said that their centre was now at Djirga, a spot at the confluence of waters.[1]

The Catholicus Nerses, here mentioned, was almost certainly Nerses III, Catholicus from 641 to 661;[2] presumably, as he gave no qualifying distinction, John meant the last Nerses to reign as Catholicus before his own time. Nerses III was a so-called Chalcedonian, an advocate of reunion with the Greek Church. As such he would be particularly stern against local heresies. That there was at this time a puritan iconoclastic anti-priestly party in the Albanian church we know from a passage in Moses of Kaghankatuk, who talks of its existence in the days of the monk Mairogometsi (about the year 640).[3] Djirga or Djrkay is impossible to identify with accuracy. Possibly the canton of Djrkan, near Bitlis, south-west of Lake Van, is intended,[4] but it is tempting to place it farther to the north.[5]

For the derivation of the name "Paulician", John offered no suggestion. He accepted it without demur. It must therefore have been generally in use by that time. But henceforward no Armenian writer mentions the Paulicians again, at least under that name.

For further information we must go to the Greeks. In the ninth century the question of the Paulicians seriously troubled the Byzantine authorities, and thenceforward various accounts of the heresy and its history were published, so that suitable steps might be taken to combat it. The relation of these accounts with each other and identification of their ultimate source have provided palaeographists with many labours; but it seems certain that they were derived from one authoritative description of the Paulicians, written at some date before the late ninth century and now partly lost. The author probably derived his information from the Paulicians themselves, whom he visited as an ambassador.[6]

[1] John of Otzun, quoted by Conybeare, *Key of Truth*, Appendix IV, p. 154.
[2] Dates given by Laurent, *L'Arménie*, p. 392.
[3] Moses of Kaghankatuk, *History of the Aghovanians* (in Armenian), pp. 211–14.
[4] Conybeare, *Key of Truth*, p. lix. He suggests as an alternative Djrbashkh, near Bayezid.
[5] See below, p. 37.
[6] For a fuller discussion of this problem, see Appendix I, p. 181. The following account of the Paulicians is based on Petrus Siculus.

The Paulicians, according to this story, take their name from a certain Paul of Samosata. He and his brother John were the sons of a Manichaean woman called Callinice, and they spread the Manichaean faith in Samosata. In the reign of Constantine, the grandson of Heraclius, that is to say Constans II, an Armenian from Mananali called Constantine met an ex-captive from Syria called Diaconus, who took him to Samosata and taught him the heresy, which he took home to Mananali. From Mananali he moved with his disciples to Cibossa, near Colonea, where he founded his church securely. For twenty-seven years he flourished there, till the Byzantine authorities ordered an inquiry. An imperial official, Symeon, arrived with full powers to deal as he chose with the heretics. Symeon ordered the Paulicians to put their leader to death, but none could be found to carry out the sentence, till at last a certain Justus, Constantine's own adopted son, consented to be the new David and overthrow the giant of heresy. But the episode was too much for Symeon's orthodoxy. Unhinged by the Paulicians' fervour, he embraced the heresy himself and stepped into their murdered leader's place.

Symeon ruled the Paulicians for three years; then he died, during a persecution ordered by Justinian II. His successor was a certain Gegnesius, the son of an Armenian called Paul, who somehow secured his elevation. Gegnesius made his centre a village called Episparis but later moved to Mananali. He ruled for thirty years, and in the course of his rule he had a disputation with the Patriarch of Constantinople.

On his death his son Zacharias succeeded him; but there was a schism. The greater part of the Paulicians followed a bastard, Joseph, whom Zacharias nearly slew, and who fled for protection to the Saracens, during one of their invasions. Joseph apparently triumphed in the end over Zacharias. He moved from Episparis, where the pious local prince Crichoraches took action against him and ended his life at Chortacopeum, apparently near Antioch-in-Pisidia. When he died—the approximate date is not indicated—the leadership was taken over by Baanes, the natural son of two of his chief disciples. But Baanes was soon overshadowed by a greater heresiarch, Sergius, son of Dryinus of Annia. Sergius had been converted to Paulicianism by a female friend. Once converted, he flung himself into the movement; and under his guidance Paulicianism reached its heyday. His letters have the true ring of the missionary. "From East to West, from North to South have I hastened, preaching the Gospel of Christ, tramping on my feet."[1]

Sergius dominated the Paulician Church for thirty-four years, from Irene's reign to that of Theophilus. There had been a schism between him and Baanes, which must have weakened the church, though the Baaniotes were apparently few. The Emperors Michael Rhangabe and Leo the Armenian both ordered persecutions; but their officials, the Metropolitan Thomas of Caesarea and the Prefect Paracondaces, were killed by the heretics, the former by a branch called the Cynochorites, the latter by the Astati. However, Sergius thought it wiser to retreat to the protection of the Saracens. The Emir of Melitene, whose patronage he sought, gave him and his disciples the villages of Argaoun and Amara near Melitene. From there they would make frequent raids into the Empire.[2]

In 835[3] Sergius was killed with an axe by a certain Tzanion of Nicopolis, while he was chopping logs on the mountain-side above Argaoun. On his death his disciples decided to have no leaders but all to be equal. They began their democracy by killing off the followers of Baanes, till Sergius's disciple Theodotus persuaded them to stop. For the next few years they lived in happy anarchy, raiding the Empire and collecting slaves to sell to the infidel.

The presence of this Paulician principality on the Euphrates was for a time to loom large in Byzantine politics. Before we trace the story of its fate, and before we examine the nature of Paulician tenets, we must estimate the historical value of the foregoing narrative.

---

[1] Quoted by Petrus Siculus, p. 1293.

[2] *Theophanes Continuatus* (ed. Bonn), pp. 165–6, in a brief account of the Paulicians mentions Amara. Petrus Siculus only mentions Argaoun.

[3] This is the date (A.M. 6343) given by Photius (p. 80). Petrus Siculus (p. 1301) gives A.M. 6303. In both texts the numbers are written out in full. Photius's date is obviously a correct emendation. Sergius is mentioned also by Matthew of Edessa (c. 1075), who anathematizes "Tychus and, by his Armenian name, Sarkis". Dulaurier's translation runs incorrectly (p. 139) "Eutyches and Sarkis who has an Armenian name". Conybeare, *Key of Truth* (p. lxviii), gives the corrected version. Tychus is also called Eutyches by Petrus Siculus.

The historical existence of Callinice and her sons, and the consequent derivation of the name Paulician must be discussed later, in
reference to Paulician doctrines. With the information given by the
Greek source of Constantine and his successors we are on securer
ground. It fits in well with John of Otzun's account and with other
known facts—except for a gap in the chronology. Constantine
preached in the time of Constans II. During the course of his career
he moved from Mananali to Cibossa. Constans II reigned from 641
to 668. His reign coincided with the rule of the Catholicus Nerses III
in Armenia (641 to 661). Nerses, John of Otzun tells us, persecuted
the heretics and drove them into hiding and into taking refuge
with the infidel. This is the reason for Constantine's migration from
Mananali, which is a canton on the upper Euphrates, just west of
Erzerum (not near Samosata, as Photius erroneously imagined),[1]
to Cibossa, near Colonea,[2] within the Imperial frontier, but in a
district which, after the close of Constans's Armenian campaign,
was perpetually overrun by the Arabs. Constantine led the Paulicians
for twenty-seven years and Symeon for three; we then find ourselves
in the reign of Justinian II (685 to 695, 705 to 711). He persecuted
the Paulicians; and under Gegnesius, who led them for thirty years,
they migrated back to Mananali. This explains the anxiety that John
of Otzun showed about the heresy and the steps to combat it at the
Synod of 719. In this case the site of Djirga must be found in the
district of Mananali.

The thirty years' rule of Gegnesius seem to be dated from his
migration to Mananali, after Justinian II's persecution. Constantine's
control of the sect must have begun not later than 660, before the
fall of the Catholicus Nerses III (661). His twenty-seven years' rule
and Symeon's three bring us to 690. Justinian II's persecutions must

[1] I prefer Conybeare's location of Mananali, as the district on the eastern branch
of the Euphrates, near the modern salt works at Kuminji—Ali (*աղ*) = salt
—to the position given by Photius, near Samosata, though Grégoire follows
Photius. Not only does it fit the story of the migrations better if Mananali is
farther to the north-east, but also if the Mananali mentioned by Aristaces of
Lastivert is the same Mananali—and there is no reason to doubt it—a situation
near Samosata is quite impossible. See Conybeare, *Key of Truth*, pp. lxix, lxxiii,
136-9: Grégoire, *Les Sources de l'Histoire des Pauliciens, passim.*
[2] Colonea in Armenia Minor, not Colonea-Archelaïs.

cover the period of 690 to 695—the Synod *in Trullo* (690) was then attempting to restore order to the Church of the Empire, and the Emperor was falling victim to the blood-lust that proved his undoing. Gegnesius's interview with the Patriarch of Constantinople took place. we are told, during the reign of Leo III (717 to 742), and it is tempting to see in it an indication of the Iconoclastic movement. The Imperial authorities might well be interested to learn the views of a notoriously iconoclastic sect. In that case, the disputation should be dated round about 727, the year of the Iconoclastic Edict. Moreover, the chronicler implies that the disputation occurred fairly early on in Gegnesius's career. There are other reasons for postponing Gegnesius's dates. The next date that we are given is that of Sergius's accession to power. We are told that his authority lasted for thirty-four years, from the days of the Empress Irene (797 to 802) to those of the Emperor Theophilus (829 to 842), and that he died in the year 835. This dates his accession to power very precisely in 801. From Gegnesius's death till Sergius's accession there were only three leaders, Gegnesius's son Zacharias who was, apparently quite soon, ousted by Joseph, Joseph himself, and his successor Baanes, who was a contemporary of Sergius. Even if Joseph had enjoyed a lengthy innings, it is difficult to assign a period of more than fifty years, at the outside, to these three heresiarchs. If the chronicler has not left out some leader—and his narrative is convincingly consecutive—Gegnesius cannot have died before the year 750. An omission must therefore have been made amongst his predecessors. Probably his father, Paul the Armenian, of whom we only hear that he secured his son's appointment to the leadership, was himself a leader and ruled for several years. Indeed, unless he had held some position of authority himself, it is hard to understand how he succeeded in elevating Gegnesius. The migration to Mananali would then have occurred under his leadership, not under Gegnesius's. But for some reason the Greek chronicler found him uninteresting, perhaps because he could not discover by what Pauline name he rechristened himself.

Whoever may have led them, during the middle of the ninth century the Paulicians seem to have prospered and to have suffered no persecution at the hands of the authorities. The Iconoclastic emperors must have felt some sympathy for them. Indeed, if the evidence of his enemies is to be believed, Constantine V held views that suggest a Paulician origin. It is just possible that he had learnt them from the Paulicians, perhaps even from Gegnesius himself at the time of his disputation with the Patriarch.[1] But their centre was always being moved. Constantine had founded the church of Cibossa, Gegnesius that of Mananali. Joseph transferred it to some unknown place. There were later Sergius's foundations at Mopsuestia, at Argaoun, and at Cynopolis (or of the Cynochorites). Moreover the Paulicians were spreading to Europe. Constantine V transplanted colonies of them to Thrace, partly as a protection to his frontier and partly as a counterbalance against the obstinate iconodules.[2]

With the triumph of the Image-worshippers, Paulician prosperity ended and a new period of persecution began. Irene, for all her piety, seems to have neglected her duty here, while Nicephorus was suspected of positively favouring the heresy,[3] but Michael Rhangabe and Leo V instituted the bloodthirsty methods that drove the Paulicians to seek Moslem protection. The Greek chroniclers bear out our basic authority, telling with pride of the achievements of the God-fearing Emperors.[4] But the work was not carried out thoroughly. Not only did Paulicians join the army of the rebel Thomas in his war against Michael II;[5] but, led by Sergius and by Carbeas after him, they built up a free-booting state on the upper Euphrates, under Arab suzerainty; and there were still many Paulicians left within the confines of the Empire.

Their subsequent history is told to us in many of the chronicles.[6] The Emperor Theophilus was an iconoclast, but his iconoclasm was only directed against the monkish party in Byzantium. He had no sympathy with the rebellious puritans on his eastern frontier. The

---

[1] See Appendix II.
[2] Theophanes, *Chronographia*, ed. de Boor, vol. 1, p. 429.
[3] *Ibid.* p. 488.   [4] *Ibid.* p. 495.
[5] *Theophanes Continuatus*, p. 55, calling them Manichaeans.
[6] Besides the authorities quoted in Appendix I, a full account is given henceforward in *Theophanes Continuatus* (pp. 165-7, 176-7, 266-76) and the other tenth-century chronicles. The account in Cedrenus is derived from them.

Paulician raids into his provinces incited him into action. In the last years of his reign he instituted a wholesale persecution of the heretics, but died before it was carried out.

The glory of the task was left to his widow, the Empress-Regent Theodora. Heartened by her success in re-establishing Image-worship, she hoped to gain equal merit by the conversion of the Paulicians. But the Paulicians would not yield to peaceful persuasion; and the officers sent out by the Empress, Leo Argyrus, Andronicus Ducas and Sudales, found the sword the better argument. With a ferocious thoroughness they fell upon the heretic churches, till, according to the chroniclers, a hundred thousand victims perished.[1]

The results were not altogether fortunate. Paulicianism within the Empire was, it was true, stamped out; but the centre of the heresy now lay in Moslem lands. Heretics fleeing before the wrath of the orthodox swelled the garrisons of Argaoun and Amara; and even in the ranks of the Imperial army secret sympathisers were shocked into declaring themselves and escaping over the frontier. Amongst these latter was the Captain of the Guard of the Stratege of the Anatolic Theme. This promising officer, Carbeas, was the son of a Paulician who was impaled during the persecution. Horrified by his father's fate, he fled across the frontier with five thousand heretic followers and joined the settlement at Argaoun. In this moment of crisis the Paulicians needed a leader; and his abilities marked him out for the post. One of his first actions was to move them from Argaoun and Amara to Tephrice, farther up the Euphrates; he found it better situated for raiding the Empire and Armenia, and for the recruitment of sympathisers from those countries, and he preferred to be farther from the control of the Emir of Melitene. There the Paulician state was more firmly entrenched than ever.

The raids of the Paulicians now grew more numerous, reaching even the towns of the Black Sea. Carbeas usually worked in with

---

[1] We cannot tell how much allowance to make for the pious exaggeration of the chroniclers. Vogt (*Basile Ier*, pp. 10–11) divides the number by ten, but any such reduction is arbitrary. Ter Mkrttschian chooses to disbelieve altogether in the persecution (*Die Paulikianer*, p. 118). It is hard to explain this disbelief except as the outcome of a charitable disposition.

the Saracen emirs of Melitene and Tarsus, so much so that he was accused of being a convert to Islam. The Imperial government was roused to military action. In 856 Petronas, the brother of the Empress-Regent, was sent to deal with an invasion of Carbeas and the Melitenians, apparently with little success. Two years later, in 858, the young Emperor Michael III himself led an army over the frontier, accompanied by his uncle and chief minister, Bardas. The Paulicians joined the Arabs against him; and one Sunday morning, as divine service was being held in the Imperial camp before Samosata, the infidel allies fell on him. According to Greek sources hostile to him, Michael and Bardas just escaped with their lives, but not less than a hundred high Imperial officers were captured by Carbeas. As no Arab mentions this victory, it probably never occurred; but at some time Carbeas took some important prisoners; for he was said to have rejected the money offered to redeem the Palatine Seon and kept him in captivity, because Seon refused to admit that he was ever moved by the lusts of the flesh.[1]

In 860 Carbeas with his Arab allies again invaded the Empire as far as the Black Sea coast, from whence Petronas, again in command of the Imperial troops, had difficulty in forcing him to retreat.[2] So dreadful was Carbeas's reputation now that, according to the Arabs, his statue was placed by the Greeks in one of their churches together with those of the Saracen leaders that most they feared.[3]

In 863 Carbeas was killed in battle with the Byzantines.[4] But the Paulicians acquired an equally formidable leader in his nephew, John Chrysocheir. Chrysocheir came of a good Greek family and, like Carbeas, had been a Byzantine officer, a Spatharius. His family

[1] Genesius, ed. Bonn, p. 91, is the source. But no Arab source mentions the Arab victory, though Ibn Tabari mentions the expedition. Seon's adventure is mentioned by Vasiliev, *Byzantium and the Arabs* (in Russian), I, p. 195.
[2] *Theophanes Continuatus*, pp. 179–83: Ibn Tabari, in Vasiliev, *op. cit.* I, p. 195.
[3] Masoudi, *Prairies d'Or*, VIII, p. 74. This is clearly an example of the στοιχεῖον superstition. The Byzantines believed that everyone had an inanimate object, a statue or a pillar, with which his life was bound up. If the statue were harmed or destroyed, similar harm would befall the man. Tsar Symeon of Bulgaria died because his στοιχεῖον, a pillar in Constantinople, had its top knocked off (*Theophanes Continuatus*, pp. 411–12).
[4] Masoudi, *Prairies d'Or*, loc. cit. p. 74.

connections predisposed him towards heresy, but his actual lapse was watched with anxiety by no less a personage than the Patriarch Photius himself. Three times Photius wrote to him, first to strengthen him in the faith, next to warn him that suspicions were being raised about his orthodoxy and he should clear himself, and finally to denounce him as an apostate and ingrate.[1] The Patriarch's efforts had been useless. Chrysocheir openly declared himself a heretic and fled to his uncle at Tephrice. Carbeas welcomed him gladly, married him to his daughter and named him his heir.[2]

Chrysocheir was a worthy successor to his father-in-law. In 867 or 868, when the Imperial Government was still disorganized by the usurpation of Basil I, he led a raid across Asia Minor to Nicomedia on the shore of the Sea of Marmora and to Ephesus where he stabled his horses in the Church of St John the Divine.[3] In 869 the Emperor, wishing to concentrate his attention on Italian affairs, decided that he must treat with Chrysocheir and sent an embassy to Tephrice, offering a ransom for his captives and gold and silk garments, and talking of the duty of Christians to be friends. His ambassador, Peter the Sicilian, collected much useful information during his visit to the Paulicians, but achieved no political result. He returned with the alarming news that the Paulicians were still in touch with their co-religionists whom Constantine V had moved to Thrace a century before, and with an insolent message from the Paulician leader. "Let the Emperor, if he desires peace, abdicate the East and retire to rule in the West", wrote Chrysocheir, mocking at Basil's

---

[1] Photius, *Epistolae*, no. 9, to John Chrysocheres, Spatharius, no. 19, to John, Spatharius, and no. 26, to John, Spatharius (*M.P.G.* vol. CII, pp. 933, 941, 945). Sathas, *Les Exploits de Digénis Akritas*, pp. lxxxiv–v, tries to maintain that all letters, written by Photius to correspondents called John, were addressed to Chrysocheir; but the three cited above are the only ones in the least relevant or appropriate.

[2] Chrysocheir's career is given in the Greek authorities quoted above, p. 39, n. 6. Sathas, *op. cit.* p. xxii, identifies him with the Chrysocherpes of the poem of Digenis Akritas, a fugitive Greek who married the daughter of the Emir of Melitene, Ambron (a historical figure, the ally of Carbeas). The identification is unlikely in view of what we know of Chrysocheir's career; but Chrysocherpes, if he was a historical figure, might well have been one of Chrysocheir's or of Carbeas's companions.　　　　　[3] Genesius, p. 121.

Italian ambitions. "If he refuses, the servants of the Lord will drive him from the throne."[1]

Basil was forced to take action. In 870 he led an army out against Tephrice. His troops destroyed many Paulician villages, such as Avara, Spathe and Coptus, but before Tephrice itself he met with disaster. His army was routed and his life only saved by the exertions of an Armenian peasant Theophylact, surnamed the Unbearable, who thus began the career that led his son Romanus Lecapenus to the Imperial throne. Chrysocheir was exultant. Next year his troops raided the Empire as far as Ancyra. Basil in despair prayed daily in his oratory to the Archangel Michael and the Prophet Elijah that he might live to see Chrysocheir's death and himself pierce his godless head with three arrows. In the meantime he sent a new army to the East. This time he did not accompany it himself, but placed it under his son-in-law, the Domestic of the Schools,[2] Christopher.

Christopher set out in 872, while the Paulicians were raiding in the heart of Asia Minor. His line of campaign followed the best canons of Byzantine strategy. He ordered the Generals of the Charsianian and the Armeniac Themes to follow the raiders as they journeyed back heavily laden with booty, with careful instructions that they should not follow too far. He himself with picked troops waited on the raiders' route. It all worked out as he had hoped. At Bathyr-rhyax at the foot of Mount Zogoloenus the Paulicians found themselves caught between Christopher's army and the armies of the Themes. They were routed. Thousands were killed, and Chrysocheir fled in panic. With him fled a few friends and servants, amongst whom was one Pulades, a Greek captured in 870, whose buffoonery amused the heretic leader. Pulades managed to approach Chrysocheir and suddenly attacked him. Though Chrysocheir's friend Diaconitzes bravely tried to save his life, others came to Pulades's help. Chrysocheir fell to the ground and was decapitated. His head was sent to the Imperial camp and thence to Constantinople. There the Emperor, after enjoying a triumph that belonged more properly to his son-in-law, ceremoniously pierced it with three arrows.

[1] For the evidence for this embassy, see Appendix I.
[2] I.e. commander-in-chief of the Imperial army.

Chrysocheir's death broke the Paulician resistance. The Imperial army arrived at Tephrice to find it deserted. It was occupied and annexed to the Empire. So the glory of Tephrice was ended.[1]

Having crushed the political power of the Paulicians, Basil does not seem to have pursued them further with persecution. Indeed he induced many of them to take service in his regiments. We find Chrysocheir's loyal friend Diaconitzes a few years later performing deeds of valour for the Empire in Italy.[2] Paulician congregations lingered on the Eastern frontiers of the Empire. About a century later there were so many of them in the districts newly added to the Empire that the Patriarch Thomas of Antioch advised in view of their doubtful loyalty their transplantation to some district farther from the Saracens. The Emperor John Tzimisces followed this advice. About the year 975 he moved as many as he could collect and settled them in Thrace, round the fortress of Philippopolis, newly reconquered from the Bulgarians, where their notorious bravery could be usefully employed to defend the Empire.[3]

There they remained down the centuries. In return for their aid against the barbarians over the frontier they were allowed the free exercise of their religion and even tyrannized over the orthodox Christians of the district. But pious Emperors yearned for their conversion; and eventually Alexius Comnenus (1081 to 1118) undertook the task. He was justifiably annoyed with them. About 2500 of their men had set out with him in 1081 to fight against the Normans in Epirus, and then, before the war was over, suddenly went home. Alexius, therefore, on his own triumphant return, summoned their officers to meet him at Mosynopolis and, on the pretext of registering them, secured their arms and horses and imprisoned them, while his police set off to incarcerate the non-belligerent members of the sect in the citadel at Philippopolis. During their imprisonment learned clerics were sent to argue with them, the Emperor, himself a fervent theologian, joining in the

---

[1] *Theophanes Continuatus*, pp. 271–6: Genesius, pp. 120 ff.
[2] *Theophanes Continuatus*, p. 313.
[3] Cedrenus, vol. II, p. 382: Zonaras, ed. Bonn, vol. III, pp. 521–2: Anna Comnena, XIV, viii (trans. Dawes, p. 385).

disputations. Several conversions were effected; but soon Alexius decided to postpone matters—he had other cares to divert him. The ringleaders were banished to the Princes' Islands; the others were allowed to return to their homes.[1] But a few years later, while waiting in Philippopolis to start a campaign against the Cumans, he came back to the charge. This time his efforts were crowned with success. Converts were made, according to his daughter Anna, at the rate of a hundred a day; and she estimated the total of souls saved at ten thousand. All these converts he settled in a town across the river from Philippopolis, and gave them lands that he confirmed to their descendants, male and female, for ever. With the Paulician leaders, Culeon, Cusinus and Pholus, he argued himself, taking them back to Constantinople with him. They riposted valiantly, always coming to each other's rescue. In the end Culeon, being, Anna says, the most intelligent, was converted, but Cusinus and Pholus remained obstinate. So they were cast into gaol and died there, with every material comfort, but in solitary confinement.[2]

These pious labours reduced the Paulicians of Thrace, but a small community lingered on. The Crusaders met them near Pelagonia as they passed by to fight in the East;[3] in 1205 the Paulician community at Philippopolis tried to surrender the city to the Bulgarian Tsar Joannitsa, and in consequence their quarter was burnt by the Frankish knight, Renier de Trit;[4] and, centuries later, in 1717, when Lady Mary Wortley Montagu paused at Philippopolis on her way to Constantinople, she wrote home to say that: "I found at Philippopolis a sect of Christians that called themselves Paulines. They show an old church where they say St Paul preached, and he is their favourite saint, after the same manner that St Peter is at Rome; nor do they forget to give him the preference over the rest of the Apostles."[5] These words show that the Paulicians had long since forgotten their original doctrines. Indeed, during the course of the

[1] Anna Comnena, IV, iv, v, iii (trans. Dawes, pp. 103-4, 120).
[2] Anna Comnena, XIV, viii-ix (trans. Dawes, pp. 383-9).
[3] *Anonymi Gesta Francorum*, ed. Lees, § 4, p. 8.
[4] Villehardouin, *La Conquête de Constantinople* (ed. Faral), vol. II, p. 210.
[5] Lady Mary Wortley Montagu, letter dated Adrianople, 1 April 1717.

seventeenth century they were gradually won over by Jesuit missionaries and the Catholic bishops Pietro Salinate and Ilya Marinov to the fold of Rome.[1] And there they remain to this day, one of the smallest but most curious of the Uniate Churches.

The history of the Paulicians that remained in Asia is more obscure. The Crusaders found a Castra Publicanorum held by Armenians near Antioch in 1097, and in 1099 another such castle, called Arche, near Tripolis. Paulician troops were also mentioned as fighting for the Infidels against the Cross.[2] The name "Publicani", which was thus introduced into Western literature, came within a century to be used fairly often to describe dualist heresies, partly because of their imagined derivation from the Paulicians and partly because the word with its New Testament associations had a good abusive ring about it. Its formation shows that the Westerners learnt of the Paulicians by word of mouth in the East. They did not associate it with the name Paul, but, rather, would sometimes write it "Telonarii" from the Greek word for "tax gatherer".[3]

Other Paulicians may have joined the kindred sect of the Thonraki —a sect that was still to be found in the highlands of Armenia at the close of the nineteenth century.[4]

III

The history of the Paulicians contains many definite unquestionable facts. Their doctrines must remain largely a matter of conjecture. None of their books survive, if indeed they used any beyond their bible. Nor do we know what apocryphal chapters that may have contained. The only full account of their beliefs is that given by the Greek authorities. This was based on information gained by Basil I's ambassador in Tephrice in 869. Photius, who claimed to have been present at disputations with Paulicians, repeated this account, confirming it therefore with his considerable theological authority.

---

[1] See Dujčev, *Il Cattolicesimo in Bulgaria nel Sec. XVII*. Salinate died in 1623 and Marinov, his successor, in 1641.
[2] *Anonymi Gesta Francorum*, ed. Lees, §§ 8, 11, 20, 21, 24, pp. 19, 25, 43, 46–7, 81.
[3] See below, p. 185.
[4] See Conybeare, *Key of Truth*, pp. xxiii ff.

There is no cause therefore to suppose it inaccurate, though it is unquestionably hostile. Subsequent Greek descriptions of the Paulicians, such as that of Euthymius Zigabenus, are re-editions of Peter the Sicilian.[1] The only Armenian writer to make any mention of the Paulicians except in passing is John of Otzun; but he, though useful with his historical information, is, as we have seen, clearly beside the mark on points of doctrine.[2] On the other hand various Armenians describe fully the sect of the Thonraki, whi h seems to have had Paulician affinities. If the identity of the Thonraki with the Paulicians could be established, the sum of our evidence would be doubled, and we could even pay attention to a manual of great antiquity known to be in use amongst the later Thonraki, called the *Key of Truth*.[3] Finally there is the information to be derived from various casual references, and the name "Paulician" itself.

This word raises fundamental difficulties. It clearly indicates a connection with Paul; but the usual adjective formed from Paul would be Pauline, or Paulian. The inserted "ic" betrays an Armenian origin. In Armenian Paulikios would be a rather contemptuous diminutive for Paul. The Paulicians must therefore be the followers of some contemptible Paul or the contemptible followers of Paul.[4] But who was Paul? The Greek story was that the Paulicians took their name from Paul and John, the sons of Callinice, a Manichaean woman of Samosata. Photius suggested that "Paulician" was really a corruption of "Paulioannian", a follower of Paul and John.[5] This suggestion is more ingenious than probable. Presumably the Greeks derived their story from a Paulician source; Callinice and her sons must have been figures of Paulician tradition.

It is tempting to identify Paul, son of Callinice of Samosata, with the heresiarch Bishop of Antioch, Paul of Samosata. His mother

[1] See Appendix I.
[2] See above, pp. 32-3.   [3] See below, pp. 55-7.
[4] Παυλικιανοί is the usual Greek form. Παυλινιάνοι is used for the followers of Paul of Samosata. But Paulicius must be the Armenian name Իազգ իկիու —such diminutives were common amongst the Armenians—e.g. Tacticius, Curticius: though they seem seldom to have been used for well-known names. Probably therefore the diminutive refers to the followers rather than to Paul.
[5] Photius, *M.P.G.* vol. CII, col. 17.

may have been called Callinice; and, though she could not have been a follower of Mani, who was born some decades after her son, Manichaeanism need only mean Dualism; she may well have been a Gnostic, possibly a Marcionite. He may also have had a brother called John. This identification was made by the learned tenth-century Arab, Masoudi. "The Paulicians (el-Beïlakani)", he wrote, "follow the heresy of Paul of Samosata, one of the first Patriarchs of Antioch; he professed doctrines which were midway between those of the Christians and those of the Magians and Dualists, for they included the veneration and worship of all the luminaries in their order."[1] Masoudi, though he had heard of Paul of Samosata, clearly knew nothing of his doctrines. Either he was proposing his own theory, or he had heard from the Greek source of Paul, the son of Callinice, and jumped to conclusions. The Armenian Gregory Magister seems to imply the same identification when he talks of the "Paulicians, who have been poisoned by Paul of Samosata".[2] He almost certainly was thus misinterpreting the Greek story.

For the reasons for rejecting this identification are strong. Unless we are prepared to admit that the Paulician church was simply an Adoptionist body and the Greek descriptions were utterly wide of the mark,[3] it is difficult to see much resemblance between the followers of the Patriarch of Antioch and the Paulicians of Tephrice. Moreover the Greeks, who knew all about the great Antiochene, clearly did not believe him to be the same person as the son of Callinice; yet they had no special interest in suppressing the identification; for Adoptionism was as awful a heresy as Dualism. On the other hand they explicitly stated that the Paulicians anathematized Paul of Samosata.[4] But probably the Greeks themselves had missed the point. In this Samosatian family-party Callinice seems to have been the dominant personage; and John was as

---

[1] Masoudi, *Avertissement*, p. 208: in *Prairies d'Or*, VIII, p. 80, he repeats: "We have spoken elsewhere of the doctrine and dogmas of Beïlaki, a sect which takes after both Christianity and Magism."

[2] Gregory Magister (see below, p. 53).

[3] As Conybeare (*Key of Truth*, passim).

[4] Petrus Siculus, Introduction, col. 1245.

important as Paul. Why should Paul's name be singled out to describe the sect that they founded? The answer must be that the sect was called after the Apostle Paul; but the original Greek investigator, hearing of this perhaps legendary family whom the sect honoured for having taught its founder Constantine, and discovering that one of Callinice's sons bore the name of Paul, decided too impetuously that he had solved the problem.[1]

It is clear that the Paulicians held the Apostle Paul in special reverence.[2] The words that Lady Mary used in 1717 would have been applicable a thousand years earlier. Lady Mary's remark that they called themselves Paulians probably presented an equally ancient truth. But their opponents in Armenia, tired of having St Paul continually thrust at them by these heretics, called them the petty followers of Paul, the Paulicians. We are told that they called themselves Christians, dismissing the Orthodox as the Romans. This does not mean that they would have disdained the name of Paulian, still less that they were Old Believers, protesting against later innovations;[3] they were merely adopting the attitude that every Christian sect must necessarily adopt, the claim to possess the only true Christian doctrine.

Nor must we make the error of taking the name *Manichaean* too seriously. Long before the ninth century the Greeks had adopted the epithet as a synonym for Dualist, to describe people with views like Mani's rather than followers of Mani: just as extreme Protestants to-day use the word Romish to describe High-Church practices, hoping to discredit them by the suggestion of the Triple Tyrant, but without imagining that their devotees are necessarily of his allegiance. The Byzantine would call the Marcionites Manichaean, though he well knew that Marcion had died before Mani was born. All the Greek sources agreed that the Paulicians anathematized

[1] Ter Mkrttschian, *Die Paulikianer*, pp. 64–5, quotes a late and worthless Armenian description of the Paulicians, which is full of fabulous details, e.g. that the Greeks drove them across the Caucasus, and somehow mixes up the Turks in the story. But an interesting fact is that it credits the origin of the sect to a woman. Some vague tradition about Callinice must have lingered.
[2] Petrus Siculus, col. 1277.
[3] As Conybeare (*Key of Truth*, p. xlix) believes.

Mani himself,[1] but they did believe them to be, like Mani, strongly Dualistic.

The Paulicians' affection for St Paul was striking. They christened their churches by the names of those that he had founded. The Church of Cibossa was called Macedonia, that of Mananali Achaea, that founded by Joseph and Zacharias Philippi, Argaoun Colossi, Mopsuestia Ephesus and Cynopolis (or the Cynochorites) Laodicea.[2] Their leaders assumed the names of St Paul's disciples; Constantine became Silvanus, Symeon became Titus (Cerus, the whale, would have been a better name, thought Peter the Sicilian), Gegnesius Timothy, Joseph Epaphroditus and Sergius Tychicus.[3] These names were probably given after a final initiation service. Carbeas and Chrysocheir never seem to have been rechristened. Presumably they remained merely military leaders and were never admitted into the grade of the Initiates.

It is, however, questionable whether St Paul would have liked the other beliefs of his new disciples. According to the Greek authorities their chief doctrines were as follows:[4] first, they believed in two Principles, the Heavenly Being, the Three in One, and the Creator, the Demiurge who made the material world and will rule it till its end; then the Heavenly Being will take control of all. Secondly, they gave no reverence to the Virgin Mary; Christ was not born of her, but acquired His body in Heaven, merely passing through her as through a pipe. Nor did she remain a virgin after His birth but had other children by Joseph. Thirdly, they would not partake of the Sacrament, to them a meaningless ritual. Fourthly, they assigned no value to the Cross, on which Christ had only seemed to die. Fifthly, they rejected the Old Testament, and retained of the New Testament only the Gospels, the Pauline epistles and the epistles of

---

[1] Petrus Siculus, introduction, col. 1245. His later remark (col. 1300), that their religion is just like Mani's, must be taken in this propagandist sense.
[2] Thus given in Petrus Siculus (col. 1297): Georgius Monachus reverses the names of the Churches of Argaoun and Cynopolis (ed. de Boor, pp. 720–1).
[3] Petrus Siculus, coll. 1276 ff. Zacharias and Baanes are given no Pauline names. But both were soon rejected by the majority of the Paulicians.
[4] Given in Petrus Siculus, coll. 1256–7: Georgius Monachus, ed. de Boor, pp. 721 ff.

James, John and Jude. They read also epistles of their leader Sergius[1] about St Paul. Sixthly, they rejected the elders of the Church and the whole ecclesiastical hierarchy. Nor would they have consecrated churches but merely meeting-houses for prayer.[2] We hear elsewhere that Baptism and Marriage were amongst the sacraments that they rejected; and their rejection of the latter justified the Orthodox in bringing charges against them of shocking immorality. They also declared that the Mother of God to be adored was not Mary but the Heavenly Jerusalem, and that the Body and Blood of Christ of which we should partake was His word. Similarly Christ Himself was the Cross that saved mankind; and Baptism should be by name only, for did not Christ say: "I am the living water".[3] On the question of their priesthood the Greek sources are not clear. We are told that they had no priests, only ministers and notaries,[4] who were not different to the ordinary people. On the other hand there seems to have been a class of initiates; the rechristening of the leaders by Pauline names indicates this; while Sergius, at least, announced that he was the Paraclete,[5] by which he probably meant that he had reached the highest rank of initiation. Their dislike of churches embraced all icons and relics. Indeed Theophanes regarded them as being akin to the Iconoclasts.[6] A final point made by the Greeks was the readiness of the Paulicians to conform outwardly. They would even be baptized by Orthodox priests quite freely. It was thus often hard to detect them. There were, however, one or two questions on which their principles would not allow them to equivocate.[7]

If we admit the Thonraki as Paulicians, the Armenian sources will amplify this somewhat meagre detail. In the first half of the ninth century, in the days of Sembat the Bagratid (826 to 855) and the

---

[1] Sergius is here (Petrus Siculus, col. 1257) called their founder.

[2] The word used is προσευχή.

[3] These are Gegnesius's arguments in his disputation with the Patriarch (Petrus Siculus, col. 1284).

[4] Georgius Monachus, ed. de Boor, p. 729.   [5] Petrus Siculus, col. 1292.

[6] Theophanes, ed. de Boor, vol. I, p. 496.

[7] Georgius Monachus, ed. de Boor, p. 723. They declare that the Paulicians make use of Orthodox baptism and the Cross as a safeguard, apparently employing captive Orthodox priests.

Catholicus John V (834 to 855), there lived in the district of Thonrak, the highlands of Ala Dagh north of Lake Van, a certain Sembat, who founded a sect, called from its habitation the Thonraki.[1] Senıbat, we are told, learnt his doctrines from a Persian doctor called Mdjusik. He himself claimed to be Christ and was eventually slain by an Arab soldier who was shocked at his presumption. The Thonraki were still flourishing in the middle of the eleventh century. Gregory Magister, an Armenian-born governor of Vaspurakan and Taron under the Emperor Constantine IX (1042 to 1055), was busily occupied at that date in stamping them out. The Thonraki leader of the moment was a blind man called Lazarus; the previous leaders had been called Thodros (Theodore), Ananias, Sargis (Sergius), Cyril, Joseph and Jesus.[2] During this period the Thonraki had often caused worry to the authorities. According to Gregory Magister each of the thirteen Catholici of Armenia that had reigned from Sembat's day to his own had anathematized them.[3] About the year 987 there was a general scare that many eminent Armenian divines were showing Thonrakian tendencies. Even the sainted devotional writer, Gregory of Narek, was suspect; to clear himself he wrote a letter denouncing such heterodoxy to the Abbot of Kdjav (in Mokh, just south of Lake Van), of whom the suspicion of heresy was only too well founded.[4] A little later, about the year 1005, the Bishop

[1] Gregory Magister, letter to the Catholicus of the Syrians, ed. Kostanianz, pp. 148–64. Conybeare's attempt to identify this Sembat with Sembat the Bagratid is unconvincing, especially as he is not clear which Sembat the Bagratid he means. Nor is Chamich's identification of him with the Paulician Sergius any more probable (*History of Armenia*, trans. Avdall, II, p. 105). The sentence in the fourteenth-century writer, Mekhitar of Airivanq, *ad ann.* 821, "Sembat Ablasay. He was the first of the heresy of the Thonraki" (Mekhitar of Airavanq, *History*, ed. Moscow, 1860, p. 54), is too late to be of importance. Conybeare, *Key of Truth*, p. lxi, incorrectly gives the date as 721.
[2] Gregory Magister, ed. Kostanianz, p. 154, ll. 28–9 (trans. in Conybeare, *Key of Truth*, pp. 144–5, in Ter Mkrttschian, p. 142). In his letter to the Thulaili he mentions also a heresiarch Esau then alive or recently dead (ed. Kostanianz, p. 166, l. 18).
[3] Gregory Magıster, ed. Kostanianz, p. 154.
[4] Letter of Gregory of Narek, translated in Conybeare, *Key of Truth*, pp. 125–30. Armenian original in Sarkisean, *Study of the Manichaeo-Paulician Heresy* (in Armenian), pp. 107–17.

Jacob of Harq (situated between Erzerum and Thonrak) went over to the heretics and consequently suffered imprisonment. He fled and escaped to Constantinople, but the Greeks would have none of him. He retired next to Thonrak, but even the Thonrakians rejected him as being too horrible; and he died in lonely neglect.[1] The Thonraki were still flourishing in the twelfth century, when the monk Paul of Taron, who died in 1123,[2] and Nerses of Claj, Catholicus from 1165 to 1173,[3] both wrote against them; and the Catholicus Isaac, who went over to the Greeks about the same time, devoted to the question a chapter in his description of the Armenian church, which though it does not mention them by name is clearly directed against them.[4]

There is no indication that any of these writers identified the Thonraki with the Paulicians, save in one sentence of Gregory Magister's letter to the Catholicus of Syria. After describing the heresy he says: "Here you have Paulicians, who have been poisoned by Paul of Samosata."[5] It is possible that he thereby intended that the names Paulician and Thonraki were interchangeable. It is far more likely that he was trying to find language that the Syrian prelate would understand. Gregory himself, as an experienced

[1] Aristaces of Lastivert, *History*, § XXII, trans. in Conybeare, *Key of Truth*, pp. 131–6; Armenian edition, ed. Tiflis, pp. 144–53.

[2] Paul of Taron, *Letters*, ed. Constantinople, pp. 259–65; trans. in Conybeare, *Key of Truth*, pp. 174–6.

[3] Nerses Clajensis, *Epistolae*, trans. (into Latin) by Cappelletti (Venice, 1833), pp. 58 ff.

[4] Written in Greek and published in Combefisius, *Historia Hereticorum Monotheletorum*, pp. 317 *seq*.: the chapter (no. VIII) is translated in Conybeare, *Key of Truth*, pp. 171–3.

[5] The Armenian text of Gregory Magister (ed. Kostanianz, p. 161, ll. 4–5) runs աւադիկ բող իկեան.քդ, որք ի բողոսէ Սամոսատացւոյ դեղեալ, i.e. translated literally: "Here (are) your Paulicians" or "here (are) Paulicians for you, who (have been) poisoned by Paul of Samosata". Ter Mkrttschian translates (p. 148): "Siehe da die Paulikianer..."; Conybeare (p. 148): "Here then you see the Paulicians...." The suffix ף is the so-called "Article distinctive of the Second Person". It can be used to mean "those", as opposed to "these of mine". The rendering "Here are Paulicians for you" or "here you have Paulicians", brings out the sense of the word rather better, and more convincingly fits the context in the letter and the circumstances in which it was written.

official of the Eastern Empire, must have known all about the Paulicians and saw how closely akin their tenets were to those of the Thonraki. There undoubtedly were Paulicians in the Syrian Catholicate; therefore when Gregory summed up the Thonrakian heresy as being really nothing more or less than Paulician, he felt that the Catholicus would now readily understand the point and not be deceived by the plausibility of the Thonraki who were seeking refuge under his wing. If the Thonrakian and Paulician churches were identical, one would have expected to find a more explicit reference to the fact.

Moreover, we are given the history of Thonraki from the days of its founder Sembat till the eleventh century. Neither the names of its leaders nor its locality coincide with those of the contemporary Paulicians. The Armenian Aristaces of Lastivert does, it is true, mention a prince Vrver of Shiri in Mananali who lived about the year 1000 and was converted to heretical doctrines which he preached widely. He got into trouble with the Church authorities and countered by bringing an action against the local bishop before the Byzantine governor. But his sins were found out. He escaped disgrace by becoming a convert to the Greek church, but even so he perished miserably of leprosy. We are nowhere told to what sect he belonged. From his teaching he might as well have been a member of the declining Paulician church of Mananali as a Thonrakian.[1]

But Gregory Magister was certainly right in noticing the resemblance of Paulician and Thonraki doctrines. The Thonraki too, though they anathematized Mani, believed in Two Principles, asserting that it was the Devil that made the earth.[2] They too paid no reverence to the Virgin Mary,[3] to the Sacraments,[4] to the Cross

[1] Aristaces of Lastivert, *History*, § XXIII, Armenian edition, pp. 154–65. Vrver's doctrines were, we are told, the rejection of Baptism, the Mass, the Cross and fasts. Conybeare, *op. cit.* p. 136, wrongly numbers the chapter XIII.
[2] Gregory Magister, ed. Kostanianz, p. 161, ll. 14–16. They are always given the epithet of Manichaean.
[3] *Ibid.* p. 157, ll. 18–19.
[4] *Ibid.* p. 157, ll. 8 ff.: Gregory of Narek (Conybeare, p. 127).

(this point is emphasized in all descriptions of them),[1] to the apostolic succession in the priesthood.[2] Their attitude with regard to the Scriptures is not made clear, but they were said to "love Paul and execrate Peter"; and to hold that "Moses saw not God but the Devil":[3] which would imply that they rejected the Old Testament and the Petrine epistles, as did the Paulicians. Like the Paulicians they disdained churches and relics and icons; they also, through a readiness to interpret everything symbolically, could pretend to conform to the orthodox Church.[4] They disallowed genuflexions, observance of the Sabbath and the use of the Font.[5] They did not apparently rechristen their leaders or their Churches by Pauline names. On the other hand they possessed a class of initiates or Perfect whose attitude seemed to Gregory Magister to be one of utter despair like the Epicureans'.[6] These Perfect conducted the ordinations of the sect.[7] Probably all the Perfect and certainly the leader of the sect claimed to be a Christ (just as Sergius the Paulician claimed to be the Paraclete). Sembat declared that he was Christ and allowed himself to be worshipped by his disciples. This boast proved to be his downfall; his persecutor murdered him challenging him to rise again.[8] Gregory Magister discovered two other grades, one of catechumens and one of mere adherents.[9] The charge brought against them of magical practices was one that almost every heresy had to answer; it means little. But there was probably some

---

[1] Gregory Magister, *loc. cit.*: Gregory of Narek (Conybeare, p. 127): Nerses Clajensis, *Epistola*, 1 (trans. Conybeare, p. 155): Paul of Taron, p. 260 (Conybeare, p. 175).

[2] Gregory Magister, ed. Kostanianz, p. 154, ll. 5 ff.: Gregory of Narek in Sarkisean, *op. cit.* pp. 108–9.

[3] Gregory Magister, ed. Kostanianz, p. 161, ll. 12–14

[4] *Ibid.* pp. 156–7.

[5] Gregory of Narek in Sarkisean, *op. cit.* pp. 109–10.

[6] Gregory Magister, ed. Kostanianz, p. 158, l. 33 to p. 159, l. 2.

[7] This is clear from Gregory of Narek (in Sarkisean, *op. cit.* p. 110): Aristaces of Lastivert (in Armenian, p. 149)—Jacob of Harq appoints his priests: Gregory Magister, ed. Kostanianz, p. 154.

[8] Gregory of Narek in Sarkisean, *op. cit.* pp. 111, 112–13.

[9] Gregory Magister, ed. Kostanianz, p. 158, ll. 32–3: cf. the three grades of the Gnostics.

rite of spiritual baptism, conducted at night and therefore savouring of occultism, that was undergone by the candidate for Perfection— a rite which in the case of the ordinary Thonraki was postponed to the last possible minute.[1]

The Thonraki still existed in the nineteenth century. At that time there was in use amongst them a manual known as the Key of Truth which is extant in a manuscript copy dated 1782.[2] The language of this manual is of a far older date. Competent scholars have considered it to be characteristic Armenian of the earlier centuries A.D., placing the ninth century as its latest limit and considering most of it to be older still. But any such dating can only be approximate, particularly in view of the strange love of liturgical authors for archaisms in grammar, vocabulary and style. It is, however, perfectly possible that the Key of Truth was extant in the ninth century and in use amongst the Thonraki of that time; it is even possible that it is a still older book taken over by the Thonraki from some earlier heretical body. We may therefore possess in it an account of Thonraki doctrines given by the heretics themselves. The theology of the Key of Truth in most cases bears out the description of the Thonraki tenets provided by the Orthodox Armenian writers. We have there the same iconoclasm, the same rejection of the Virgin Mary, the same elevation of a Perfect or Elect caste who claim to be Christs. In other cases we find the doctrines modified. The Sacraments of Repentance, Baptism and the Body and Blood of Christ are allowed; in the Eucharist the bread and wine are changed by the blessing invoked, though a false priest can only change it into his own body

---

[1] This is obviously the sense to be derived from Gregory Magister (*loc. cit.*) and the frequent references to re-baptism in all the sources, to their "nightly crimes", their tendency "to perform by night their worthless ordinations" (Gregory Magister, ed. Kostanianz, p. 153, ll. 23, 24). The Thonraki also disapproved of the *Matal* or animal sacrifices that were regularly performed by the medieval Armenian Church. Aristaces of Lastivert, § XXII, *ibid.*: Paul of Taron, p. 243 (Conybeare, p. 176).

[2] See Conybeare, *Key of Truth, passim.* Conybeare discovered the MS. at Etchmiadzin in 1891, and translated it into English in 1896 from a copy made for him by Ter Mkrttschian. The dating given below is his. As an Armenist Conybeare was excellent, and careful as a theologian. But his use of historical evidence sometimes betrays more hasty enthusiasm than judgment.

and blood. No disrespect is paid to Peter nor are his epistles rejected, but he has no special power. The ritual name of Peter is given to all candidates for Election, for all the Elect can bind and loose. But there is one fundamental difference between the doctrine attributed to the Thonraki by the heresiologues and the doctrine of the Key of Truth. To the heresiologues the Thonraki were Dualists. Gregory of Narek talks of Cumbricius (Mani) their master; Gregory Magister and Paul of Taron call them Manichaeans. But the Key of Truth is an Adoptionist document. The Devil is the enemy of God but not the Creator of the World, which God created by a single word. Jesus was only a created man till His Baptism when He became the Messiah. There was no Docetism about Him; His sufferings were insupportable. If the Elect become Christs, it is not because they are purified from the bonds of matter, but like Jesus they are adopted as Christs through their baptism. The teaching of the Key of Truth about the Trinity is unfortunately obscure, owing to mutilations in the text.[1]

It is possible that the heresiologues were mistaken all along about the Thonraki, that Gregory Magister was in spite of himself speaking the truth when he called them "Paulicians who received their poison from Paul of Samosata". The Thonraki may perhaps have been merely the survival of an Adoptionist church in Armenia, refurbished in the ninth century or earlier. If this is so, it would indeed be tempting to equate them with the Paulicians and derive the latter name from Paul of Samosata. But the temptation should be resisted. The Key of Truth is probably an ancient work of early Armenian Adoptionists, and was probably at some much later date taken over by the Thonraki, who found most of its teaching closely akin to their own; and its influence may have inclined them out of Dualism into Adoptionism. Heretical Churches do not, any more than orthodox Churches, remain rigid in their faith down the centuries. Possibly even in Gregory Magister's time a section of the Thonraki may have been Adoptionist. He tells us of several daughter-Churches, the Kaschetzi, the Thonraki of Khnun who

---

[1] I have extracted these articles of faith from Conybeare's résumé of the Key's doctrines (*Key of Truth*, pp. xxxiii *seq.*).

declared that Christ had been circumcised, and the Thulaili who declared that He had not. It was this last body that fled on Gregory's persecutions to try to find refuge with the Catholicus of Syria.[1] There may have been many variegations in their views; and though Adoptionism may seem to theologians a vastly different thing from Dualism, to simple mountain-peasants the difference would not be so striking. There is, however, no cause to suppose that Gregory Magister or Paul of Taron hurled the epithet Manichaean at the Thonraki as a meaningless term of abuse. There were indeed truer Manichaeans in Armenia, as Gregory knew, the Arevordiq, who called themselves Christians but worshipped the sun and execrated darkness;[2] but the fact that he distinguished them from the Thonraki does not mean that he considered the Thonraki not to be Dualist; rather, he mentioned them in the same paragraph as the minor Thonraki sects. It seems simpler to assume that he and Paul of Taron used the epithet Manichaean, quite consciously, in its usual medieval sense. Nor, even if the Thonraki could be proved not to be Dualist, would that necessarily disprove the Dualism of the Paulicians, for the Paulicians were a separate, if very similar, sect.

It would, therefore, be unwise to credit the Paulicians with those embroideries to their doctrines that the Thonraki displayed. Probably their Elect or Perfect were organized along similar lines as those of the Thonraki, but further assumptions are unsafe. Moreover, while it is just possible to doubt whether the Thonraki were Dualists, the Dualism of the Paulicians is unquestionable. Not only are the Greek authorities positive on the subject, but even the Arabs agreed; to Masoudi, who must have known them, the Paulicians stood half-way between the Christians and the Zoroastrians;[3] and there are reasons

---

[1] Gregory Magister, ed. Kostanianz, p. 161. His 68th letter is addressed to the Thulaili.

[2] Gregory Magister, *loc. cit.*: Nerses Clajensis, *Epistola*, xx, ed. Cappelletti, pp. 239 ff. In view of the little evidence about them we cannot decide if the Arevordiq's parentage was Manichaean or merely Zoroastrian, as Gregory says. See Ter Mkrttschian, *Die Paulikianer*, pp. 101–3. Thomas Metzob refers to them much later in his history of Tamurlane: ed. Nève, pp. 58–9.

[3] See above, p. 48, n. 1. The Arabs had had frequent relations with the Paulicians within half a century of Masoudi's birth.

for believing that Paulician Dualism was as fundamental as Marcion's and Mani's; the Monarchianism of most of the Gnostics would never have satisfied them, as their influence in Bulgaria was later to show.[1]

IV

It is easier to describe a heresy than to discover its origins. Traditions unencased in the written word are mutable; they often arise from a misunderstanding of earlier traditions, they often acquire a character that their founders would not recognize. It is difficult therefore to decide to which of the earlier heresies Paulicianism should ascribe its paternity.

The resemblance of the Paulicians to the Thonraki suggests either a common ancestry or that the Thonraki learnt their creed from the Paulicians. But we are told categorically that Constantine of Mananali, the first Paulician, was taught his heresy in Samosata, and Sembat of Zarehevan, the first Thonraki, was taught his heresy by a Persian physician. The only stated point of contact between the two churches was that both received recruits from Albania (Aghovania). John of Otzun says that Albanian iconoclasts had already before his day joined the Paulicians. Gregory Magister declares that every Albanian as well as every Armenian Catholicus had denounced the Thonraki. Aristaces of Lastivert tells us that the early eleventh-century heretic prince Vrver of Mananali derived his views from an Albanian monk.[2] That an Albanian church of iconoclastic tendencies, disapproving of baptismal and marriage ceremonies, existed in the seventh century is told us by the Albanian chronicler Moses of Kaghankatuk;[3] but he refers to it once only and without much emphasis. If it was an enduring church then it must have flourished in obscurity. But Albania is situated on the north-east of Armenia, where the narrow valleys widen out into the Caspian plain. It looks towards the East. Persian ideas could travel easily there. When triumphant Islam drove Zoroastrianism from the Iranian plateau, it

[1] See below, pp. 88–9.
[2] See above, p. 54.
[3] See above, p. 34, n. 2.

was to such outlying districts that the old religion fled. Albania must have absorbed many Persian Dualists, coming in a thin stream for several centuries; and their descendants would be willing recruits to any Dualist church.

Paul of Taron compared the Thonraki to the Marcionites;[1] and it is not impossible that they and the Paulicians owed much to the Marcionite church. The grades of initiation, the postponement of baptism, the rejection of the Old Testament and the stress laid on the Pauline epistles and finally the identification of the Elect with Christ or the Paraclete, all are Marcionite doctrines; indeed the Paulicians seem to have taken over the whole Marcionite canon;[2] and the crude Dualism of the Paulicians, though unlike Marcion's own Dualism, was similar to that which the Marcionite church soon acquired. The Marcionites of whom Bishop Esnik tells[3] may well have lingered on to inspire later heresy. But there were differences between the Marcionites and the Paulicians, especially in their respective Christology. In Marcion's theories Christ only appeared in the fifteenth year of Tiberius Caesar, and he rejected any of the scriptures that gave Christ a childhood on earth. Moreover, Christ's death was to Marcion the price of the world's salvation. To the Paulicians Christ was an angel sent down from Heaven to be born through the Virgin Mary, to grow and seemingly to suffer and to die; His function on earth lay not in His death but in His teaching They could accept the Gospels in their entirety, if they interpreted one or two statements symbolically.

Such divergencies need not be taken too seriously.[4] It is unlikely that all Marcionites adhered with absolute rigidity to their founder's doctrine. Indeed Marcion's chief disciple, Apellas, promulgated the idea of Christ receiving flesh from the elements. Doubtless many Marcionites followed other teachings not strictly Marcion's. It is

[1] Paul of Taron, p. 263 (Conybeare, p. 175).
[2] See Grégoire, *Les Sources de l'Histoire des Pauliciens*, p. 104.
[3] See above, p. 27.
[4] Friedrich, *Bericht über die Paulikianer*, pp. 93–8, makes the most of these differences. He considers Constantine of Mananali to have evolved an entirely new faith.

noticeable that Paul of Taron mentions Apellas as a heresiarch with views similar to the Thonraki.

The Marcionites were not, however, sole purveyors of Gnostic ideas. The later Gnostic sects that flourished in Armenia may have evolved doctrines of their own, though Marcion almost certainly influenced them. Unfortunately we do not know of what the Christology of the Archontics consisted—merely their opinion as to the number of heavens—nor do we know anything of the theology of the Borborites, who are probably a far more important link in the chain. They may well have followed a simplified form of Gnosticism—their name tempts one to regard them as a sect of humble people—which was developed into Paulicianism.

The Eastern Patriarchs of the ninth century identified the Paulicians with the Montanists, considering them both, with reason, as extreme Iconoclasts.[1] They were not altogether unjustified. Sergius the Paulician wrote a letter to Leo the Montanist which implies that the Churches were in close relations with each other.[2] There cannot have been many Montanists left after their final persecution in A.D. 722; possibly the remnant joined up with the Paulicians. The Montanists had popularized the notion of women-priests and the claim of the Elect to be Paracletes. The Paulicians were suspected of the former and certainly guilty of the latter. But in the realms of strict theology the Montanists gave little to the Paulicians.

The Messalians seem closer akin to the Paulicians. They possessed a class of the Elect who became Paracletes, a Dualist creed and a hatred of the Old Testament. But their Dualism was not so thorough as that of the Paulicians. Fundamentally they were Monarchian. Moreover, we have a positive statement from Anna Comnena. She tells us that Bogomilism was a combination of two evil doctrines, "the impiety, as it might be called, of the Manichaeans, which we

---

[1] Letter of the Eastern Patriarchs to Theophilus, published among John Damascene's works (*M.P.G.* vol. xcv, coll. 373-6).
[2] Quoted by Petrus Siculus (col. 1297). He accuses Leo of rending the faith —a task which would be hard unless he and Leo were officially of the same faith. But Leo's surname of "the Montanist" may refer to views that he had held earlier in his life.

also call the Paulician heresy, and the shamelessness of the Messalians".[1] Anna was proud of being a well-educated theologian. Had she detected Messalianism amongst the Paulicians she would have said so; but to her the two sects were definitely distinct.

We must abandon without result the search for the parent-sect from which, if the stories are true, a housewife in Samosata, a Persian physician and a monk from Albania could extract such similar false doctrines with which to poison the Armenians. John of Otzun declared that the Paulicians thought that they had discovered something great and new. Perhaps they were right; perhaps Constantine, who rechristened himself Silvanus, was a remarkable original thinker who evolved the heresy from his own inspiration. But John of Otzun added that really their teaching was old and obsolete; and this is the more convincing theory. The old and obsolete teaching is the Gnostic teaching, the answer that the Gnostics gave to the problem that tormented them: "Whence came Evil, and in what does it exist?" This answer lay in Dualism. The Paulicians accepted the Dualist tradition from the Gnostics, whether Marcionite or Borborite we cannot know; and by simplifying it, ridding it of much of its Gnostic elaboration, they preserved it, to hand it on themselves to the West.

[1] Anna Comnena, xv, viii (Dawes, p. 412). Zigabenus also distinguished the Messalianism of the Bogomils (see below, p. 79).

CHAPTER IV

The Bogomils

I

GEOGRAPHY has provided an easy land-route from Western Asia to Europe; and in the Middle Ages men made full use of it. The great Byzantine roads ran from Armenia and the Saracen frontier over the highlands of Asia Minor, then still fertile and flourishing, down to the narrow sea and the Imperial City. Beyond they ran on again, through the wilder Balkans, to the Danube and to the Adriatic Sea. Along these roads year after year journeyed Armenians, crowded out from their own narrow valleys, eager to join in the busy life of the Capital or to find fresh lands for exploitation amongst the guileless peoples of Europe.

The Balkan peninsula in the ninth century was fit ground for them. In the days of the old Roman Empire it had been amongst the richest provinces of Europe, its countryside studded with busy market-towns and breeding a sturdy peasantry. Its inhabitants, Latin-speaking except in the mountains of the West where a primitive tongue now called Albanian lingered and in the coastal ports of the Greeks, formed the best soldiers in the Roman army. When the Visigoths crossed the Danube and Valens fell at Adrianople this prosperity declined. Invader after invader, Goth, Hun or Avar, overran its pastures; its harvests seldom were allowed to ripen. The population grew smaller, and retired more and more to the mountains, to Pindus in the south and, in greater numbers, to the Carpathians beyond the Danube, to emerge, as Vlachs or Roumanians, after very many centuries. But few of the warlike raiders from the East remained; the empty places were taken by a gentler race, the Slavs.

The Slavonic invasions of the Balkans began in the latter half of the sixth century. A century later only the Greek peninsula[1] and the

---

[1] The Greek peninsula itself was soon to be partially overrun.

Albanian hills and a few isolated ranges were left to the earlier inhabitants. The Slavs were not a nomad race. They had left their former homes away in the plains of Poland only because their own increasing numbers and pressure from outside had forced them on. Once they had found new lands they settled there happily and resumed their pastoral life, soon taking to agriculture and acquiring an ever greater love for their soil. But they were a chaotic disorganized people. Occasionally some outside influence would urge them to combine to raid a great city, such as Thessalonica, which St Demetrius himself had to descend from Heaven to save. But for the most part they remained in little quarrelsome clans, too full of local patriotism to build a nation.

The political organization that the Slavs lacked was given them by later invaders, a branch of the Finno-Ugrian nation of the Bulgars.[1] A large section of the Bulgars crossed the Danube in 679 A.D. and began to build up a kingdom on its southern bank towards the Black Sea, defying all attempts of the Imperial armies to reject them. It is probable that there were not many Slavs settled in the original Balkan lands of the Bulgars; but as the power of Bulgaria spread it embraced more and more territory peopled with Slavs. Over them now ruled a caste of military Bulgar nobles, owing a rather turbulent allegiance to the Great Khan at Pliska near the Danube.

In the eighth century, Constantine V crippled the Bulgarian Kingdom so that its end seemed imminent; but at the close of the century it revived, chiefly, it seems, owing to a junction with another branch of the Bulgars settled farther up the Danube. A new dynasty was started under the terrible Khan Krum, whose armies soon thundered at the gates of Constantinople. In the middle of the ninth century the Bulgarian realm spread from Carinthia to the Black Sea, from the boundaries of Poland to the hills above the Aegean. In this vast realm the Bulgar soldiers still lorded it over a population of Slav peasants, but already intermarriage was beginning to blur the line between the two races. The Bulgarian language had

---

[1] For early Bulgarian history (of which I give a very brief résumé below) see Zlatarsky, *History of the Bulgarian Empire* (in Bulgarian), *passim*; Runciman, *First Bulgarian Empire*: Jireček. *Geschichte der Bulgaren, passim.*

died out; the nobles were called by Slavonic names. In the Eastern Balkans the blend was almost complete. Farther West the Slavs resented the sprinkling of orientals sent to govern them, and this alien domination gave them a greater sense of unity than any that they had felt before. At the first opportunity the Croats and the Serbs threw off the yoke and began their lives as nations. But there remained a certain uniformity throughout the Slav world. The Slavonic language that the Bulgarians now spoke by the Black Sea was intelligible to the Slavs of Macedonia, the Slavs of Croatia and even the Slavs of Moravia, far away to the North.

Armenians soon sought employment under the Bulgar Khan. Bulgarian architecture of the ninth century shows an Iranian influence that was doubtless supplied by Armenian architects. Whether these Armenians came from the Paulician colonies that Constantine V had planted in Thrace or whether they came from Armenia itself we cannot tell; but doubtless some of them were Paulicians.

It was impossible for a self-respecting monarch in the mid-ninth century to remain heathen; and the Bulgarian Khan Boris, seeing that the Church might buttress his autocracy, decided to embrace Christianity. At once missionaries of all sorts flocked to the country. It is unnecessary here to trace the struggle between the Patriarch of Constantinople and the Pope of Rome to secure the allegiance of the new converts. In the end the former won, conceding to the Bulgarians the right to employ the Slavonic liturgy that had been prepared for the Moravians by St Cyril and St Methodius and been rejected when the German party in the Moravian Church triumphed.

In 867 Pope Nicholas I, writing to his then dutiful son Boris of Bulgaria, noticed with disapproval that there were Armenian as well as Greek missionaries in his country.[1] A little later the Greek Abbot Peter the Sicilian dedicated to the Archbishop of Bulgaria, by now a servant of the Patriarchate of Constantinople, his treatise against the Paulicians, warning him that they intended to send missionaries into the country.[2] It is therefore probable that the missionaries mentioned by the Pope were Paulicians. The official

---

[1] *Responsa Papae Nicolai* in *M.G.H.*, *Epistolae*, vol. VI, § cvi, p. 599.
[2] See Appendix I.

Armenian church was too proudly nationalist to trouble itself over missionary work; but the Paulicians in Thrace might well feel alarmed at the prospect of enjoying no longer the freedom of frontiersmen but becoming squeezed between the Orthodox Empire and the new Orthodox Kingdom. Propaganda was their natural weapon.

But the propaganda was not at first very successful. When St Clement, the first Slavonic bishop of the Bulgarian church, died in Macedonia in 916, Paulicianism had made no headway.[1] But as the century advanced conditions favoured the spread of heresy. The new hierarchy of the country became grander and more luxurious, seeking vainly to copy the majesty of the Byzantine Church. It was used politically as the tool of the monarchy by the great Tsar Symeon,[2] son of Boris, and Symeon's son Peter.[3] Despite its new Slavonic liturgy it never reached down to the souls of the poorer people, save perhaps in Macedonia where the best Slavonic missionaries had worked.[4] The aristocracy was divided into two groups, the old Bulgar-born warriors resentful of the monarchy and contemptuous of the Slavs, and the new Court-nobility clustering round the Capital and copying as best it could the usages of Byzantium. The oppressed Slav peasantry had little sympathy from either of these parties. To it the creed of the Armenian exiles, democratic and insistent on the wickedness of things, was far more friendly and attractive.

The Bulgarian John the Exarch, writing of the glories of Tsar Symeon's latter years, told ominously of the presence of Manichaeans amongst the Tsar's subjects.[5] But it was a few decades later, in the middle of the tenth century, that the peasantry became articulate.

---

[1] See Appendix I. St Clement's biographer says that there was no heresy in the country at the time of St Clement's death. Does he mean in all Bulgaria or only in St Clement's district, Macedonia? It was anyhow his policy to show that so long as the great saint lived, heresy could not flourish.

[2] Reigned 893–927. [3] Reigned 927–69.

[4] The lives of Clement and Nahum suggest a more popular backing to their churches.

[5] John the Exarch, *Shestodniev*, ed. Moscow, 1879, book 4, p. 115 (ρει), coll. 3 and 4.

II

"In the days of the Orthodox Tsar Peter there lived in the land of
Bulgaria a priest called Bogomil (loved of God) who in reality was
not loved of God (Bogu ne mil), who was the first to sow heresy in
the land of Bulgaria."[1] These words, written before the end of the
century by the priest Cosmas, contain almost all that we know of the
greatest popular heresiarch of the Middle Ages. Where or when he
was born or died, by whom he was taught, how widely he preached,
all must remain unanswered. Now and then in after years an
anathema is hurled against his name, unreliably crediting him with
twelve apostles[2] or with the authorship, under the name of Jeremiah,
of heretic apocryphal stories.[3] But the apostles seem rather to have
been later leaders of his sect; and the evidence that he and the priest
Jeremiah were one is inadequate. His whole existence is shrouded in
mystery. Yet he gave his name to a Church that lasted for centuries
and influenced most of the countries of Europe.

Bogomil's heresy must have been well under way by the year 950.
About that year the Patriarch Theophylact of Constantinople, uncle
of the Bulgarian Tsaritsa Maria-Irene, received from her husband,
Tsar Peter, two anxious letters describing a new religious but anti-
clerical movement that had arisen in his country and asking how best
to suppress it. Theophylact, though more interested in horseflesh
than in theology, looked into the matter and decided that this was a
revival of Paulicianism. He replied that he knew the symptoms well,
and he sent the Tsar a catechism to apply to the heretics and arguments to persuade them back to Orthodoxy. His methods seem to
have been copied from those applied to the Paulicians in the previous
century. But while he explained the movement away as a familiar
heresy he was clearly impressed by its new appearance in Bulgaria.[4]

---

[1] *Slovo Kozmyi*, ed. Popruzhenko, p. 2. The pun between *Bogomil* (Богумилъ)
and *Bogu ne mil* (Бгу не милъ) shows that Bogomil was the founder's proper
name, not merely the name of the sect (the lovers of God, or, loved by God).
Cosmas uses the form *Bogumil* to make the pun more effective.

[2] *Sinodik of Tsar Boril*, ed. Popruzhenko (1928 edition), pp. 42, 82.

[3] The first identification of Bogomil with Jeremiah occurs in an Index of the
Russian church, dated 1608. See below, p. 82.

[4] The MS. of this letter is in the Ambrosian library at Milan (No. 270 E. 9);

Theophylact's letter was written before A.D. 954. That year the Patriarch met with a severe riding accident and thenceforward he was incapable of work, dying two years later. The next mention of the new religion comes from an angry Orthodox Bulgarian priest called Cosmas. Some time after A.D. 977, probably about 990, he published a book[1] denouncing the heresy of Bogomil and upbraiding the laziness and luxury of the Orthodox that permitted such a heresy to flourish. To Cosmas the heresy was a recent invention, and he knew of it first-hand. If, therefore, his attack on it resembled earlier Greek attacks on the Paulicians, it is not because he copied such attacks but because the Bogomils themselves genuinely resembled the Paulicians; and Theophylact's assumption was justified.

The political basis of Bogomilstvo, the faith of Bogomil, was the reaction of the Slav peasants against their Bulgar or Graecized overlords. It was a negative, defeatist reaction; but it undoubtedly helped in the decline of Bulgaria under Peter and his sons. When Cosmas wrote, the numbers of Bogomils were considerable. Shortly before, the Emperor John Tzimisces had carried out his great transplantation of Paulicians to the Slavonic districts round Philippopolis. This advent of a sympathetic people must have strengthened the Bogomils and perhaps explains Cosmas's alarm. But in the days of Tsar Samuel, when Bulgaria was gloriously defying Byzantium and almost recovering her glory, little is known of the Bogomils. Their passivity was not in tune with the time. A dubious legend declared that the great Tsar's daughter and his brother were Bogomils and even, in secret, his son John Vladislav. But the true Bogomils were unwilling to shed blood. It is unlikely that the last warrior prince of old Bulgaria was of their number.[2]

Zlatarsky (*History of the Bulgarian Empire*, I, pt. II, pp. 840–5) gives a facsimile and Bulgarian translation. Spinka (*Christianity in the Balkans*, p. 63) assumes that because Theophylact does not mention Bogomil's name, Bogomil cannot yet have taken control of the sect. But Cosmas definitely regards Bogomil as its founder. Nor is there any reason why Theophylact should have mentioned Bogomil, especially if he considered the sect merely as a revival of Paulicianism.

[1] *Slovo Kozmyi*, ed. Popruzhenko. For the date of its composition see Popruzhenko's preface, and Trifonov, *The Discourse of Kosma and its Author* (in Bulgarian), *Proceedings of the Bulgarian National Academy*, vol. XXIX, pp. 37–77. But see below, p. 87, n. 6.

[2] The assertion of heresy in the Greek life of John Vladimir ('Ακολουθία τοῦ

The years that followed, when Bulgaria was a Byzantine province, were more fruitful for Bogomil expansion; for hated masters, Greek or Graecized, domineered over the peasantry. It was probably during these years that the great schism of the Bogomils occurred. Besides the official Bogomil or "Bulgarian" church we find a church known as the "Dragovitsan", from the village of Dragovitsa, on the borders of Thrace and Macedonia.[1] Dragovitsa was not far from the Paulician colonies at Philippopolis; and probably the doctrines of its church, which were more completely dualist than those of the "Bulgarians", represent the earlier Bogomil views, such as Bogomil himself had adopted from their Paulician neighbours. There seems to have been no animosity between the two branches. In the face of perpetual persecution the heretics knew better than to advertise any disunion. Subsequent daughter-churches of the heresy followed at their pleasure one or other of the two schools of thought; and even in Western Europe the names, sometimes varied or corrupted, of "Dragovitsan" or "Bulgarian" were used to describe the two categories.

The schism in no way limited the missionary activity of the Bogomils. They sought converts with fervour. By the end of the eleventh century they were well established in Macedonia, alongside of the Paulicians. The branch of the sect known as the Phundaites was already spreading along the coasts of Asia Minor.[2] Already not only the principalities of Serbia but Bosnia beyond were infected by the

---

ἁγίου 'Ιωάννου τοῦ Βλαδιμήρου, publ. Venice, 1858) is suspect. According to Professor Adontz Samuel was of Armenian origin. If he were of Paulician Armenian origin, that would provide the combination of bellicosity and heresy in his family. See Adontz, *Samuel l'Arménien, roi des Bulgares*.

[1] This schism is dated by Rački in the tenth century, the Dragovitsan being a Paulician church preceding Bogomil's. Jireček (*Geschichte der Bulgaren*, p. 176) follows him. I think Rački is right in making the Dragovitsan the older church, but I believe it to have been actually Bogomil's church and the schism to have occurred later. Cosmas mentions no schism. It seems likely, therefore, that the schism post-dated his time. See below, p. 79. Incidentally Rački identifies Dragovitsa with Dregovicha between Berrhoea and Thessalonica. I prefer Golubinski's location of it nearer to Philippopolis (*History of the Old Slavonic Churches*, p. 707). For the name "Drugunthian" (or Dugunthian or other variations) by which the sect was known in the West, see below, p. 100.

[2] See below, p. 71.

heresy. Soon it was to reach Croatia and Dalmatia and the great countries of the West. Meanwhile it spread south-eastward also, to the great city of Constantinople.

Byzantine society at the time was in a state of religious ferment. Various heterodox leaders in their turn gathered congregations—John Italus with his Metempsychosis and Platonic Ideas, Nilus with his reformed Monophysitism, and, more ominously, Blachernites with his sect of Enthusiasts.[1] But none were so successful as a Bulgarian ascetic called Basil, a renegade monk from Macedonia, who had learnt the Bogomil heresy in his own country and had come to popularize it in Constantinople. Whether or no he had found a Bogomil church already established there, we cannot tell. Probably he built it up himself by the force of his personality. Certainly he had soon attracted a vast congregation, including some of the greatest names in the Empire.

The pious Emperor Alexius I, who had been so successful in converting the Paulicians, made, it seems, little attempt to deal with this worse heresy in Bulgaria. He was a realist, and doubtless the magnitude of the task appalled him. But he decided that the Bogomil church in Constantinople could and must be crushed. But it was some time before the authorities could discover the truth about its organization and its doctrines. At last the Emperor learnt that Basil was its leader and summoned him to the Palace, treating him with every honour, even inviting him to his table and pretending to desire conversion to his faith. Basil, after some hesitation, fell into the trap and began to expound his tenets. A secretary hidden behind a curtain took down all that he said; and when he ended his discourse, the curtain was drawn back and there were all the dignitaries of the Empire assembled. Basil's heresies were read out, just as he had uttered them, to the horror of the assembly. But Basil himself was unrepentant. The Emperor imprisoned him; but, despite the activities of a poltergeist in the prison (it was, thought Anna Comnena, the Devil avenging himself on a disciple that had betrayed his secrets), and despite frequent visits from the Emperor, who hated to fail in

[1] Anna Comnena, v, viii, x, i (Dawes, pp. 132–6, 235–6). Blachernites's "Enthusiasts" were Messalians (see below, p. 91).

the task of saving a soul, Basil remained obdurate: till at last the Holy Synod urged that so wilful a heresiarch must be burnt, and Alexius had to agree. Their leader taken, it was easy to arrest the other members of the Bogomil church. But when they were gathered together, some recanted, some denied that they had ever lapsed from orthodoxy, some remained obstinately silent. To distinguish the innocent from the guilty the Emperor ordered two stakes to be erected, the one with a cross attached to it, the other without. Each prisoner was to choose at which stake he would prefer to die. Those that chose the cross were recognized as true Christians and set free. The others were treated to further missionary attentions. But very few renounced their errors. The rest of them were burnt.[1]

The Emperor's fires for a time purged his capital. But within a few decades the Bogomil church was again prominent. Leading theologians such as the Patriarch Germanus II and the Monk Euthymius of the Peribleptos monastery took up their pens against the Phundaites of the Mediterranean seaboard of Asia Minor.[2] Soon after the accession of Manuel I, in 1143, new scandals broke out. In August of that year a synod at Constantinople denounced two "false bishops", Clement of Sosandra and Leontius of Balbissa, as Bogomils.[3] In October a second synod sentenced the Bogomil monk Niphon, who was probably the leader of the Byzantine heretics, to confinement in the monastery of the Peribleptos. But from there he was able to continue his activities, so he was brought again before a synod, in February 1144, and condemned to a stricter imprisonment.[4] Unfortunately the next Patriarch, Cosmas Atticus, fell under his spell and insisted not only on releasing him but also, to the horror of the Orthodox, on offering him the hospitality of the Patriarchal Palace. At last a synod convened by the Emperor in

---

[1] Anna Comnena, xv, viii–x (Dawes, pp. 412–19): Zonaras, 18, § 23, ed. Bonn, vol. III, pp. 743–4.

[2] Texts given in Ficker, *Die Phundagiagiten*.

[3] Allatius, *De Ecclesiae Occidentalis et Orientalis Perpetua Consensione*, p. 674: Thallóczy, *Acta...Res Albaniae*, I, no. 85. The date of the synod was 28 August 1143.

[4] Allatius, *op. cit.* pp. 678, 681—the dates being 1 October 1143 and 22 February 1144.

February 1147 rearrested Niphon and deposed Cosmas for his sympathies;[1] and a synodicon was published denouncing the errors of the heresy.[2] If a Patriarch could dare to support the Bogomils their strength must have been considerable. Later rumour even accused the Emperor Manuel himself of Bogomil tendencies;[3] but though his theology was shaky, despite his passion for the subject, it is improbable that he erred in that direction.

Even these synods could not stamp out the Bogomils of Constantinople. By the middle of the century their influence had spread to the West. In 1167 the heretics of Southern France held a Synod at St-Félix-de-Caraman, and there appeared there a certain Niquinta or Nicetas, who called himself Bishop of the heretics of Constantinople. He at once was allowed to take charge of the whole proceeding.[4]

The story of this Synod shows Nicetas to have been a thoroughgoing Dualist. The doctrines of the heretics of Constantinople must therefore have changed since the days of Zigabenus, who describes them as Monarchian; or else Nicetas must have been an impostor.[5] The former theory is probably true. Many of the French twelfth-century heretics were known as Poplicani, a name clearly derived from the Greek word for the Paulicians.[6] This suggests Dualist, Paulician-Bogomil missionary activity, based originally at Constantinople. The persecutions of Alexius Comnenus probably achieved their object. It is noticeable that the next known heresiarchs, Clement and Leontius, were not residents of Constantinople; while Germanus gives the heretics the alternative name of Phundiates, or Scripbearers,[7] a name that implies an itinerant rather than a resident church. It seems, therefore, that the heretic church of the city had to be rebuilt; and its second founder was doubtless the monk

---

[1] Allatius, *op. cit.* p. 683: Cinnamus (Bonn edition), p. 65. The date was 26 February 1147.

[2] The anathemas are given in Uspenski, *Synodicon for the First Sunday in Lent*, pp. 19–20. See below, p. 79.

[3] *Life of Ilarion*, by Euthymius of Bulgaria, in Kalužniacki, *Werke des Patriarchen von Bulgarien Euthymius*, p. 52.

[4] See below, pp. 123–4. The acts of the Synod mention the existence of seven heretic churches in 'Romania' (the Byzantine Empire).

[5] See below, p. 74.   [6] See below, pp. 122–3.   [7] See Appendix III, p. 184.

Niphon, who gave to it a more Dualist doctrine than Basil had favoured. This change-over was probably not complete in Nicetas's time, as we hear from a French source of a certain Petracus, who 'came from overseas' and 'who made a bad report of Bishop Simon, of whom Nicetas received his order of Drugarie which was the cause of the division of Italy into two parts'.[1] The passage is not clear, but it indicates that about this time Dragovitsan influences were gaining control of the church; and it is possible that 'Bishop Simon' should be identified with Niphon. The significance of this variation in doctrine will appear when we examine Bogomil theology.

III

There are two full accounts of early Bogomil doctrines, both hostile but both authoritative. The one is that of Cosmas the Bulgar priest, who was almost contemporary with Bogomil; the other is contained in the *Dogmatic Panoply* of Euthymius Zigabenus. At the behest of the Emperor Alexius Comnenus Zigabenus, a theologian well-known to the Emperor's mother-in-law, wrote a description of the various heresies of his time and the recent past. For his chapter on the Bogomils he was given, so Anna Comnena tells us, the notes taken down from Basil the Bogomil's own words.[2]

Cosmas was more interested in the habits of the Bogomils than in their theology. To his mind they were simply Dualists. He did not inquire into their beliefs as to the origin of the Devil. It was enough for him that they said that the Devil created the world.[3] This naturally involved them in rejecting the Old Testament, which assigned the role of Creator to God.[4] It also made them interpret Christ's miracles in the New Testament in a purely allegorical sense, for Christ would not touch Devil-created matter; for instance the five loaves with which He fed the multitude in the desert were taken

[1] Nazarius, in Vignier, *Recueil de l'Histoire de l'Eglise*, p. 268.
[2] Euthymius Zigabenus, *Panoplia Dogmatica* (*M.P.G.* vol. cxxx): Anna Comnena, xv, ix (Dawes, p. 415).
[3] *Slovo Kozmyi* (ed. Popruzhenko), pp. 28, 37.
[4] *Ibid.* pp. 25, 31.

to mean not loaves of bread but the four Gospels and the Acts of the Apostles.[1] The Virgin Mary was paid no reverence; Cosmas was deeply shocked at the language that they used about her;[2] or else she too became an allegory. The Sacraments were all rejected as useless, for they dealt with material things. Icons were equally debarred; feast days were pointless.[3] The Cross should be detested, not worshipped. Not only was it a material object, but it was the instrument of Christ's murder.[4] The Orthodox Church in all its branches they considered a false church. Particularly they loathed its liturgy and its vestments. The Lord's Prayer was the only prayer that they permitted. This they repeated four times daily and four times nightly.[5]

For themselves they demanded as complete a renunciation of the world as was possible. They drank no wine and ate no meat. Marriage was discouraged. They confessed and gave absolution to each other, both sexes alike.[6] Socially they adopted a policy of passive resistance, maddening to the authorities. "They teach their people not to obey masters", complained Cosmas: "they denounce the wealthy, loathe the Tsar, ridicule the elders, condemn the nobles, regard as hateful in the eyes of God those that serve the Tsar, and they forbid all slaves to do their masters' bidding."[7] On the other hand Cosmas was impressed by their quiet, meek and sober demeanour—"like sheep"—though he regarded it as hypocritical.[8] It is doubtful if Cosmas believed there to be two grades in the heresy; he nowhere clearly mentions a caste of the Perfect.

Zigabenus wrote at the request of the Emperor Alexius Comnenus. He was a trained theologian and was well supplied with material and could therefore be more explicit. It is to be remembered that he was describing the Bogomils of Constantinople as they taught in the early twelfth century. His description may only have applied to that one local branch of the sect. It is probable, however, that it would have fitted the whole Bulgarian Bogomil as opposed to the Dragovitsan Church.

According to Zigabenus the Bogomils were Monarchian; they

[1] *Slovo Kozmyi* (ed. Popruzhenko), p. 37.　　　[2] *Ibid.* p. 22.
[3] *Ibid.* p. 45.　　　[4] *Ibid.* p. 6.　　　[5] *Ibid.* p. 45.
[6] *Ibid.* p. 45.　　　[7] *Ibid.* p. 40.　　　[8] *Ibid.* p. 3.

did not believe in complete Dualism. Satan had not always been the Prince of Evil. God alone had reigned at first over a spiritual universe. The Trinity existed in Him; the Son and Holy Ghost were emanations that took a separate form. They were only sent forth to deal with the created world. When it is liquidated they will resolve back into Him. The Father begot the Son, in this sense of emission, the Son the Holy Ghost; and the Holy Ghost begot the twelve apostles, including Judas—in this last sentence Zigabenus probably travestied their doctrine; he said that they quoted Matthew i, 2[1] to support it. Satan was also the Son of the Father; he was in fact the elder son, and called Satanael (the suffix "el" indicated divinity); and he was Steward in Heaven. From pride he revolted against the Father, as Isaiah describes;[2] and angels joined him believing that under his rule there would be less work for them to do.

The rebellion failed and Satan with the rebel angels was cast forth from Heaven. In order to have a realm where he might be God, he created the Earth[3] and a second Heaven. Then, to people his dominion, he made Adam out of earth and water. But some of the water trickled from Adam's right foot and forefinger and made the serpent. Satan then breathed his spirit into Adam, but this too trickled out by the same way into the serpent. So Satan sent an embassy to the Father to ask for a little life for Adam, promising that man, thus vivified, should be held in common between them. God breathed a little life into Adam, and the process was repeated later for Eve.

All might have been well and Adam and Eve have inhabited the Earth in solitude, had not Satan in the form of the serpent seduced Eve and begotten Cain and a daughter Calomena; and Adam, roused

---

[1] "Abraham begat Isaac; and Isaac begat Jacob; and Jacob begat Judas and his brethren"; Zigabenus probably considered that the Bogomils muddled Judah (the Judas of this verse) with Iscariot. He had a slight justification for the whole statement (*Panoplia*, bk. 27, § 5, col. 1293), in that the Bogomils paid special reverence to the Old Testament figures named in these New Testament genealogies (see below).

[2] Isaiah xiv, 12–14. Zigabenus tells us that the Bogomils quoted in particular Isaiah xiv, 14.

[3] There was apparently a divine earth already created (*Panoplia*, bk. 27, § 7, col. 1296). Its functions are not quite clear.

by jealousy, did likewise and begot Abel—and later Seth. As a punishment for causing this fall from chastity, Satan was deprived by God of his divine form and apparel and his power to create; but God tempered His wrath so far as to allow Satan to remain lord of what he had created already—or else He could not depose him. But, as a remnant of God's condominium, the souls of a few men (those mentioned in the Gospel genealogies) managed to reach Heaven and begged for help for mankind. So, after 5500 years, God sent the Son, the Word, who is the same as the Archangel Michael and the Counsellor of Isaiah,[1] to go down into the world as Jesus, to cure all ills,[2] and as Christ, the Anointed by the Flesh.[3] The Son entered the Virgin through her ear, took flesh there and emerged by the same door. The Virgin did not notice but found Him as an infant in the cave at Bethlehem. He lived and taught and, by seeming to die, was able to descend into Hell and bind Satan and took the divine suffix from his name. Then He returned to the Father.[4]

This theory of the Cosmogony naturally involved a rejection of most of the Old Testament, especially the Pentateuch. Cosmas declared that the Bogomils only admitted the New Testament; but Zigabenus learnt from Basil the Bulgar's testimony that they read the Psalter, the sixteen-fold book of the Prophets,[5] the Four Gospels and the Acts. These seven books they accepted because of the words of Solomon: "Wisdom hath builded her house, she hath hewn out her seven pillars."[6] But they also revered the Epistles and the Book of Revelation.[7] As with the Gnostics, so with them the Old Testament heroes tended to become villains. Moses was the dupe of Satan. The Flood was sent by Satan to wipe out the race of giants

[1] Isaiah ix, 6.
[2] Ἰησοῦν...Ἰώμενον, an intentional pun.
[3] Christ means the Anointed.
[4] Euthymius Zigabenus, *Panoplia*, §§ 6–8, coll. 1293–1304. The doctrine of Christ's entry into the Virgin through her ear is often found in early Christian writers and is depicted on many Eastern icons. Originally it was a symbolical doctrine, the ear being the natural entrance for the Word, but the average Bogomil probably took it literally.
[5] I.e. the sixteen books of the Prophets, from Isaiah to Malachi. The Greek word is Ἑξκαιδεκαπρόφητον.
[6] Proverbs ix, 1. [7] *Panoplia*, § 1, col. 1292.

born of the fallen angels and the daughters of men described in Genesis.[1] The only saints of the Old Testament were those mentioned in the genealogies in Matthew and Luke, and those few characters who were martyred for refusing to worship images.[2]

The Bogomils naturally denounced the Orthodox Church as being in every way false. When Basil the Bulgar was asked why he rejected the holy priests and fathers whose relics performed miracles, his answer was that they had possessed demons who looked after them while they were alive and now performed the miracles after their deaths; for demons can perform miracles to the end of the seven ages.[3] He added that demons fly around everywhere, single demons inhabiting single men—a Messalian trait, Zigabenus considered it.[4] The Bogomils hated the Cross as the instrument of the Saviour's murder; and when Basil's cross-questioners triumphantly asked why then did people possessed of demons always rush to a Cross, he answered that demons loved the Cross and therefore urged their victims towards it.[5] In particular, demons lived in churches. The Temple at Jerusalem was once their principal home; now it was St Sophia at Constantinople.[6] But it was necessary to honour demons; Our Lord had recommended this, lest they should harm one. This also Zigabenus considered Messalian.[7] Church Baptism and the Communion they alike rejected, justifying the latter rejection by quoting Isaiah lxv, 11.[8]

Zigabenus described their own ceremonies and practices somewhat briefly. The catechumen seeking admission was first taught to believe in the Father, Son and Holy Ghost and to follow the Gospel, to pray and fast, to keep from all wickedness and possess nothing and be kind and humble and truthful. So far, Zigabenus thought, all was excellent, and the very excellence led poor innocents on. Then

---

[1] *Panoplia*, § 9, col. 1305. The reference is to Genesis vi, 4.
[2] *Ibid.* §§ 10–11, coll. 1308–9.
[3] *Ibid.* § 12, col. 1309.   [4] *Ibid.* § 13, col. 1309.
[5] *Ibid.* §§ 14–15, coll. 1309–12.
[6] *Ibid.* § 18, col. 1313.   [7] *Ibid.* § 20, col. 1316.
[8] *Ibid.* § 17, col. 1313. The verse in Isaiah runs: "But ye are they that forsake the Lord, that forget my holy mountain, that prepare a table for that troop and that furnish the drink-offering unto that number."

the poison began to be administered.[1] The baptismal ceremony required a careful initiation. It was, the heretics declared, Christ's baptism, baptism by the spirit, as opposed to Orthodox baptism which was John's baptism, baptism by water.[2] The candidate had first to make confession and spend some time in self-expurgation and continual prayer. Then St John's Gospel was placed on his head and the Holy Ghost was invoked and the Pater Noster repeated. After this first baptism further time was set aside for living more soberly, praying more purely and learning more of the faith. When men and women could testify that this had been done, then the candidate was brought forward and stood facing towards the East and again the Gospel was put on his head; and men and women took his hands and sang a hymn of thanksgiving. Thenceforward he ranked among the Elect.[3]

The claims of the Elect distressed Zigabenus. They declared that each of them deserved the title of the Mother of God, for in each of them the Holy Spirit resided and each therefore gave birth to the Word. The Virgin Mary was no better than any of the rest.[4] Also, when an Elect apparently died, he did not really die but changed in sleep, easily putting off the mantle of the flesh and putting on the stole of Christ, and took his place amongst the angels, his earthly body crumbling into dust.[5] The Elect boasted, too, that they had seen God, not merely in dreams; God the Father was an old man with a beard, the Son a youth just grown up and the Holy Ghost a beardless boy.[6] They dressed like monks and they fasted till the ninth hour on Mondays, Wednesdays and Fridays; but, remarked Zigabenus, they ate like elephants if they were invited out.[7] Such dissimulation was, indeed, their practice. They maintained that Our Lord bade them save themselves by what means they could, by art or by deceit.[8]

---

[1] *Panoplia*, § 26, col. 1320.   [2] *Ibid.* § 16, col. 1312.
[3] *Ibid.* § 26, col. 1320.   [4] *Ibid.* § 22, col. 1317.
[5] *Ibid.* § 22a, col. 1317.   [6] *Ibid.* § 23, col. 1320.
[7] *Ibid.* §§ 24, 25, col. 1320. It is not absolutely clear whether Zigabenus means that only the Elect or all the heretics kept these fasts.
[8] *Ibid.* § 21, col. 1316. Their justification was probably the text "Render unto Caesar...".

The only prayer that they permitted was the Pater Noster. This they said on seven occasions every day and five occasions every night. On each occasion they would repeat it as many as ten times, with genuflexions.[1]

Zigabenus ended his description by a quotation of various Biblical texts used by the Bogomils, showing how they perverted them and allegorized their meaning to attack the Orthodox. For example when we read[2] that Christ left Nazareth for Capernaum, Nazareth is interpreted as the Orthodox Church, Capernaum as the heretics themselves: or, to "cast pearls before swine" was taken to mean to cast secret truths before the Orthodox.[3] And so they went on, even falsifying texts. It was, said Zigabenus, a lengthy, stupid and useless task to try to argue with them.[4]

The one great difference to be noticed between the accounts of Cosmas and Zigabenus is that to the former the Bogomils are merely Dualist, to the latter they are Monarchian. This seems to show that Bogomil himself taught a Paulician dualism, and that the Dragovitsan school represented the original views of the sect, whereas the Monarchianism of the official Bogomil or "Bulgarian" church was an eleventh-century innovation, due to the connection with Byzantine Messalianism.

No other Greek source described the Bogomils so fully. The Synodicon of 1143 merely echoed Zigabenus. It anathematized them on five counts:[5] because they did not recognize the Trinity, calling the Word an angel, not equal with the Father, and saying that it was only an angel that was incarnated and adopted;[6] because they declared the Creator to be the Prince of Evil; because, like the Messalians, they described Baptism and the Eucharist as valueless; because they would not adore the Cross, calling it the weapon of Satan,[7] and because they would not adore icons, calling them idols. The treatises of the Patriarch Germanus II of Constantinople and the

---

[1] *Panoplia*, § 19, col. 1313.
[2] Matthew iv, 13.   [3] *Panoplia*, § 44, col. 1328.
[4] *Ibid.* § 27, col. 1321.   [5] See above, p. 71, n. 3.
[6] The Greek word employed is ἐπείσακτος. This doctrine is not the Adoptionism of Paul of Samosata, where it is a man, not an angel, that is adopted.
[7] The Greek phrase for Satan is ἀντικείμενος ἄρχων.

monk Euthymius attack them along the accepted lines, and contribute no new theological evidence.[1] Of the Byzantine historians, Anna Comnena referred her readers to Zigabenus's work. She herself, like Zigabenus, considered the Bogomil faith to be a compound of Paulicianism and Messalianism; and she would like, she said, to give a complete account of the heresy, but being a woman and a Princess she could not so far defile herself. Indeed she implied that the Bogomils indulged in practices much more horrible than anything that Zigabenus described. This impression may merely be due to her much advertised modesty; but it is possible that she actually possessed more details of their rites than Zigabenus knew of, and there was something about them that genuinely shocked her. Her only useful contribution to our knowledge is that Basil the Bogomil took about with him twelve "apostles", as well as a number of disreputable female followers.[2]

Anna's fellow-historians, such as Zonaras or Cinnamus, though they mention the Bogomils, have no additional information about the Bogomil creed. Nor do the later Bulgarian accounts give further enlightenment. The Council of Tirnovo of 1211, which condemned Bogomil doctrines along with those of other sects, mentions no beliefs that were not already described by Cosmas or Zigabenus.[3] St Hilarion, Bishop of Moglen, who died in 1164, found in his Macedonian diocese large numbers of Paulician and Bogomil heretics with whom he held many triumphant disputations. But his arguments, as presented by his fourteenth-century biographer the Patriarch Euthymius of Bulgaria, seem to have been those regularly used against the Dualists.[4] Nor are the homilies of the monk Athanasius of Jerusalem written later in the twelfth century more helpful. One is addressed to a certain Pank who apparently read forbidden Bogomil literature; but what poison he derived from it is unspecified.[5]

---

[1] Ficker, *Die Phundagiagiten*, gives the texts. He discusses the name on pp. 192 ff.
[2] Anna Comnena, xv, viii, ix (Dawes, pp. 412–15).
[3] See below, p. 95.
[4] Kalužniacki, *Werke des Patriarchen von Bulgarien Euthymius*, pp. 33 ff.
[5] Given in Pypin, *False and Rejected Books* (in Russian) and edited by Leonid in the *Moscow Diocesan Reports*, no. 3.

A little addition to our information can be extracted from Western writers. The Italian ex-heretic, Rainier Sacchoni, writing about the year 1230, declares that the Bulgarian church had been Dualist but now was Monarchian, thus confirming the impression to be derived from a comparison of the accounts of Cosmas and Zigabenus. He adds that some of the Bulgarian heretics believed Mary to have been a real woman and Christ really to have taken flesh from her and been crucified.[1] But a little later he says that the Italian heretic bishop Nazarius, who had been educated in Bulgaria, told him that he learnt there from the bishop and the Elder Son of the Bulgarian church that the Virgin was an angel.[2] Another Italian writer, Moneta, confirms this latter view. The Slavs declare, he said, that God the Father sent three angels into the world, Mary, Christ and John the Evangelist.[3] From this we may deduce that the Mariology of the Bogomils was very vague, as it was later amongst the Cathars. The line drawn between angels or eons and the Elect was somewhat indistinct and it was hard to decide on which side of it Mary was placed. Sacchoni's evidence is further valuable because it gives us the only known details of the organization of the Bulgarian heretic church. From it we can tell that it had a bishop, like the Bosnian heretic church, and the bishop had an Elder Son and presumably, therefore, a Younger Son, like the heretic bishops of the West.[4] This was probably a later development.

The only evidence that the Bogomils themselves supply is in their apocryphal literature. Doctrinally it is not very clear-cut evidence but it carries certain important implications. By the time of Athanasius of Jerusalem the Bogomils were known to be reading works by a certain priest Jeremiah. "If you have read", said Athanasius to the wavering Pank, "the homily of the priest Jeremiah, the one on the Holy Wood and the Holy Trinity, of which you used to talk, then you have read lying fables."[5] The Orthodox Church

---

[1] Sacchoni, *Summa de Catharis et Leonistis*, in Martène et Durand, *Thesaurus Novum Anecdotum*, vol. v, p. 767.
[2] *Ibid.* pp. 1773–4.
[3] Moneta, *Summa contra Kataros et Valdenses*, bk. III, § 2, pp. 226 ff.
[4] See below, pp. 161–2.
[5] Leonid, *op. cit.* For Athanasius's further remarks, see below, p. 92.

was repeatedly worried by the number of apocryphal books in circulation. For the welfare of the Slavs an Index, called "Of True and False Books", was published by the Russian Church. The oldest text of it that survives is found in a Nomocanon of the fourteenth century, but the list probably was compiled before that time and applied to other Slavonic Orthodox Churches, and was frequently re-edited and republished.[1] In a late sixteenth-century edition we read that "The founders of heretic books in the Bulgar land were Priest Jeremiah and Priest Bogomil and Sidor Friazin (and Jacob Tsentsal[2]), but Fryazin and a multitude of other names are recorded in the great Manakanun".[3] An edition of 1608 identifies Jeremiah with Bogomil;[4] and the identification has been accepted by most historians.[5] It is certainly possible that Bogomil adopted a new name on his initiation; it is certainly strange that if Jeremiah was contemporary with but different from Bogomil, Cosmas should never have mentioned him. But there is no need to regard the two as being exactly contemporary. More probably Bogomil's teaching was purely oral, while Jeremiah a little later enriched the heresy with a literature, and in so doing altered its theology.

The part that Jeremiah played becomes clear when we examine the writings attributed to him. In the Index he is condemned as the author of works on the following subjects: *The Wood of the Cross; How Christ became a Priest; The Holy Trinity; How Christ ploughed with the plough; How Christ called Probus His Friend; The Questions of Jeremiah to the Mother of God; The Questions and Answers of how many particles became Adam; Falsehoods about Fever and Other Illnesses* (the

---

[1] Pypin and Spasowicz, *Histoire des Littératures Slaves* (trans. into French by Denis), pp. 116 ff. The Indices are given in Gorskii and Nevostruev, *List of Slavonic MSS. in the Synodical Library of Moscow* (in Russian). Ivanov gives the Fourteenth-Century Index in *Bogomil Books and Legends* (in Bulgarian), pp. 52–3.

[2] "Jacob Tsentsal" is Ivanov's emendation for obscure contractions in the text (коβцейцд^т) (Ivanov, *Bogomil Books and Legends* (in Bulgarian), p. 50).

[3] Gorskii and Nevostruev, *op. cit.* II, p. 641.

[4] *Ibid.*

[5] See above, p. 67, n. 3. Ivanov does not identify Bogomil with Jeremiah but believes them to be contemporary (Ivanov, *op. cit.* pp. 50 ff.).

Story of St Sisinnius and the daughters of Herod).[1] Athanasius had already mentioned the first and third of these; and a *Slovo Ieremieia* of the fourteenth century includes the same two with a work on *The Remembrance of Moses*.[2] In addition to those mentioned as being of Jeremiah's hand, the Indices denounce various other apocryphal books that were studied by the heretics.[3]

It is highly improbable that any of these works were original contributions on the part of Jeremiah and his followers. The story of *How Christ became a Priest* was well known to the Greeks long before his day. Suidas refers to it in his Lexicon.[4] The story of the *Wood of the Cross*, later to be one of the most famous of early medieval legends, first appears in the apocryphal *Gospel of Nicodemus*, a Greek work of Gnostic origin.[5] St Sisinnius had featured largely in semi-heretical writings since his reputed lifetime. He was supposed to have been a Parthian knight who became a friend and disciple of Mani. He then was converted to Christianity and supplied Bishop Archelaus with the information about Manichaean lore that enabled the bishop to defeat the heresiarch in argument. For this he was a popular saint to invoke against demons.[6] The other stories of Christ are to be found in the apocryphal gospels.[7] That about Adam is certainly a version of the legends of the Creation, which, with their insistence on Adam's creation out of the elements, date back to the pre-Christian Judaeo-Greek embellishment of Genesis known as the *Book of Jubilees*.[8] *The Remembrance of Moses* contains nothing original. Only the treatise on the Trinity is unidentifiable, from the vagueness

[1] Pypin and Spasowicz, *loc. cit.*: Gorskii and Nevostruev, *loc. cit.*
[2] Popov, *First Supplement to the List of MSS. belonging to A. Y. Khludov* (in Russian), pp. 31–44. The MS. comes from Novgorod.
[3] Gorskii and Nevostruev, *loc. cit.* Jeremiah possibly wrote a Probus legend (see Pypin and Spasowicz, *op. cit.* p. 115, n. 1).
[4] Suidas, *Lexicon*, under Ἰησοῦς. Vassiliev prints a Greek text with a discussion of the date in his *Anecdota Graeco-Byzantina*, pp. 58–72 and xxv–xxvii.
[5] See M. R. James, *The Apocryphal New Testament*, i, pp. 94 ff.
[6] See Perdrizet, *Negotium Perambulans in Tenebris*, pp. 15 ff.
[7] They are to be found in many forms in such collections as M. R. James, *The Apocryphal New Testament*.
[8] Or Leptogenesis. *The Book of Jubilees* has been fully edited by Charles.

of its title. It may therefore be an exposition thought out by Jeremiah himself.

Nor can we even be certain that the heretical elements shown in the Slavonic versions now extant of the apocryphal legends were due to Jeremiah, though he may have amplified them. *The Wood of the Cross* in itself was harmless enough to inspire later such pious writers as Godfrey of Viterbo and Calderón; but the Slavonic version begins with the ominously Bogomil sentence: "When God created the world, only He and Satanael were in existence...."[1] It is quite possible that here we have Jeremiah's own words. Jeremiah's function was in fact to adapt and if necessary to colour Greek popular legends of Gnostic origin, to suit his own heretical views and so to give a solid Gnostic, rather than Paulician, foundation to Pope Bogomil's oral teaching. His followers copied him, and thus a literature of Slavonic translations arose, with a strong heretic tinge.[2]

But it would not be accurate to call this literature a Bogomil literature. To judge from extant manuscripts, it flourished most richly in Russia, a country into which the Bogomil heresy never penetrated. It is possible that in the Balkan lands zealous inquisitors destroyed any doubtful manuscripts with a thorough success, whereas in Russia the absence of such heresy made the authorities less severe, till at last, centuries later, the wealth of doubtful apocryphas made an Index necessary. Even so, many of the works permitted by the Church show Bogomil tendencies. For instance in the Slavonic version of Josephus, in the chapters already interpolated by the early Christians, the locusts of John the Baptist's diet are altered to more vegetarian dishes, cane and roots and wood shavings;[3] for the Bogomil adept could not touch flesh. Or in a version of the *Apocalypse of Baruch* the forbidden tree, a tree of lasting evil, is the vine; for the Bogomil adept could not touch wine.[4] The versions of

[1] Text given in Veselovsky, *Investigations* (in Russian), x, pp. 367 ff. This beginning seems to be Dualist, rather than Monarchian like most Bogomil legends.
[2] Bonwetsch in Harnack, *Altchristliche Literatur*, vol. I, p. 902, gives the names of forty-five Slavonic apocryphal stories.
[3] See Grégoire's article on John the Baptist's diet in *Byzantion*, vol. v, pp. 109 ff.
[4] In the Serbian version, given in Ivanov, *Bogomil Books*, p. 196.

the Slavonic *Book of Enoch* show sometimes seven, sometimes ten heavens, following the patterns of the Gnostics.[1] The *Palea*, the great popular Old Testament of medieval Russia, is the most striking illustration of this influence.[2] It retells the narrative given in Genesis and Exodus, with a brief summary of events till the time of David, but it retells it with a luxuriant embroidery of apocryphal legend in which all the old Judeo-Gnostic and Dualist-Gnostic stories reappear.[3] Moreover it is arranged in such a way as to show that every event in the New Testament was foreshadowed in the Old Testament. Now the Bogomils particularly disapproved of the Pentateuch, which they found inconsistent with Christian doctrine. The *Palea* seems to be a deliberate attempt to provide an Old Testament which would not be liable to that objection. It is, with the same object, punctuated throughout with abusive evocations of the Jews—"I ask you, O Jew", or "O sinful Jews." Like the individual legends it was either the translation of a Greek version or was compiled from various Greek versions; and it was almost certainly disseminated at first by Bogomil sympathizers, but eventually circulated on its own merits as a story-book. Theologically, however, it does not reproduce strict Bogomil truths. To the Bogomils Satanael was the elder son of God.[4] In the *Palea* he is merely the head of the fourth group of angels.[5] It is possible that the Bogomils, despite their taste for details, were not particular about the origin of Satan, the origin of evil, that question over which their Gnostic predecessors worried so minutely. Certainly their two schools, Monarchian and Dualist, seem with rare exceptions to have worked in conscious harmony.

The only extant apocryphal book which we know positively that the Bogomils used exists in a Latin translation. The Inquisitors in Southern France found a heretical work, which they copied out, writing on the manuscript: "This is the Secret Book of the Heretics

[1] See the edition by Charles.
[2] For the *Palea* see Popov, *The Book of Heaven and Earth* (*The Palea*) (in Russian): Speranski, *The Historical Palea* (in Serbian): Vassiliev, *Anecdota Graeco-Byzantina*, pp. 188–292. See also Gaster, *Greeko-Slavonic Literature*, pp. 150ff.
[3] Even Pseudo-Areopagite material is used in the description of the hierarchy of angels.   [4] See above, p. 75.   [5] Vassiliev, *Anecdota*, p. 189.

of Concoresso, brought from Bulgaria by Nazarius, their bishop, full of errors."[1] This book is a dialogue between St John the Evangelist and Christ about the origin of the world. It includes all the usual stories of Satan's fall, of Enoch's rise, of the Wood of the Cross; and passages are almost identical with passages in the *Palea*, in the *Apocalypse of Baruch* and in the old Bulgar version of *The Wood of the Cross*;[2] and part of the text is a word for word translation of the Slavonic *Questions of John the Evangelist*.[3] But its theology is strictly Bogomil. Satan was next after God the Father before he fell (though Christ sat by God the Father's side). Mary was an angel sent down to earth, and Christ entered and left her through her ear. John the Baptist, who is Elijah, was also an angel. Man has holy spirit derived from the angels imprisoned in him. The whole book is a popular allegorized summary of Bogomil doctrine. But here again we cannot tell if this is an original Bogomil work or a translation from the Greek. Probably, to judge from its doctrine, it represents a compilation made by some Bogomil author or some Messalian author out of the apocryphal material at hand.

The evidence supplied by popular folklore still extant amongst the southern Slavs is similarly inconclusive. Most of their legends are frankly heretical and are dualist in their essentials.[4] It is therefore reasonable to assume that they are Bogomil in origin. But they display a remarkable diversity. In the legends of the Cosmogony sometimes God and Satan existed for all time as comrades, as

---

[1] "Hoc est secretum haereticorum de Concorezio, portatum de Bulgaria a Nazario suo episcopo, plenum erroribus"—added to the Carcassonne MS. of the book, published in Benoist, *Histoire des Albigeois et des Vaudois ou Barbets*, vol. I, pp. 283–96. Another almost identical but incomplete version, entitled "Joannis et Apostoli et Evangelistae Interrogatio arcana sancti regni coelorum de ordinatione mundi et de Principe et de Adam", exists at Vienna and is published in Döllinger, *Beiträge zur Sektengeschichte des Mittelalters*, II, pp. 85–92. Nazarius was a heresiarch known to Rainier Sacchoni, and had been educated in Bulgaria. (See below, p. 170.)

[2] Ivanov, *Bogomil Books and Legends* (in Bulgarian), pp. 68–71, gives parallel passages.

[3] Given in Tikhonravov, *Materials* (in Russian), vol. II, pp. 174–92.

[4] The fullest collection is given in Ivanov, *op. cit.* pp. 327 ff. The legends there come mostly from Bulgaria, Macedonia and Bessarabia.

brothers or as associates;[1] sometimes God created Satan from His shadow; sometimes Satan is a fallen angel.[2] The exact roles of God and Satan in the act of Creation differ from legend to legend.[3] Adam is usually God's creature but enters into Satan's power, sometimes because he has to work on the earth, which is Satan's, sometimes so as to obtain light which he cannot otherwise acquire after his expulsion from Paradise. Subsequent mortal men are the possessions of Satan up to the Redemption.[4] The person and achievements of Jesus are explained in many ways. It is impossible to say how far any of these stories represent genuine Bogomil beliefs. Occasionally there has been a clear invasion of pre-Christian folklore, as when the man created by Satan turns into a wolf, or when the bee whispers Satan's secrets to God.[5]

Probably the other divergencies are best explained as local variations inevitable when stories are carried down by oral tradition.

IV

All the doctrinal evidence about the Bogomils is perhaps a little inconclusive; and there are several points on which exactitude is impossible. But it is sufficient to enable us to guess at the sources of the heresy.[6]

The first obvious source is Paulicianism. Colonies of Paulicians had been settled on the Bulgarian frontier since the eighth century. Already in the ninth century they were indulging in missionary enterprise. In the tenth century their colonies were reinforced. If at

---

[1] Ivanov, *op. cit.* pp. 329, 333, 343, 348.   [2] Ivanov, *op. cit.* pp. 337–8, 346.
[3] Ivanov, *op. cit.* pp. 329–36—three similar but not identical legends.
[4] Ivanov, *op. cit.* pp. 338–9, 350, 351–2.   [5] Ivanov, *op. cit.* pp. 335, 347, 348, 349.
[6] The fullest modern account of Bogomil doctrines is given in Puech and Vaillant, *Le Traité contre les Bogomiles de Cosmas le Prêtre*, Paris, 1945, which contains a translation of the Discourse of Cosmas, with a careful commentary. I have seen this book too late to make full use of it. I am in the main in agreement with the authors' findings, though I cannot accept their refusal to allow Messalianism any part in the development of Bogomilstvo, in view of the clear evidence provided by the Greek sources. Incidentally they produce strong arguments for dating the publication of Cosmas's work in 972 (*op. cit.* pp. 19–24).

about this time another Dualist heresy came into existence just across
the frontier, it is reasonable to ascribe its birth largely if not wholly
to Paulician influence.

This was the opinion of the contemporary Patriarch of Constantinople, Theophylact. Moreover, in the brief outline of tenth-
century Bogomil doctrines given by Cosmas, there is nothing that
might not equally, as far as we know, be applied to Paulician
doctrines. The rejection of the Old Testament, the disrespect paid
to the Virgin and the Saints, the existence of a class of Initiates,
might all, quite apart from the basic dualism, have been bodily
copied from Paulician teachings. The differences between Paulicianism and early Bogomilstvo were in language and in habits. The
former was natural and unimportant at first; the latter was due to
the differing social conditions. The Paulicians had long been a
fighting community, keeping close-knit for protection. It was their
military prowess that had enabled them at all to survive; and in
Europe they seem to have preserved the traditions of life that had
made them formidable in Asia. Thus they did not fully follow out
the implications of their doctrine of the wickedness of matter. They
had sufficient truck with matter to use material things in self-defence.
The Bogomils were differently placed. They were not a centralized
body but were scattered in villages over a wide empire. They
therefore found it a more useful weapon to adopt a practice fully
consistent with their doctrines, that of passive resistance. Or again,
the Paulicians were nationalists, Armenians fighting against the
Orthodox cosmopolitans of Byzantium; the Bogomils might be
nationalists in origin, Slav peasants struggling against Bulgar or
Greco-Bulgar landowners, but their struggle was visibly one of
class, peasant against landowner, not Slav against Bulgar; and in
class-warfare the strike rather than active hostility is the weaker
side's better policy.

Thus it is likely that Bogomil himself learnt his heresy from the
Paulicians and adapted it and organized it to suit the social conditions
of his time. But very soon new elements crept in. The Bogomils
somehow came into contact with Gnostic elements within the
Byzantine Empire. A Bogomil literature in Slavonic sprang up,

based on the apocryphal books of the Gnostics and associated with the name of a priest Jeremiah. At the same time Gnostic traditions modified the crude dualism of Bogomil theology. Certain branches of the Bogomil church, coming from districts near to the Paulician settlements, remained faithful to the uncompromising "Manichaean" Dualism of the Paulicians. This was the school of Dragovitsa, a school which even preserved the Paulician name.[1] But the bulk of the Bogomil church adopted a Gnostic conception of the origin of evil. By the end of the eleventh century the main body of the Bogomils was definitely Gnostic in its ideas.

Whence did this Gnosticism come? It was not from the Paulicians, though they themselves were partly Gnostic in origin. The Paulicians seem to have used practically no literature beyond the Bible and the commentaries of Sergius. The *Key of Truth*, the only extant book that they may possibly have possessed, was certainly not of their authorship. They ignored the Gnostic legends. It is remarkable how few apocryphal books of any sort have survived in the Armenian language.[2] The simplicity of their theology is testimony to their dependence on oral tradition backed only by the Bible. The main Gnostic stream flowed in a different channel.

To Zigabenus and to Anna Comnena the answer was clear. The Bogomils, they said, were derived from a blending of the Paulicians with the Messalians or Euchites.[3] Zigabenus's account of Bogomil theology bears out his contention. He cites as being peculiarly Messalian the Bogomil beliefs that a demon dwelt in every man and that this demon must be placated.[4] He might have added the claim

[1] See below, p. 122.
[2] The few Armenian apocryphal books that exist, as collected in the Թանգարան Հին և Նոր Նախնեաց (The Treasury of Old and New Stories), seem to me to have no Gnostic affinities. Even the legends about Adam (nos. 11 and 12 in the collection) are perfectly orthodox in doctrine.
[3] Zigabenus, *Panoplia*, bk. 27, preface, col. 1289: Anna Comnena, xv, viii (Dawes, p. 412). For the Messalians, see above, pp. 21–5. Cedrenus (I, pp. 514, 547) when talking of the origin of the Messalians says that they are also called Euchites, Enthusiasts or Bogomils. The *Synodicon* of Tsar Boril, published in Bulgaria in 1211, repeats the charge, calling the heresy a blend of Manichaeanism and Messalianism. See below, p. 95, n. 1.
[4] *Panoplia, ibid.* § 13, col. 1309: § 20, col. 1313.

that initiates could see God Himself.[1] Indeed the initiation practices of the Bogomils of his time were Messalian rather than Paulician. The fundamental article of faith that separated the "Bulgarian" from the Dragovitsan heretics, the doctrine that Satan before he fell was the elder son of God, was a Messalian doctrine.[2] The whole description of the heresy that Zigabenus gives is one of a late Gnostic heresy that might be that of the Messalians themselves. It is even rather difficult to see where any Paulicianism came in. Probably Zigabenus, who knew the Paulicians quite well as a separate heresy, realized that the Paulician contribution was in the foundation of the movement. It is doubtful if he was informed of the Dragovitsan church.

Zigabenus and Anna were trained theologians. There is no reason to doubt their assertion, especially as we know that there were Messalian churches flourishing in their time.[3] The Messalians re-emerge from obscurity in the middle of the eleventh century, when Psellus treats of them as being extant but a little recondite and very sinister. His treatise on Demonology takes the form of a dialogue between two friends, one of whom has visited a Euchite (Messalian) community and describes it to inform the other of its devilish practices.[4] But his book is not a serious attempt to expound Messalian doctrines. Rather, the Messalians serve as a peg on which Psellus can hang his own views on demonology. A few decades later, under Alexius Comnenus, a certain Blachernites popularized a form of the heresy in Constantinople itself.[5] These Messalians were almost certainly the spiritual descendants of the Messalians of the fourth century. The accusation of magic brought against them by Psellus implies that they kept a secret Tradition and probably had secret books. These books may be assumed to have been heterodox Gnostic legends.

When exactly the Bulgarian heretics came into contact with the Messalians we cannot tell. The main Messalian communities were in

---

[1] *Panoplia, ibid.* § 23, col. 1320.
[2] Psellus, *De Daemonum operatione* (M.P.G. vol. CXXII, coll. 824–5), says that the Manichaeans (by whom the Paulicians were usually meant) believed in two First Principles, but the Messalians in three—the Father and two Sons. See above, pp. 74–5.
[3] See above, p. 70.   [4] Psellus, *op. cit., passim.*
[5] See above, p. 70 and note 1.

Thrace. Psellus in the dialogue on Demonology gives the name of Thrax, the Thracian, to the disputant who describes the Messalians.[1] From Thrace, Messalian doctrines could easily infect the Paulicianized Bulgarians. The Patriarch Germanus describes Thrace as having been the centre of Bogomilism in the eleventh century. It was the home of the arch-heretic John Tzurillas.[2] Probably the contact took place early in Bogomil history; and the man that effected it was the Bogomil priest, Jeremiah, who was the first to translate Messalian-Gnostic books into the Slavonic. Thus Jeremiah was, with Bogomil, co-founder of the Bogomils. Indeed, with the irony of history, Bogomil founded the Dragovitsan church, while the later Bogomil church was founded by Jeremiah. It was therefore an easy error to make to identify the two heresiarchs as one.

Once the Bogomils had acquired a taste for apocryphal stories, there were many ways of adding to their store. Such legends were eagerly retailed at Byzantium. Orthodox chroniclers, not only the popular writers such as Joel or Manasses, but reputable historians like Cedrenus and Zonaras, made use of them in their world histories. Into some of them Gnosticizing scribes would instil little drops of heterodoxy; others, for all their wide circulation, were frankly heretical. They could be used to supplement Messalian teaching or to give precision where it was vague. For instance, while we do not know the Messalian view about the relations of the Persons in the Trinity, the Bogomil doctrine, as described by Zigabenus, is exactly like that given in the *Ascension of Isaiah*, a Gnostic work that dates probably from the late first century A.D. The influence was mutual. Bogomil taste certainly inserted Gnostic emendations into innocent apocryphas, but the Bogomils themselves largely owed their theology

[1] Psellus, *ibid.*, *passim*. He describes (coll. 853–7) the magical powers of a Messalian from Elasone. I have not been able to identify where Elasone is. But the Initiation ceremony that he gives there is probably not intended to represent the ordinary Messalian ceremony but is, rather, a special act of devil-worship.

[2] Ficker, *Die Phundagiagiten*, p. 249. Ficker considers that the words "ἐν τοῖς τῶν Θρακῶν μέρεσιν" mean the Thracesian Theme in Asia Minor. That seems to me to introduce a quite unnecessary complication. The word Thrace was still used in literary circles in its old geographical sense; and Psellus was particularly accurate in his classicism.

to these books that medieval Byzantium had inherited from the Christians of the first few centuries, when Christian doctrine was still imperfectly circumscribed and Gnostic tendencies were rife.

Certain of the orthodox gave yet another source for the heresy. Athanasius of Jerusalem, in his homily to Pank, accuses him if he has read Jeremiah's works of following a Latin heresy.[1] The Russian Index in the Synodical Library at Moscow condemns along with Jeremiah and Bogomil a certain "Sidor Fryazin"; and from the Index we learn that Jeremiah is now in the Underworld in the circle of "Verziul".[2] It is possible that by "Sidor Fryazin" we should understand "Sidor the Frank". It is almost certain that for "Verziul" we should read "Virgil". The poet had already become the arch-magician of Western medieval lore, and the implication must be that Jeremiah learnt his heresy from magicians of the West.

All this was probably propaganda, to save the good name of Eastern Christendom. When Athanasius wrote, the Bogomils were already linked up with the heretics of the West; and he therefore sought to discredit Bogomil doctrines by denouncing them as Western. The theologians of the Russian Church doubtless had similar motives. They would remove from the Eastern congregations the stigma of founding the heresy and fasten it on to the hated Latins.[3]

Their loyalty was in vain. Zigabenus and Anna Comnena were closer to the truth. The Bogomil heresy was born amidst peasants

---

[1] See above, p. 81, n. 5.

[2] Gorskii and Nevostruev, *op. cit.* vol. II, p. 641.

[3] Till recently it was held that Dualist tendencies were inherent in the Slavs and that the Bogomils thus derived their basic doctrine from native sources (Gieseler, *Über den Dualismus der Slaven* (*Theol. Studien u. Kritiken*, vol. II), pp. 357 ff.: Schmidt, *Histoire des Cathares*, vol. II, pp. 271 ff.: Rački, *Bogomili i Paterini* (Rad. vol. X), p. 260, and others). This argument was based on Helmold of Lübeck's description of the Slavs in Germany in the twelfth century. He says that they worshipped a good God and a bad God, calling the latter *Zcernebog*, the Black God. (Helmold, bk. I, chap. 52—p. 125 in Bangert's edition.) Jireček doubted this, but it was left to Mochulski to prove, in his work *On the Supposed Dualism in Slav Mythology* (in Russian, Warsaw, 1889), that there is no trace of Dualism in pre-Christian Slav religion, as far as the Russian and Balkan Slavs are concerned; Helmold's words apply only to a local branch of the Slavs and at an irrelevant date. It is easier to assume that Helmold's Slavs were infected with Bogomilism.

whose physical misery made them conscious of the wickedness of things. The Christianity imposed upon them by their masters seemed alien and without comfort. The creed of the Paulicians, settled near by, was fitter; it taught a simple Dualism and explained the misery of the world. An unknown priest called Bogomil adapted it for the Slavs, damping its militarism into a more formidable passive resistance. But as time went on the new faith developed; the heretics came into touch with the Messalians, who gave them access to all the wealth of Orientalized Gnostic tradition. And thus a new Christianity was founded, based on early Christian legend and Eastern Dualism, and answering to the needs of the medieval peasantry, to become very soon one of the great religions of Europe.

CHAPTER V

The Patarenes

I

HERESIES, like civilization itself, are apt to spread Westward from the East. The Gnostic seeds were to flower most richly not in Armenia nor in Bulgaria but in the Westernmost country of the Balkan peninsula and in Latin countries more Western still. By the end of the twelfth century the greatest centres of Bogomil activity were in Bosnia, in Lombardy and in France.

Nevertheless the heresy remained strong in its original birthplace; and the Balkan peninsula was regarded, even by the Western heretics, as its home. During the twelfth century the churches of Constantinople and Bulgaria still ranked as the chief heretic congregations. It was there that Bogomil doctrine had been fully evolved. Bulgaria was Bogomil's country; and Constantinople was still the greatest city of the Christian world The career of Nicetas, self-styled bishop of the heretics of Constantinople, in France in 1167 shows the respect that Constantinople still commanded. But it is doubtful if there was in fact a strong heretical body resident there. The city was well policed and the Emperors dangerously interested in theology. If there had been much heresy there would have been heresy-hunts, and some record would almost certainly have survived.

With the political decline of Constantinople the prestige of its heretical church faded. The centre of gravity of the heresy was moving westward, while after the Fourth Crusade the city was in full decay. In 1230 the Bogomils still formed a flourishing congregation in the Capital, side by side with a small Latin heretical church which was introduced almost certainly after the Latin conquest of 1204.[1] But that is the last information that we possess of the heresy in Constantinople. Probably it had been a passing fashion and soon faded out under the dominion of the Latin Emperors, when religious dissidents found a better cry in attacking the alien tyranny of the

---

[1] Rainier Sacchoni, *Summa*, in Martène et Durand, *Thesaurus*, vol. v, p. 1767.

Church of Rome. After the restoration of the Greek Empire, no more is known of the Bogomils of Constantinople.

In Bulgaria, Bogomil's own home, his heresy had a longer and more turbulent history. In 1186 the Asen brothers freed their country from the Imperial yoke and set up its Second Empire. It seems likely that this nationalist resurgence had the full support of the Bogomils. The first Asens showed them tolerance. But the dynasty was too warlike to approve of their passive nationalism. Moreover it liked to flirt with Rome; and Rome recommended strong measures against heresy. It was not long before the government took action.

On 11 February 1211 a Council of the Bulgarian church, summoned by the Tsar, Boril, opened its sessions at Tirnovo. Its main work was to condemn the Bogomils and their teaching. The various heretic doctrines were in turn denounced and their holders anathematized, some by name. All heretics were to be arrested. Those that were incorrigible were to be exiled, the rest to suffer varying terms of imprisonment.[1]

This Council was probably inspired by the presence in Bulgaria a few months previously of a Cardinal-legate from Pope Innocent III.[2] The foreign backing to it can only have made the ensuing persecution the more unsuccessful. Boril's fall a few years later, in 1216, may have been largely helped by the hostility of the Bogomils, who preferred his rival John Asen.[3] John Asen II, as King, recognized the strength of the sect. The heretics, so Pope Gregory IX complained to the King of Hungary, enjoyed perfect toleration and protection in Bulgaria.[4] But the Bulgarian King was rewarded; the greatness of Bulgaria under his rule was undoubtedly helped by this policy.

Meanwhile in Macedonia, Bogomil congregations still flourished, to the distress of the Patriarchs of Ochrida. Demetrius Chomatianus, Patriarch from 1217 to 1234, wrote anxiously of them in his letters.[5]

[1] *Sinodik of Tsar Boril*, ed. Popruzhenko (Sofia, 1928), *passim*, esp. pp. 42 ff.
[2] See Drinov, *Historical Survey* (in Bulgarian), p. 83.
[3] Jireček, *op. cit.* pp. 244 ff., 258.   [4] Theiner, *Monumenta Hungarica*, I, 160.
[5] Ed. by Pitra, *Analecta*, vol. VII, pp. 261, 302, 325, 390, 438. 'Messalianism', i.e. Bogomilism, existed still in Macedonia in the early XIVth century, when Palamas sojourned there. (Philotheus of Constantinople, in *M.P.G.* vol. CLI, col. 562.) But this clearly was not the simple Bogomilism of earlier days.

For a century after John Asen II's reign we hear little of the Bogomils. When Rainier Sacchoni described the state of the various heretic communities in about 1230, the Bulgarian church was still among the most important.[1] The Cardinal Conrad, writing in 1223, believed that in Bulgaria there lived the Pope of all the heretics. He was mistaken, for the heretics had no supreme Pontiff; but his opinion shows the high prestige of Bulgaria amongst their sects. But the Kingdom of Bulgaria was declining. Perhaps the passive doctrines of the Bogomils helped in the decline, but the Bogomils themselves were entering into decay. When next they became prominent, in the mid-fourteenth century, they no longer enjoyed the monopoly of heresy. The Hesychast controversy was raging and providing an outlet for would-be dissidents. Fortified by a Jewish Tsaritsa Judaizing sects were appearing in the country. Even amongst the Bogomils themselves, extremists were breaking off from the main body. The development of these sects was due to the increased influence of the heretical traditions of Byzantium.

In the early fourteenth century the Bogomils had achieved a sensational triumph. They penetrated to the Holy Mountain of Athos itself. There was a pious lady in Thessalonica called Irene, who ran some sort of a hostel where Athonite monks would stay when visiting the city. She embraced the heresy; and thanks to her missionary skill her visitors carried it back with them to the Mountain. The authorities took firm action against it, and in the course of its suppression they banished its leading devotees, two monks called Lazarus and Cyril, surnamed the Barefooted. The exiles came to Tirnovo, the Bulgarian capital, and there founded their own sects. Lazarus inclined towards nudism, in a desire to return to the happy days before the Fall; he also preached that men should be castrated so that no further material bodies should be brought into the world. Cyril seems to have been less exacting. He attacked the cult of icons and the Cross, like any good Bogomil; he claimed to have visions, and he denounced marriage. Married couples, he considered, should live apart from each other. But though his doctrines could be claimed as purely Bogomil, he was apparently disconnected from

[1] See below, pp. 162, 170.

the old-established Bogomil church. At the same time a third sect was arising, led by an itinerant preacher called Theodosius. He too seems to have favoured nudism, but the essence of his message was to encourage men to sin that the grace of repentance might be given them. His followers therefore indulged in orgiastic excess.

These heresiarchs taught nothing new. Such doctrines were all in the old Gnostic tradition and had been preached and practised before. But just as the more extreme Ophites and the Carpocratians had by their doctrines and habits brought discredit on the early Christians, so these exaggerated Bogomils must have weakened and distressed the main Bogomil church and given a handle to its enemies. For some time past it seems that no Bulgarian king had ventured to persecute the Bogomils. But now they were weak enough to be repressed with impunity. Two great Councils of the Bulgarian Church were held at Tirnovo, one in 1350 and the other a few years later, probably in 1355. At both of these Bogomilstvo and its daughter-sects were anathematized, their wilful adherents being threatened with exile, branding and imprisonment; and at the former council the heresiarchs Cyril and Lazarus were tried and found guilty. Cyril repented and abjured his errors. Lazarus and his leading disciple Stephen remained obdurate. They were therefore condemned by the Tsar, in conformity with the laws of the Church, to be branded on the face and banished from the kingdom.[1]

In the early fifteenth century there were still Bogomils in Macedonia. The Metropolitan Symeon of Thessalonica noted their presence there. He called them Kudugers, probably from the name of the village which was their centre. But the fact that they were given so local a name shows that they were only a small community now.[2] The stern measures of the authorities had been effective. We hear nothing more of the Bogomils of Bulgaria. The country had worse, more sensational problems to face. The Ottoman Turks had crossed into Europe first in 1308. In 1356 they came there to settle

---

[1] Callistus, Patriarch, *Life of Theodosius of Tirnovo* (in Slavonic), ed. Zlatarsky, § 14, pp. 19–20, § 15, p. 22.
[2] Symeon, Archbishop of Thessalonica, *On All the Heresies*, chap. 1, ed. Skatharos, pp. 17–20.

and to conquer. Next year Adrianople fell into their hands, and they reached the Bulgarian frontier. In 1361 they intervened in the dynastic quarrels of the Bulgarians. The Bulgarians in vain allied themselves with the Serbs. During the next few years the allies fought a losing war; and finally, after the Serbian rout on the Maritsa in 1371, Bulgaria passed under Turkish domination. The last Tsar of Tirnovo died in 1395, two years after the capture of his capital. His brother, the Tsar of Vidin, followed him some three years later; and Bulgarian independence was ended for five centuries.

During these tribulations the Bogomils faded away. It was the Orthodox Church that took the lead in preserving Bulgar nationalism against its new masters There was no role for the Bogomils to play. In obscurity Bogomil's creed vanished from the country of his birth, leaving its trace only in the legends and fairy stories which the Bulgarian peasant told and still tells to his children.[1]

II

To what extent the Bogomils spread into the countries north of Bulgaria it is difficult to tell. Their doctrines show themselves now and then in both Roumanian and Russian folk-lore. In Russia, indeed, Bogomil literature circulated in large quantities; and the *Palea*, the great bible of medieval Russia, shows considerable Bogomil influence. But of an actual Bogomil sect there is no trace. The Pneumatic sects of more recent Russian history, such as the Dukhobors or the Molokany, cannot be traced so far back into the past. Both these churches in many ways resemble the Bogomils. The Dukhobors have much the same Dualist beliefs on a Monarchian foundation, and in consequence similarly despise matter; but their Christology is Adoptionist. The Molokany, who though sternly puritan are less dualist, hold a Docetist view of Christ similar to the Bogomils'; and their "Bishops" have two coadjutors, just as the Cathar Bishop had his two "sons". But the Molokany date the origin of their church in the sixteenth century; and it is doubtful if the Dukhobor church is as old. There was probably no continuous heretic church in Russia,

[1] For these legends see above, p. 86.

but when circumstances brought about the birth of heresy, many of the heresiarchs made use of the Bogomil traditions embodied in the *Palea* and other old Slavonic sacred books.[1]

Though thus the Northern Slavs may have preserved the Bogomil tradition longer than many of their brothers, the Bogomil movement spread far more vehemently towards the West. Serbia, Bulgaria's neighbour in the West, was soon reached by Bogomil missionaries. Of their earlier successes we know nothing; but by the latter half of the twelfth century there was a sufficient number of Bogomils in the country for the Grand Zhupan, Stephen Nemanya, himself for political as well as religious reasons a champion of the Eastern Orthodox Church, to find it necessary to take stern action. Some time towards the end of the century, encouraged by his revered son, St Sava, he held a great council to condemn their teachings. The heresy was forbidden and stern measures, probably the regular penalties of branding and exile, were to be taken against its adherents. But the Serbians are a warlike race. Even their Bogomils rejected the policy of passive resistance that their doctrines enjoined, and, led by a number of the nobility, took to arms. Stephen replied with arms, and after a short campaign crushed out the heresy and drove its leaders into exile.[2]

Stephen's measures seem to have been successful. Probably the very bellicosity of the Serbians made them on the whole little susceptible to such a religion. Certainly it was not till the days of King Stephen Dushan, in the middle of the fourteenth century, that Bogomilstvo, under the name of the Babun doctrine,[3] is heard of again in Serbia. Dushan, in his great code of laws, put particular penalties on Bogomil or Babun heretics. A noble who preached

---

[1] For the Dukhobors and Molokany, see Conybeare, *Russian Dissenters*.

[2] *Lives of Saint Symeon and Saint Sava* (in Slavonic), ed. (in Serbian), Belgrade, 1860.

[3] "Babunska Vjera." Probably the name was given to the heretics because of a Bogomil colony on the River Babuna in Macedonia. It is usually used in fourteenth-century Serbian texts and in some Bosnian texts. There is no reason to suppose that the Babuni were either a different or a daughter-sect to the Bogomils; but the lack of organization amongst the Bogomils led frequently to the use of local names to describe them.

Bogomil doctrines was to be fined a hundred gold pieces, a commoner ten but was also to be flogged. Wilful heretics were, as usual, to be branded on the face and exiled. Anyone who protected or gave refuge to a heretic was to suffer the same punishment.[1] The need for these measures was due probably not so much to the rebirth of the heresy in Serbia proper as to the extension of Dushan's dominions, into Macedonia where it lingered still and into Bosnian territories, the centre at the moment of the heretics. The shrinking of the Serbian Empire after Dushan's death solved this particular problem for its monarchs. In their long tragic struggle against the Turks they had at any rate an Orthodox country behind them.

The same could not be said of their cousins across the Western frontier. There the Bogomil heresy reached its apogee.

III

Between Rascia, or Serbia proper, and the Adriatic lay the ancient kingdom of Dioclea or Zeta, the later Montenegro. The Diocleans temperamentally resembled the Serbians, whose political lead they usually followed; as with the Serbians, the Bogomil heresy made only spasmodic incursions into their land. But to the north-west of Dioclea was the land of Hum, Zachlumia or Chelma, which later, under the Dukes of St Sava, became known as The Duchy or, in a Germanized form, Herzegovina. And north of Hum was the great province of Bosnia.

It is unknown at what date Bogomil doctrines first entered Hum and Bosnia. They came through two distinct channels. In the thirteenth century the heretic church that embraced the Dalmatian and Istrian coast was known as the church of Drugucia or Drugunthia, and its centre was the town of Tragurium or Trau. Its doctrines were not Monarchian like the true Bogomils' but were fundamentally Dualist.[2] Clearly here there has been a confusion. The name Drugucia is a debased form of Dragovitsa, and the fact that the town of Tragurium was a heretic centre merely has added to the muddle.

[1] Stephen Dushan, *Code*, article 85 (ed. Novakovic, p. 67), article 10 (*ibid.* p. 14).
[2] Sacchoni, *Summa*, in Martène et Durand, *Thesaurus*, vol. v, p. 1767.

The truth almost certainly is that the missionaries to the Dalmatian coast-line came from amongst the Dualist Dragovitsans, possibly working from Macedonia, or perhaps by sea from Constantinople, which seems to have produced, in the middle of the twelfth century, a Dualist missionary school.[1] The second channel was by land from Bulgaria through Serbia. The Bosnian heretic church, called by the heretics the Church of Sclavonia, was in close touch with the Bulgarian church and shared its Monarchian principles.[2] The Churches of Drugucia and Sclavonia seem to have been on good terms with each other, despite their divergent views over Satan's origin. Indeed, with persecutors all round, they could not afford to be otherwise.

About the year 1150 the Emperor Manuel, displeased with King Radoslav of Dioclea, divided up his lands between princes of the old Serbian family of Zavida, and Stephen Nemanya secured the land of Hum. In 1168, with Manuel's favour, Stephen was raised to the Serbian throne, and Hum passed to his brother Miroslav. About the same time under Manuel's suzerainty a certain Kulin acquired the throne of Bosnia, to reign there as an independent Ban after Manuel's death in 1180.[3]

Miroslav married Kulin's sister, and the two brothers-in-law started on a policy that was to cause deep distress to the authorities of the Orthodox and the Catholic churches. Both rulers had a similar religious problem. Their subjects included both Catholic and Orthodox, the former originally converted from the towns of the Dalmatian coast, the latter from the Balkan hinterland. But till recently Bosnia and Hum had been fought over by the Kings of Hungary and Byzantine Emperors. The Catholic hierarchy supported the former, the Orthodox the latter; and though Byzantium was now sinking in a fast decline, its place as local Orthodox champion was amply filled by Stephen Nemanya's new Serbia. To a nationalist monarch either church was suspect. A support of the growing heresy seemed to Kulin the best solution of his troubles; and Miroslav, rather more half-heartedly, followed his example.

[1] See above, p. 72.   [2] Sacchoni, *ibid.*, *loc. cit.*
[3] See Klaić, *Geschichte Bosniens*, pp. 76 ff., 131 ff.

In 1180 Miroslav started on a feud with the Latin Archbishop Rainier of Spalato, the ecclesiastical superior of Hum. He refused to allow Rainier, whom he regarded as an agent of the Hungarian king, to consecrate a bishop for the town of Stagno in his dominions. Moreover he confiscated a large sum of money due to the Archbishop. Rainier complained to the Pope, Alexander III, who sent a nuncio, Theobald, to report on the matter. Theobald found Miroslav quite obdurate and in addition a patron of heretics. So he placed the prince under a ban. Miroslav remained unmoved, even when next year the Pope wrote to him in person. Furious, Alexander next wrote to King Bela III of Hungary, telling him as overlord of Hum (an overlordship that Miroslav did not recognize) forcibly to see that Miroslav performed his duty.[1] We do not know if Bela tried to carry out the Pope's behest. In any case Miroslav was unabashed. He was still flourishing and making commercial treaties with Ragusa in 1186 and 1190.[2]

But the Latin vengeance came in time. By March 1198 Prince Andrew of Hungary was enjoying the title of Prince of Dalmatia, Croatia and Hum.[3] By 1199 Miroslav was dead, and his wife living in exile at her brother's court in Bosnia.[4]

This court was now openly heretical. The growth of Hungarian power coinciding with the rise of Serbia confirmed Kulin in his Bogomil policy. The Bogomils, exiled by Stephen Nemanya, found a welcome in Bosnia, and Bogomil missionaries were given every encouragement. Kulin had moreover a grievance against the Papacy. In 1191 the bishopric of Bosnia was removed from the jurisdiction of the Archbishopric of Ragusa, a city with which he was on the best of terms owing to their mutual commercial interests, and given to the control of the see of Spalato, whose Archbishop at the time, Peter Ugrin, was a Magyar and an agent of the Hungarian king.[5] It seems that this wrong was righted by 1196,[6] but the incident

---

[1] Correspondence given in Kukuljević, *Codex Diplomaticus*, II, p. 121.
[2] *Ibid.* pp. 137, 157–9.
[3] *Ibid.* p. 191.   [4] See below, p. 103.
[5] Kukuljević, *Codex Diplomaticus*, II, pp. 147–8, 162.
[6] *Ibid.* p. 175. See Klaić, *Geschichte Bosniens*, p. 78.

rankled; and Kulin was further influenced by the anti-Hungarian sentiments of his dispossessed sister, the Princess of Hum. Finally in 1199, the Ban, his wife, his sister, various others of his kin and ten thousand of his subjects openly avowed their adherence to the Bogomil faith.[1]

The emergence of Bogomilstvo as a state religion in Bosnia inevitably encouraged its adherents in the neighbouring countries. The news of Kulin's conversion was first given to the Pope in an alarmed letter from the King of Dioclea, Stephen Nemanya's son, Vukan,[2] and more and more reports came in of the spread of heresy. In these reports the heretics were usually called Patarenes or Paterenes, an Italian name probably derived originally from the Latin *Patera* or cup and already used in the mid-eleventh century to describe the Low-Church party at Milan. It is as Patarenes that the Bogomils of Bosnia and Dalmatia won notoriety in the West.[3]

Whatever their name their presence was infuriating to Pope Innocent III. In 1200 he wrote to King Emmerich of Hungary, whom he considered as overlord of Bosnia, complaining of Kulin's behaviour and citing the protection that he gave to heretics from Spalato and Trau, where the sect seems to have been numerous. Emmerich was to see that Kulin returned to the Catholic faith as soon as possible, and if he did not Hungarian troops must depose him. A similar threat was to be made to the Bishop of Bosnia, Daniel, who too had lapsed into heresy.[4] But Emmerich was unable to take action at first; and meanwhile the heretics were allowed to spread. Two goldsmiths, Matthew and Aristodius, Italians by birth who had lived many years in Bosnia, founded a flourishing school of heresy at Spalato.[5] About the same time the heretics destroyed the cathedral of Kreshevo and kept the bishopric vacant for thirty-five years.[6]

---

[1] Letter of Vukan of Dioclea to Pope Innocent III, in Theiner, *Monumenta Slavorum Meridionalium*, vol. I, p. 6.
[2] See note above.   [3] See below, p. 184.
[4] Letter in Theiner, *Monumenta Slav. Merid.* vol. I, pp. 12–13; Farlati, *Illyricum Sacrum*, vol. IV, p. 55.
[5] Thomas Archidiaconus, *Historia Salonitanorum...*, § 24.
[6] Farlati, *Illyricum Sacrum*, vol. IV, p. 46.

In 1202 the Latin Crusaders, on their way to their orgy of destruction at Constantinople, sacked the Dalmatian city of Zara, a domain of the King of Hungary, and claimed as an excuse that it was riddled with heresy.[1] Emmerich was thus reminded of his duty to the Church and advanced on Bosnia. Kulin saw the folly of resistance to the great Hungarian army. He wrote to Rome saying that he had been deluded into thinking the Patarenes good Christians, and offered to send a mission of Patarenes to Rome that they might learn there what their errors were. At the same time he asked for a Papal mission to Bosnia. In 1202 the Archbishop of Ragusa and his Archdeacon Marinus conveyed a Patarene delegation to Rome; and a little later, the Papal mission, Bernard, Archbishop of Spalato, and a Papal chaplain, John de Casamaris, arrived in Bosnia.[2]

Kulin gave in with a good grace. On 6 April 1203, at Bjelo Polje on the river Bosna, before the Papal legate, John, and the Archdeacon Marinus, Kulin and his leading subjects abjured their heresy. Their particular promises show what were considered by Rome to be the main errors of the Patarenes. First they promised in every way to acknowledge full Roman supremacy, to accept Catholic priests and in all things to be obedient to Rome. Then they promised to restore altars and crosses to their places of worship, to adopt the confessional and penitence, to accept the Roman calendar of feast and fast days, to communicate at least seven times a year on the major feasts of the Church. Finally they must not arrogate to themselves alone the name of Christians, nor must they shelter heretics; and the sexes must be kept apart in monasteries.[3]

It is interesting that the Roman legates insisted not on questions of doctrine but solely those of usage. Rome was too careful to risk a long theological debate such as Greek churchmen would have loved. Complete submission and the abandonment of bad habits were all that she demanded.

---

[1] This is, I think, what the Doge means when he says to Innocent III that he never expected the Pope to count it as a Christian city (Innocent III's letter, VII, 202, in *M.P.L.* vol. CCXV, col. 511).

[2] Theiner, *Monumenta Slav. Merid.* vol. I, p. 15.

[3] *Ibid.* p. 20.

To make their submission the more binding the Patarenes were further required to send two leading representatives with the Papal legate to the Hungarian court, where Kulin's son already was staying as a hostage. There, on the Royal Isle at Budapest, before the King and the Archbishop of Kolosz and other eminent ecclesiastics, the Patarene magnates swore to abide by their submission, and Kulin's son undertook that his father should pay a thousand silver marks as forfeit, were the agreement of Bjelo Polje ever broken.[1]

John de Casamaris hoped to follow up the Papal victory by reorganizing the Bosnian church. The only bishopric then existing was in fact, so John wrote to the Pope, lifeless. He suggested that three or four more bishoprics should be created and filled with good Latins.[2] But his recommendations were not carried out, apparently owing to Hungarian opposition. To King Emmerich and the Archbishop of Kolosz, a weak Bosnia with a weak church was infinitely more attractive.

We must hope that Kulin abode by his promise. But there was no decrease in the number of Patarenes in his dominions. He himself died in 1204. His son and successor Stephen was, it seems, personally a good Catholic, but he took little or no steps to persecute his heretical subjects, calculating no doubt that that would cost him his throne. But neither the Popes, faced with heresies nearer home, nor the Hungarian king, Emmerich's successor Andrew II, faced with an unruly nobility seeking to limit his power, could enforce the agreement of Bjelo Polje on him. Moreover the Hungarian triumph in Bosnia had provoked a reaction in the land of Hum. There the Hungarian prince Andrew fades out of history. By 1218 the throne of Hum was firmly in the hands of a heretic magnate called Peter.[3]

In 1221 Pope Honorius III sent his chaplain Acontius to look into Bosnian affairs. Acontius's report was not encouraging. Heresy was rampant; and despite the free hand that Honorius had given him and the letters that he had written to the Hungarian authorities, Acontius could achieve nothing. He preached vainly for three years, and he tried to organize a Crusade. But King Andrew could not help him.

---

[1] Theiner, *Monumenta Slav. Merid.* vol. I, p. 20.   [2] *Ibid.* p. 22.
[3] Thomas Archidiaconus, *Historia Salonitanorum...*, § 29.

The only support came from the Archbishop of Kolosz, Ugolin, who in 1225 agreed to finance a Crusade if in return Bosnia and the outlying provinces of Usora and Soli were put under his ecclesiastical jurisdiction. The Pope consented; and the Archbishop looked round for a leader. There happened to be at the moment in Hungary an impoverished Byzantine prince, John Angelus, son of the Emperor Isaac Angelus and of King Andrew's sister Margaret. He was to command the Crusade, and was advanced 200 silver marks by the Archbishop. But together with the money John Angelus disappears from history, despite an angry letter from the Pope. After this fiasco the scheme was dropped.[1]

The Bosnians went on their own heretical way. In 1232 they deposed their Catholic Ban Stephen, and set up in his stead a Patarene magnate, Matthew Ninoslav. Stephen and his son Sebislav were only able to retain the little district of Usora. Under Ninoslav Patarenism was definitely the state religion. Twice he had to simulate conversion, first in 1233, after the Papal legate in Hungary, Cardinal Jacob of Penestrino, had toured the country backed by the force of Hungary,[2] and again in 1237 after a two years' Crusade led by Coloman, Duke of Croatia, King Andrew's son. But on each occasion, though he asked for Dominican preachers to set his people right, his repentance was short-lived. In 1237 he had been reduced to strict subservience,[3] but in 1239 he was again an independent monarch, strengthening his position by an alliance with Ragusa next year.[4] The Hungarian disasters of 1241 at the hands of the Mongols saved him from the fear of reprisals. By the year of his death, in 1250, Bosnia was in a state of great prosperity. Its church, so Pope Innocent IV had written three years before, had "totally fallen into heresy".[5]

The land of Hum was meanwhile even more prosperous and more Patarene. The heretic, Prince Peter, managed to force Spalato to accept him as its overlord from 1222 to 1225. His nephew and

[1] Theiner, *Monumenta Hungarica*, vol. I, pp. 55, 72.
[2] *Ibid.* vol. I, pp. 113, 120.
[3] Theiner, *Monumenta Hungarica*, vol. I, pp. 147, 162–3, 168–9.
[4] Miklosich, *Monumenta Serbica*, pp. 24, 28–9.
[5] Theiner, *Monumenta Hungarica*, vol. I, pp. 204–5.

successor Tolen, though not so triumphant against the Spalatans, was even more hated by them. He for a time had to acknowledge the suzerainty of first the King of Serbia, then the King of Hungary, but in fact he ruled independently. He too favoured the Patarenes. Tolen died in 1239. His successor Andrew and his son Radoslav were better friends to the coastal cities, and their reigns were periods of peaceful prosperity. But from 1254 onwards we hear no more for a period of Hum, its rulers or its heretics. That year Radoslav acknowledged himself a vassal of Hungary; but probably soon afterwards his land was absorbed into Serbia.[1]

Of the organization of the heresy we unfortunately know nothing. Some sort of ecclesiastical organization had developed. From Western heretic sources it is clear that the Bosnian heretics together with those of Slovenia and other neighbouring inland districts formed a unit, known in the West as the church of Sclavonia.[2] This church had its bishop or Father,[3] who is usually referred to by contemporaries as the Bishop of Bosnia, thus causing confusion with the Catholic bishop who at times was permitted to reside in the land. The residence of the Patarene bishop was apparently at Janici, in north-east Bosnia.[4] At times it seemed that the Catholic bishop himself lapsed into heresy;[5] but we must presume that if so he did not automatically become Patarene bishop. But the whole question of the Catholic church in Bosnia is obscure. In the twelfth century it was notorious that Bosnian bishops seldom could speak Latin,[6]

---

[1] See Klaić, *Geschichte Bosniens*, pp. 134–8. Radoslav's submission is given in Miklosich, *Monumenta Serbica*, vol. i, p. 44.
[2] Sacchoni in Martène et Durand, *Thesaurus*, vol. v, p. 1767.
[3] The Slavonic word *Djed* was employed. We know the names of three *Djede*, Miroslav (1303), Radomir (1404) and Miloie (1446). See Klaić, *Geschichte Bosniens*, p. 287.
[4] It is from Janici that the Djed Radomir writes his letters; see below, p. 108, n. 1.
[5] The early thirteenth-century Bishops of Bosnia, Daniel and the Bishop at the time of Jacob of Penestrino's tour (1233), were both apparently heretics. (Farlati, *Illyricum Sacrum*, vol. iv, p. 45; Theiner, *Monumenta Hungarica*, vol. i, p. 113.)
[6] E.g. Bishop of Radogost (*c.* 1197) who "non sapeva lettere latine, ne altre eccetto le slavoniche". (Gondola, *Chron.* MS. quoted by Jireček, *Geschichte der Serben*, vol. i, p. 224, n. 4.)

herein showing the influence of the neighbouring Orthodox Church
and its vernacular liturgy; and Bosnia had at all times a large
Orthodox "schismatic" population. The perpetual inter-transference
of the jurisdiction over Bosnia between the Archbishoprics of
Ragusa, Spalato and Kolosz shows how difficult and unsatisfactory
Rome found the whole of the Bosnian bishopric.

If the Bosnian ruler were a Bogomil, it was presumably he that,
with the Bishop's advice, controlled the Patarene community. But
we find the Patarene bishop acting himself as a political authority,
writing, for example, letters of recommendation for members of his
flock to the Republic of Ragusa, and having those letters given full
attention.[1] There were probably other bishops under the chief
bishop; and each bishop had his Elder Son and his Younger Son, as
in the older Bogomil churches. The bishops were known as the
Strojnici, the Slavonic word for "Leaders". Beneath them was the
grade of the Elect or Perfect, which was probably very limited if
one disregarded the many believers who entered its ranks on their
death-beds.[2] The creed of the Bosnian Patarenes seems, from the
little evidence that we have, to have been that of any of the Monarchian Bogomil churches.[3]

The heretics of the coastal districts were also increasing in number.
The laws and diplomas of the various Dalmatian cities throughout
the thirteenth, fourteenth and fifteenth centuries, often refer to
them. But they formed a distinct Church, the Church of Tragurium,
different in origin and more Dualist in creed.[4] Its organization,
however, was probably similar. It is uncertain to which of these two
churches the heretics of Hum belonged. Most probably they were

[1] *Acta Bosnae, Monumenta Spectantia ad Historiam Slavorum Meridionalium*,
vol. XXIII, no. CCCLXXIX, p. 71.

[2] Sacchoni estimated in *c.* 1230 that there were about 500 Perfects in the
four churches of Sclavonia, Bulgaria, Tragurium and Philadelphia (Sacchoni,
loc. cit.).

[3] Such works as the "Herrores quos communiter Paterini de Bosna credunt",
publ. by Rački in *Starini*, vol. I, pp. 138 ff., or the *Quinquaginta Errores* written
by Torquemada, *ibid.* xiv ff., 5 ff. contain nothing novel and deal chiefly with
usages.

[4] Rainier Sacchoni, *loc. cit.*; *Summa Auctoritatis*, ed. Douais, p. 121.

of the Sclavonian body. Both Churches had strong missionary traditions, working in Italy and even in France.[1] But the coastal Church was probably the more effective in mission work, as the Sclavonians were largely occupied in making their Church a national church for Bosnia.

In 1250 their task seemed complete. But Ninoslav's death for a time ruined the Patarenes. A disputed succession and civil war followed, till in 1254 King Bela IV of Hungary took over the whole country. To weaken it he divided it into two halves, the north, Machva-Bosnia, going to princes of his own family, his daughter Agnes and her husband, the Russian Rastislav, the southern half to native Catholic nobles. By 1272 there were three Bosnian bans, two Hungarian palatines sharing the northern half, and a Bosnian lord ruling the south. In 1280 the north had passed again to the Hungarian royal house, to the Queen-Mother Elizabeth. The Patarenes had been left largely to themselves during these years; but Elizabeth was a dutiful daughter of the Roman Church and undertook their persecution. On her death, in 1282, her son-in-law the Serbian ex-king, Stephen Dragutin, succeeded to her lands.[2] Stephen was a Catholic convert and eagerly sought to convert others. His zeal with regard to the Patarenes was particularly admired by the Holy See, which gladly acceded to his request to send Slavonic-speaking Franciscan missionaries to the country.[3] But it seems that Dragutin was too wise to attempt any severe persecution. On the contrary, the Patarene bishop, Miroslav, served on his council.[4]

Dragutin retired into a monastery in 1312, to mortify his flesh by sleeping nightly in a coffin filled with thorns. Bosnia then fell for a few years under Mladen Shulich of Croatia and Dalmatia, an eager persecutor of heresy. But in 1322 Hungarian influence replaced him by Dragutin's son-in-law, Stephen Kotromanich, who in 1325

[1] The Concoresso Church claimed a Sclavonian and Bulgarian origin (*Summa Auctoritatis*, p. 123). The Albigeois are said (*op. cit.* p. 121) to have had their doctrine from the Church of Tragurium, which certainly sent missions to Italy also. But see below, p. 170.
[2] See Klaić, *Geschichte Bosniens*, pp. 112–17.
[3] Theiner, *Monumenta Hungarica*, p. 378.
[4] Miklosich, *Monumenta Serbica*, p. 69.

annexed Hum and soon afterwards became lord of most of Dalmatia.[1]

With Stephen Kotromanich begin the greatest days of Bosnia. But his reign illustrated the religious difficulties that beset any Bosnian ruler. Stephen was born Orthodox, but in 1340 he joined the Catholic Church. Till that date he had shown the greatest toleration to the Patarenes. Pope John XXII tried to make him resume persecution; but his attempts failed, chiefly because the Franciscans whom he sent to conduct the Inquisition found that the right of Inquisition had been given in Ninoslav's time to the Dominicans, who refused to yield it. It was some time before the Papal Court could enforce a decision in favour of the Franciscans.[2] But eventually fear of the Orthodox champion, Stephen Dushan of Serbia, and a consequent desire for a Hungarian alliance drove the Bosnian Ban into the Catholic Church; and henceforward, though he would not actively proscribe the heretics—he had told the Franciscan Minister-General Gerhard in 1339 that he could not afford to alienate so powerful a section of his subjects[3]—he encouraged Slav-speaking Franciscan friars to preach the true faith throughout the country. Meanwhile, under Franciscan influence, the Church in Bosnia was reorganized and split into three bishoprics.[4]

This happy period, rich, it was claimed, in conversions from heresy, came to an end with Stephen Kotromanich's death in 1353. His nephew and heir, Stephen Tvrtko I, who in 1376 assumed the title of "King of Serbia and Bosnia, the Coastal Provinces and the Western Lands" and in 1390 added Croatia and Dalmatia to his kingdom, was Orthodox by conviction and a friend of the Patarenes from policy. The Patarene Church, known now usually without qualification as the Bosnian Church, recovered all its strength. It

[1] For Kotromanich's reign, see Klaić, *Geschichte Bosniens*, chap. VII.

[2] Nicholas IV confirmed the office of Inquisition to the Dominicans in 1291; Boniface VIII began to use the Franciscans. John XXII sent the Franciscan Fabian in 1326, but in 1327 confirmed the Dominicans' rights. The question was eventually settled in 1330 (Theiner, *Monumenta Hungarica*, vol. I, pp. 513, 514, 526).

[3] Theiner, *Monumenta Hungarica*, vol. I, p. 632.

[4] See Klaić, *Geschichte Bosniens*, pp. 161–2.

enjoyed complete civil equality with the Catholic and Orthodox Churches in the land. In vain Pope Innocent VI told the Bishop of Bosnia to ask for governmental help in the suppression of heresy,[1] and Pope Urban V tried to restrict its spread by ordering the excommunication of anyone in the Dalmatian cities who should show hospitality to a heretic.[2] In vain in 1360 King Louis of Hungary made Tvrtko promise to exile all Patarenes.[3] Bosnia remained, in Urban's bitter words, the "cesspool of heresy of all parts of the world".[4] The strength of the heretics is illustrated by such incidents as the retreat of the Prior of Aurana from his monastery to Nin, because of the number and power of the Patarenes in the countryside.[5]

In 1391 Tvrtko died, leaving Bosnia at the height of its glory. The Turkish danger had not yet come. Indeed the defeat of the Serbian King, Lazar, by the Turks at Kossovo in 1389 had merely enabled the Bosnians to annex part of his territory. But after Tvrtko's death the Bosnian kingdom crumbled. Two Turkish incursions, a disputed succession, jealous magnates and an ambitious king-maker, the noble Chervoya Vukchich, contrived within twenty years to make the country once more a Hungarian province. But the Hungarian monarch, the Emperor Sigismund, could not govern the country himself. His nominee, Tvrtko's son, Tvrtko II, was displaced in 1415 by a former king, Stephen Ostoya, who had since 1408 ruled in Hum. Ostoya only won the throne with Turkish support, but his overlord, the Turkish sultan, allowed him and, after his death in 1418, his son Stephen Ostoyich, to reign unmolested.[6]

The weakness of Bosnia had not meant the weakness of the Patarene church. Vukchich had been a Patarene[7] as was his kinsman

---

[1] Letter no. 327 in Theiner, *Monumenta Slav. Merid.* vol. I, p. 240, dated 1360.
[2] Letter no. 366 in Theiner, *Monumenta Slav. Merid.* vol. I, p. 265, dated 1368.
[3] *Acta Bosnae*, no. CLXXXIV, p. 3.
[4] Letter to King Louis in Theiner, *Monumenta Hungarica*, vol. II, p. 91, dated 1369.
[5] *Acta Bosnae*, no. CCXLV, p. 46, a letter from the Prior to the citizens of Spalato, dated 17 Nov. 1387.
[6] For the history of these years see Klaić, *Geschichte Bosniens*, chaps. IX and X.
[7] Matthew of San Miniato, in *Acta Bosnae*, no. CCCLXV, p. 68; Rački, *Pokret na Slavenskom Jugu, Rad. Jugoslav. Akademi*, vol. IV, p. 59.

and slightly younger contemporary, the great noble, Sandal Hranich. King Stephen Ostoya and his son both gave the heresy their full patronage.[1] The Doge of Ragusa, giving instructions to his ambassadors in 1404, tells them to pay full attention to the assembly of the Patarenes; and the Ragusans provided the Patarenes with safe hospitality within their walls.[2] Huge areas of the country, such as the great silver-mining district of Srebrenica and almost the whole of Hum, had a purely Patarene population. Indeed, with the perpetual quarrels of the magnates and the weak evanescent monarchs, the Patarene church must have seemed the most stable institution in the land.

Tvrtko II regained his throne in 1421. But, good Catholic though he was, he could not enforce his religion on his people. The Council of Bâle, which met in 1431, was very much occupied over the question of heresy, being especially anxious to suppress the Hussites. The Bosnian Patarenes were now an isolated church; their fellow-heretics, in the West and even in the Eastern Balkan peninsula, had died out long since. But their missionary zeal remained. They attempted to send a delegation to address the Council, but it was not permitted.[3] On the other hand, the Bosnian and Serbian rulers, despite an eager invitation to be represented at the Council, merely ignored it. The Council, however, did not ignore Bosnia. In 1432 Pope Eugenius IV sent a friar, Jacob de Marchia, to revive the Franciscan organization in Bosnia, and the Council gave him full authority as an Inquisitor.[4] For four years the Inquisitor worked in the country; but his energy merely made him hated by his subordinates. The Grand Master of the Franciscans wrote from Toulouse to beg him to be less severe with his friars.[5] Eventually Jacob gave up the task, citing the apathy of King Tvrtko as the cause of his failure. But King Tvrtko was hardly in a position to be helpful.

---

[1] Klaić, *op. cit.* pp. 286 ff.

[2] *Acta Bosnae*, no. CCCLXXIX, p. 71. Letter written by the Djed Radomir from Janici. Pučić, *Spomenici Srbski*, vol. I, pp. 50–1.

[3] Farlati, *Illyricum Sacrum*, vol. IV, p. 660. Theiner, *Monumenta Slav. Merid.* vol. I, p. 375.

[4] Klaić, *op. cit.* p. 251.

[5] *Acta Bosnae*, no. DCCLXIX, p. 168.

From 1433 to 1436 he was a refugee at the Court of the Emperor Sigismund,[1] while the great Patarene nobles, Sandal Hranich and the Voyëvod Radosav Pavlovich, who for several years forced Ragusa to pay him tribute,[2] dominated the country. Even Sandal's death in 1435 did not ease Tvrtko's position. His vast estates in Hum and Southern Bosnia passed to his nephew Stephen Vukchich, who by 1448 was wearing the title, confirmed to him by the Emperor Frederick III, of Duke of St Sava; and his lands were known as the Duchy or Herzegovina.[3] Moreover from 1436 onwards the Turk was taking an embarrassing interest in the country; and Tvrtko found himself obliged to pay 25,000 ducats annually to the Sultan.[4]

Eventually in 1443 Tvrtko was put to death by his own magnates.[5] But when they elected to the throne in his stead Stephen Ostoyich's illegitimate son Stephen Thomas, they overreached themselves. Thomas had been born and bred a Patarene; but he soon renounced his heresy and in September 1444 became a Catholic, in the hope of securing the support of the Western powers against both his unruly nobility and the encroaching power of the Turks. The Pope in return annulled his marriage with his low-born Patarene wife and cancelled his unfortunate illegitimacy. Stephen Thomas then married the Duke of St Sava's daughter Catherine, who gave up her Patarene faith in return for a crown.[6] In 1446 the Pope and the Hungarian general John Hunyadi put pressure on Stephen Thomas to persecute his Patarene subjects. He agreed to forbid them to build more churches or to repair old churches. In 1450, spurred on by the Papal nuncio, he forbade them the right of holding services.[7] Though a few eminent nobles had followed their monarch into the Catholic

---

[1] Klaić, *Geschichte Bosniens*, pp. 353–4, quoting the chronicler Simeon Klimentovich.

[2] *Acta Bosnae*, DCLXXXIX, DCXCII, DCCLXXX, pp. 132, 133, 171.

[3] Thallóczy, *Geschichte Bosniens und Serbiens im Mittelalter*, pp. 146 ff.

[4] Laonicus Chalcocondylas (ed. Bonn), p. 248.

[5] Simeon Klimentović, *loc. cit.*

[6] Theiner, *Monumenta Slavorum Meridionalium*, vol. I, p. 388; see Klaić, *Geschichte Bosniens*, pp. 368–75 (with references).

[7] Theiner, *Monumenta Hungarica*, vol. II, pp. 255–6.

fold, these decrees alienated a far greater number and vast sections of the poorer population; who either took refuge with the heretic Duke of St Sava or plotted with the Turks. Bosnia was split between two warring religions, with a third party, the Orthodox "schismatic" Slavs, siding against Catholicism.

With Bosnia so divided there was nothing to check the Turks as soon as they chose to advance farther. Of the many Crusades suggested to combat them, none materialized. Stephen Thomas had alienated his former co-religionists for nothing. For his remaining years he vainly plotted and intrigued, meanwhile paying the Sultan the heavy tribute that was demanded. In 1461 he was murdered by his son, Stephen Tomashevich, who, relying on Papal help, refused to pay, the Turkish tribute. The Sultan Mohammed the Conqueror awaited his opportunity. In 1463 he invaded Bosnia. The key fortress of Bobovats was held by an officer called Radak who had been forcibly converted from Patarenism to Catholicism. He surrendered it at once, from hatred of the Catholic king. Within a few days all Bosnia was in the Sultan's hands.

Herzegovina, protected by its high mountains and its religious unity, remained independent for twenty more years. But after 1483 only the little Orthodox state of Zeta or Montenegro survived the onrush. The Turks never conquered it.[1]

The Patarenes rejoiced in the fall of the Catholic kings; but Turkish rule was to prove their ruin. According to the Sultan's orders, only such nobles as would embrace Islam could keep their estates. A large number of the Patarene nobility, men who had undergone exile rather than become Catholic, hastened to join their new master's creed. Possibly its Puritanism and its simple fatalism appealed to them. But the more obvious conclusion is that their religious fervour had only been disguised patriotism. When they no longer had a country for which to fight but still inherited a hatred for the arrogant Hungarians and the greedy Dalmatians and their Latin church and culture, then they were ready to take up a new faith that was sufficiently sympathetic and that brought great material advantages.

[1] See Klaić, *op. cit.* chap. XIII.

The people followed their nobles' lead. By the end of the fifteenth century Bosnia was a predominantly Mohammedan province.

In Bosnia the Bogomil religion had its longest and most successful innings. But its whole history and the bathos of its end shows that the motive force there was not any inherent virtue of Bogomilstvo, except perhaps its Puritanism, which was a welcome change from the magnificence of the Orthodox and Catholic churches. It had been carried on by the forces of nationalism, as a national alternative to Orthodoxy with its Byzantino-Serbian influence and the Catholicism of Hungary and Dalmatia. The heretic church had been probably much modified during the centuries of its life, losing its old simplicity. A hierarchy had arisen. Special ecclesiastical buildings were used. There were monasteries in which, however, the sexes were not separated.[1] The ambitious quarrelsome Bosnian nobles could not be expected to retain Bogomil's ideas of passive resistance. Moreover Bosnian Bogomilstvo seems to have developed no esoteric thought nor tradition that could survive its loss of material power. It remained a superficial thing, a national dress that could be easily taken off and forgotten. And so it perished, its sacred legends fading, as elsewhere amongst the Slavs, into a set of improbable popular fairy-stories.

[1] See above, pp. 106, 110, 112.

CHAPTER VI

The Cathars

I

IN Bosnia Dualism nearly reached the triumph of permanence, but its most spectacular achievements were made in Italy and in France. It was there that its growth most alarmed the Roman Church, and it was there that the Roman Church evolved the means for its suppression. The Inquisition fulfilled its object, but only as the result of careful organization and preparation; for which historians must be grateful. For, though the books of the heretics perished by its labours, the records of its trials and the inquisitors' manuals give us a far clearer picture of the Dualist Church than can be found elsewhere. It may be questioned how far evidence about the French or Italian dualists can be held to apply to the dualists of Bosnia, Bulgaria or Constantinople. The answer to that lies in the history of the spread of Dualism and in the words of contemporary writers.

It is probable that certain traditions of the Early Church died out slowly in the West. The career of Felix of Urgel in Charlemagne's days shows a lingering Adoptionism.[1] Moreover many people were predisposed to heresy by a growing dislike of the luxury and the political activities of the Church. This attitude, which found legitimate expression in the asceticism of Peter Damian and his school and, a little later, in the Cistercian movement, led also to heretical teaching of a purely anti-clerical nature, such as that of the Netherlander Tanchelm or Tanquelin, who died in 1115,[2] or that of Peter Valdes, founder of the Waldenses or Vaudois, who combined it with a desire for voluntary poverty.[3]

[1] Alcuin, *Contra Felicem, passim, M.P.L.* vol. CI, coll. 83 ff.
[2] *Acta Sanctorum*, June, vol. I, pp. 843 ff. Robertus de Monte (of Torigny) in Bouquet, *Recueil des Historiens de la France*, vol. XIII, p. 328.
[3] For Peter Waldo, see Guiraud, *Histoire de l'Inquisition*, vol. I, chap. VIII.

Manichaean memories, too, may have lingered on and combined with this anti-clericalism to bear fruit in the eleventh century. In 991 Gerbert of Aurillac, as Archbishop-Elect of Reims, made a declaration of faith that showed him to be suspected of decidedly Manichaeo-Gnostic doctrines, including Dualism and a rejection of the Old Testament.[1] In 1022 King Robert the Pious sent several Canons of Sainte-Croix at Orleans to the stake for their doctrines of the wickedness of matter.[2] The Canons were not, however, isolated heretics. In about 1015 the Bishop Gerard of Limoges had essayed a determined drive against "Manichaean" heretics.[3] In 1022 several were discovered and put to death at Toulouse.[4] In 1028 the Duke of Aquitaine, William V, summoned a council of the bishops of his duchy to Charroux to discuss plans for the crushing of the heresy.[5] Rumour maintained that it spread from Italy.[6] It was an Italian woman and a peasant from the Périgord who were said to have carried it northward to Orleans.[7] And it is remarkable that one of the leading heretics of Sainte-Croix was Stephen, sometime confessor to the Queen, Constance of Aquitaine.[8] In 1025 Italian missionaries led by a certain Gundulf introduced heresy into the diocese of Arras, whose bishop Reginald, together with Bishop Gerard of Cambrai, brought the offenders back into the fold.[9] It seems clear therefore that the "Manichaean" tendency came from Italy. Certainly it was in Italy that the first explicitly Cathar Church appeared.

In 1030 there was at Monteforte an organized heretic community, to which the epithet Cathar was applied.[10] This name was probably

---

[1] Gerbert of Aurillac, *Epistolae*, no. 180, ed. Havet, pp. 161–2.
[2] Ademar, in Bouquet, *Recueil des Historiens de France*, vol. X, p. 159: Radulf Glaber, in Bouquet, *op. cit.* vol. X, pp. 35–6. Their doctrines were dualist—they disapproved of marriage—docetist and anti-clerical. Ademar adds: "Probati sunt esse Manichaei."
[3] Ademar, *ibid.* p. 154.   [4] Ademar, *ibid.* p. 159.
[5] Ademar, *ibid.* p. 164.   [6] Radulf Glaber, *ibid.* p. 35.
[7] Ademar, *ibid.* p. 159.   [8] Ademar, *loc. cit.*
[9] Mansi, *Concilia*, vol. XIX, pp. 423 ff. Gundulf does not appear explicitly as a "Manichaean", but his condemnation of marriage, of the Cross, etc., show him to have held all the usual Cathar tenets.
[10] Landulphus Senior, *Historia Mediolanensis*, in Muratori, *Rerum Italicarum Scriptores*, vol. IV, pp. 88–9.

a heretic term in origin, derived from the Greek word for "pure" and given by the heretics to their class of Elect or Perfect. The self-confessed doctrines of this community show them to have been in the great Gnostic tradition. During the next few decades there was apparently a certain spread of such doctrines through Italy, though its history is somewhat difficult to trace. Probably missionaries from the Balkans were definitely operating in and from Italy; and it is possible that occasional pilgrims to the East came back imbued with heterodox opinions acquired in Bulgaria or in Constantinople.

At the end of the century this pilgrim-movement culminated in the Crusades, and contact between Western Europe, in particular France, with Constantinople became closer than ever before. This contact must explain the sudden growth of "Manichaean" ideas in France. At Toulouse, in June 1119, Pope Calixtus II held a Council to anathematize certain heretics in that district who denied the Sacraments of the Holy Communion, baptism and marriage, and disbelieved in the Priesthood and the ecclesiastical hierarchy.[1] It is possible that these heretics merely belonged to the anti-clerical group; but their disapproval of marriage suggests that they were Dualist. Calixtus's anathemas did little good. A few years later the same district was being perverted by a certain Peter de Bruys and his disciple an ex-monk Henry. Peter was burnt at St-Gilles about the year 1126, but he had already committed his doctrines to writing; and they were amplified by Henry. The Cluniac monk, Peter the Venerable, found in existence a year or two later a definite sect which he called the Petrobrusians.[2]

The Petrobrusians' most emphatic trait was their disapproval of child-baptism; but they also forbade the worship of the Cross—it should rather be hated as the instrument of Christ's suffering; they considered that churches should be destroyed, not built, for God is everywhere and has no need of them; they denied the Eucharist and the Mass, and saw no value in prayers for the dead. Their positive tenets have unfortunately not survived; but these negative views are

---

[1] Mansi, *Concilia*, vol. XXI, p. 226.
[2] Peter the Venerable, *Tractatus adversus Petrobrusianos*, in *M.P.L.* vol. CLXXXIX, coll. 719 ff.

reminiscent of any sect in the Gnostic tradition.[1] It seems probable that Peter de Bruys originally learnt his doctrines from an Eastern missionary, though he may have developed them himself.

In 1147 Pope Eugenius III, who had come to France to preach the Second Crusade, was horrified at the number of heretics now living in the South. He summoned his great master, St Bernard of Clairvaux, to deal with them. Bernard found there not only Petrobrusians but other kindred sects, centred in particular round Albi. The most active workers in heresy seemed to be weavers, and the name given locally to the heretics was *Arriani*, from a village near Toulouse that was especially heretic-ridden. He also discovered that the local nobility favoured the heretics, apparently less from theological conviction than from hatred and jealousy of the Church.[2]

Bernard's mission was not a great success. At Albi, indeed, he had a remarkable personal triumph; but at Verfeil, another great heretic city, he was not allowed a hearing. He himself was not dissatisfied with his work. But what little good it achieved soon vanished. A few years later the Church was again in a state of alarm, all the greater because of the failure of its most distinguished preacher.[3]

Meanwhile heresy was burgeoning in Northern France, in Flanders and in Germany. As early as 1116 Le Mans was perverted by a hermit called Henry, of a very holy exterior but, it was suspected, of a shocking private life. He claimed to be inspired by God, as were the Prophets of old, and he always sent two disciples before him to prepare the way for him. For a time he practically ruled Le Mans. The Bishop could do nothing against him. But eventually he took flight and his sect dispersed. But soon after, one of his disciples, Pons, appeared at Périgueux, with a following which claimed to live as the Disciples had done, there being twelve chief Apostles. They were ascetic in their habits, wholly vegetarian, almost teetotal, and owning no money. They performed a hundred genuflexions every day. They rejected not only the Mass and the

---

[1] *Ibid.* col. 722.
[2] St Bernard, letter 241 in *M.P.L.* vol. CLXXXII, col. 434: Geoffrey of Auxerre, *S. Bernardi Miracula*, in *Acta Sanctorum*, August, vol. IV, pp. 349 ff.
[3] Geoffrey of Auxerre, *loc. cit.*

Cross but also alms-giving, as they disapproved of private property. They called themselves *Apostolics*, and won many converts, even from amongst the clergy. They were believed to indulge in magic. Indeed it was impossible to keep them confined in prison, as the Devil always released them.[1]

In 1125 a peasant of Bucy near Soissons called Clementius was gathering round himself a following whom he taught that Christ was but a phantasm, that the altar was the "mouth of hell" and its Mysteries valueless, and that marriage and generation were crimes. His followers therefore, according to Guibert of Nogent, only cohabited with fellow-believers of their own sex, except for occasional promiscuous orgies. Babies conceived at these orgies, Guibert added, were burnt as soon as born and a communion-bread was made from their cinders. Guibert of Nogent considered these heretics to be without doubt the Manichaeans described by St Augustine. Clementius, though the Count of Soissons declared him to be the wisest man that he knew, was eventually imprisoned for life, along with his father. Two of his leading disciples, unluckier than he, were lynched by the crowd at Soissons while awaiting their sentence.[2]

A little later, in about 1140, an illiterate Breton called Eudes de l'Etoile, was preaching heresy in the country round Saint-Malo, and used to hold secret meetings in the forest of Broceliande. He changed his name from Eudes to Eon and announced that he was the Messiah whom the Church itself foretold would come to judge the quick and the dead. He called his disciples by the names of Manichaean *eons*, Justice and Wisdom and Science, and he declared that others of them were angels or *eons*. He founded his own hierarchy of archbishops and bishops and a class of initiates who were to lead chaste and severe lives. His ordinary followers were allowed all sorts of food, so long as they were fed also with spiritual food. He himself was said to live in the greatest luxury owing to the money that he raised from his flock. His success was attributed generally to the use of magic. To his contemporary Robert of Torigny he was certainly a Manichaean. Eventually in 1148 a Council was held at

[1] *Gesta Pontificum Cenomanensium* in Bouquet, *Recueil des Historiens de la France*, vol. XII, p. 548.
[2] Guibert of Nogent, *De Vita Sua*, ed. Bourgin, bk. III, p. 215.

Reims to condemn him. He was captured and brought before it, and on his refusal to abjure his heresy, was sent to prison, to die there soon afterwards.[1]

It is clear that all these heresiarchs, Henry of Le Mans, Pons of Périgueux, Clementius of Bucy and Eudes de l'Etoile represent a rebirth of the Gnostic tradition, even more than does Peter de Bruys. Pons's *Apostolics* with their hatred of material things, Clementius's disapproval of marriage, and still more Eudes with his paraphernalia of *eons* all to some extent deserve the epithet of Manichaean hurled at them. Somewhere they must have met with Manichaean-Gnostic lore. But they were all men of humble birth; Clementius was a peasant, Eudes was known to be illiterate. They must have therefore acquired their doctrines orally. This oral background would explain the eccentricities of their particular heresies. Probably their teachers were not organized missionaries sent out by the Eastern heretics, but itinerant preachers or, still more, itinerant weavers who had learnt from the regular missions and retailed a garbled version to these outlying districts.

Soon more organized heresy was to appear. In 1144 the Bishop of Liège was alarmed by the spread of heresy in Flanders.[2] In 1157 Archbishop Samson of Reims complained that Manichaeanism was being disseminated throughout his diocese by itinerant weavers, who condemned marriage and encouraged sexual promiscuity.[3] The presence of these "Poblicani" was discovered by the refusal of a girl to submit to the attentions of a young cleric. Such chastity was considered ominous, and the girl, when questioned, admitted that she believed virginity to be obligatory, and called in her friends to support her, thus revealing a whole nest of heresy. His successor, Henry, brother of King Louis VII, wrote soon after his elevation in 1162 in alarm at the number of heretics to be found in Flanders. He called them "Manichaeans who are known as Populicani". They

---

[1] William of Newburgh, *Historia Anglicana*, I, § xix (ed. English Historical Society, pp. 51-5): Robertus de Monte (of Torigny), p. 291: Otto of Frisingen, *Chronicon Frederici I*, bk. I, § 54, p. 225.
[2] *Epistola Ecclesiae Leodensis* in Martène et Durand, *Veterum Scriptorum Amplissima Collectio*, vol. I, p. 777.
[3] Radulf of Coggeshall, in Bouquet, *Recueil des Historiens de France*, vol. XVIII, p. 92: Mansi, *Concilia*, vol. XXI, coll. 843 ff.

were rich enough to attempt to buy his protection.[1] About the same time they were rampant in Germany. Eckbert, Abbot of Schönau, met with so many heretics on the Rhine, that he thought it worth while to write a treatise against them, and he secured in 1163 a wholesale burning of Cathars at Cologne.[2] From Germany they spread to England. In 1160 a certain Gerard crossed over at the head of some thirty illiterate persons, who denied Baptism, Marriage, the Eucharist and Catholic unity. They refused to argue and welcomed persecution. A Council was held at Oxford against them and sentenced them to be branded on the forehead. Gerard himself was branded on the chin also. William of Newburgh called them Publicani.[3] In 1167 a group of heretics was rounded up in Burgundy and tried at Vézelay. These were called Deonarii or Poplicani, and were convicted, in spite of their refusal to talk, of denying all the Sacraments and in particular the value of baptism, the Eucharist, the sign of the Cross, holy water, churches, oblations, marriage, the priesthood and monastic life. The ordeal by water was applied to them; one was scourged and set free, and seven were burnt.[4]

The origin of these Flemish and Burgundian heretics is obvious. The name Populicani or Poplicani is the name Paulician, debased by Westerners who perhaps tried to affiliate it to the word "populus", or, more probably, to the "Publicans" of the New Testament. But clearly they learnt the word from the Greeks, who called the sect the Pavlikianoi, rather than from the Armenian sectaries to whom it was the Poghikeanq.[5] It seems therefore that it was the

[1] Letter of Henry, in Bouquet, *Recueil des Historiens de France*, vol. xv, p. 790.
[2] Eckbert, *Sermones contra Catharos*, in *M.P.L.* vol. cxcv, coll. 11–98: Godofredus, *Annales*, in Freherus, *Scriptores Rerum Germanicarum*, vol. i, p. 336. "Manichaean" heretics had been hanged at Goslar by the Emperor Henry III in 1052 (Hermannus Contractus, *Chronicon* and *Addenda ad Chronicon Saxicon* in Bouquet, *Recueil des Historiens de France*, vol. xi, p. 642). Did these heretics learn from Hungary and Slav countries?
[3] William of Newburgh, *Historia Anglicana*, ii, § xiii, pp. 120–3.
[4] *Historia Vizeliacensis* in d'Achéry, *Spicilegium...veterum aliquot scriptorum*, vol. ii, pp. 536 ff. These punitive measures were probably undertaken by the lay authorities to whom the Church preferred to pass the responsibility of persecution. See Herbert of Bosham's letter to the Abbot of Vézelay, written about now, advising him to hand the heretics over to the French King (Herberti de Boscham *Epistolae*, in *M.P.L.* vol. cxc, coll. 1462–3).
[5] The Greek word is Παυλικιανοί. The *u* was pronounced as a *v*, and careless

Paulicians of Constantinople who were chiefly responsible for this missionary work; and the Paulicians of Constantinople represented the strictly Dualist or Dragovitsan branch of the Bogomil Church. The freer intercourse between East and West since the first Crusade made the missionaries' task easy. The itinerant weaver seems still to have been their channel of communication.

The Dualists of Constantinople showed their hand in the spread of heresy in Languedoc also. There heresy was more triumphant than anywhere else in France, but the history of its growth, almost unchecked since St Bernard's unsuccessful tour, remains unknown. During the middle of the twelfth century it must have been rapid. In 1163 Pope Alexander III held a Council at Tours and at King Louis VII's request issued an anathema against all who sheltered or had any dealings with the heretics of the Toulousain and Gascony.[1] In 1165 the bishops of the south of France held a council at Lombez, where the heretic doctrines, the rejection of the Sacraments and of the Old Testament, were once more condemned. But the heretics, sure of noble support, defied the council, even though the Countess of Toulouse herself, King Louis VII's sister, was present. Their leader Oliver took the opportunity of addressing the assembled crowds, explaining his doctrines, so successfully that the bishops dared not take steps against him; and nothing was done.[2] Two years later the heretics themselves publicly held a great council at Saint-Félix-de-Caraman, near Toulouse. The events at this council enable us to guess at the past history of the heresy. Heretic bishops were there in full force, Sicard Cellerien of Albi, Marcus of Lombardy, Robert of Sperona, head of the French church in Italy, while the vacant sees of Carcassonne, Toulouse and the Val d'Aran in the Spanish Pyrenees sent representatives; but its president was a Greek Niquinta or Nicetas, who came from Constantinople, claiming, perhaps untruthfully, to be the head of the heretic Constantino-

Greeks might therefore write it Παβλικιανοί, which would be transliterated into Latin as "Pablicani". Early Armenian writers such as John of Otzun had written Պաւլիկեանք (Païlikeanq), but in the eleventh century Gregory Magister uses Պողիկեանք (Poghikeanq), which does not admit of the insertion of a *h*.

[1] Mansi, *Concilia*, vol. XXI, p. 1177, canon 4.
[2] Mansi, *Concilia*, vol. XXII, pp. 157 ff.

politan Church. Nicetas was a thoroughgoing Dualist. He made it his business to consecrate new bishops for the heretics, but he found their churches almost all Monarchian and insisted on forcing new Dualist bishops on them to rescue them from error. The bishops elected for the vacant sees were Bernard-Raymond for Toulouse, Guirald Mercier for Carcassonne and Raymond de Casalis for the Val d'Aran. At the same time the boundary between the sees of Toulouse and Carcassonne was fixed, the agreement being signed by the leading Perfects of either see.[1]

It seems therefore that Languedoc had been converted by Monarchian missionaries. These almost certainly came from the great heretic church of Lombardy, the church called de Concoresso, a Monarchian church which in its turn claimed to have learnt its doctrines from "Sclavonia" and from Bulgaria. The Church of Concoresso, whose obscure name some have derived from the village of Concorès in the Rouergue, was always in close touch with the Languedoc heretics and must have greatly influenced them.[2] But the history of the Italian heretics in the twelfth century is even more obscure than that of the French.

Nicetas on the other hand, like the Poplicani of Burgundy and Flanders, belonged to the strictly Dualist school now dominant in Constantinople and allied with the great Dalmatian church of Tragurium. Though Italy seems to have remained predominantly Monarchian, Nicetas apparently won his way in Languedoc. As a result of the Council of Saint-Félix, his disciple Barthélemy of Carcassonne, heretic bishop of Agen, was transferred to the see of Albi.[3] The previous bishop, Sicard, was probably a Monarchian. The Albigensian church, which grew so powerful as to give its name popularly to the whole heretic movement, was therefore the direct child of Nicetas and his council, and always retained his doctrines.[4]

But the Poplicani farther north soon were dissipated. A Dualist

[1] The Acts of this heretic council were written down. A copy dated 19 August 1222 exists, published, amongst other places, in Bouquet, *Recueil des Historiens de France*, vol. xiv, p. 448. For Nicetas, see above, p. 72.
[2] Sacchoni, *Summa*, in Martène et Durand, *Thesaurus*, vol. v, pp. 1767 ff. Guiraud, *Histoire de l'Inquisition*, vol. i, pp. 197–8.
[3] Reference above, n. 1.
[4] Sacchoni, *Summa, loc. cit.*

Church, the Cathar Church de Francia, lingered on to be rooted out by St Louis;[1] but the subtleties of neo-gnosticism had no permanent appeal to the northern peasants. Cruder heresies attracted them more. The twelfth century was a great age of heresy. Apart from the Gnostic strain, there were sects arising tinged with Judaism; there was, more emphatically, a strong anti-clerical movement, directed against the wealth and over-organization of the Church and expressed in a desire for ecclesiastical individualism and anarchy and in poverty. This movement found its popular leaders in Peter Valdes of Lyon and in Arnold of Brescia, and a little was guided back into the fold by St Francis. Peter Valdes preached from 1161 to 1180, when his doctrines, at first regarded as legitimate and never entirely condemned by certain churchmen, were officially discountenanced by the authorities. But by then his followers formed a numerous sect spreading from the Lyonnais across the Alps into Italy. Farther north heresy was kept in check. There such heretical traditions as lingered were of a Waldensian, not a Cathar, complexion; and the great movement of Lollardy that emerged a little more than a century later showed a kinship to Valdes's teachings rather than to any other. And the Waldensian church, though contemporary theologians usually treated it alongside of the Cathar churches, had in fact nothing to do with them, except in so far as both were affected by the ascetic anti-clericalism of the time. The Waldenses were Protestant Christians, striving to return to the purity of the early Church. They had no concern with the Dualism of the Cathars. When they preached asceticism and practised continence it was due to a Puritan taste for self-discipline and hatred of luxury, not to a philosophic conception of the fundamental wickedness of matter and the desirability of race-suicide. Even where their organization definitely copied that of the Cathars, in having a class of initiates or the Perfect, so made by a Consolamentum, the initiation had nothing of the same esoteric quality. It was merely a process for obtaining ministers whose ordination should in no way savour of clerical tradition.[2]

Along with the Waldenses other minor sects grew up, like them

[1] Sacchoni, *ibid.*, *loc. cit.*
[2] Guiraud, *Histoire de l'Inquisition*, vol. 1, chap. VIII, *passim*.

preserving basic Christian doctrine. Their history is of no importance, but their existence helped to narrow the range of the Cathar churches. By the end of the twelfth century the Cathars of the West were almost entirely concentrated in Languedoc, Provence and Lombardy, with a small community in central France and two in central Italy.[1]

In England Cathar heretics were to be found as late as 1210, when one was burnt in London.[2] In Germany they had a longer history. About the year 1200 Bavaria was full of heresy; there were said to be forty communities in the diocese of Passau alone.[3] The Rhine cities were also badly affected. But the Cathars were probably much less numerous than the Waldenses, and both sects together were not powerful enough to survive a few years of concentrated persecution begun in 1231 under the patronage of the Emperor Frederick II.

The Cathar churches kept in touch with each other. But their circumstances were often very different. Little is known of the history of the Italian Cathars. In 1184 Frederick Barbarossa and Pope Lucius III introduced at Verona the Constitution known as the *Ad Abolendam*, which set up an Inquisition against the Italian heretics. But it seems to have had little effect. In 1250 there were six Cathar churches there.[4] The two greatest were the *Ecclesia Albanensis* or *de Desenzano* and the Ecclesia *de Concoresso*. The former, possibly so named because its founders came from Albania, consisted of communities round Milan, Verona and Desenzano and numbered then about 500 Perfects or initiates. About the year 1200 its bishops lived at Sorano and Vicenza; their names at that time were Marchisio and Nicolas.[5] The latter was scattered throughout Lombardy and contained 1500 Perfects. The origin of its name is unknown. Its bishop (in 1200 he was a certain Garatus) lived at "Coresso", and one of his deputies at Brescia.[6] It claimed to have learnt its doctrines

[1] Rainier Sacchoni, *Summa*, pp. 1767 ff.

[2] Baleus, *Centuria 3, Catalogus Scriptorum Majoris Britanniae*, p. 258.

[3] *Addenda* to Reinerius, in Gretser, *Opera Omnia Theologica*, vol. XII, p. 27.

[4] Rainier Sacchoni, *Summa, loc. cit.*

[5] Bonacorsi, ed. Baluze, in d'Achéry, *Spicilegium*, vol. XIII, p. 581.

[6] Vignier, *Recueil de l'Histoire de l'Eglise*, p. 268. Casciono, heretic bishop of Sclavonia, was living at Mantua at this time, Alberic, his *filius major*, lived at Milan, and Otto, his *filius minor*, at Bagnolo (*loc. cit.*).

from the Slavs and the Bulgars. Like the true Bogomils it was Monarchian.[1] The Albanensis church on the other hand had been at first purely Dualist, but by the thirteenth century it was changing over to Monarchianism. There were two other Cathar churches in Lombardy, the *Baiolensis*, whose adherents were found also in Tuscany and Romagna—it had some 200 Perfects, and was probably differentiated from the other Lombard churches by its doctrine, which was definitely docetist: and the *Vicentina* or *de Marchia*, which comprised the heretics of the Eastern marches. It had been protected in the early thirteenth century by Ezzelino the Monk, the tyrant of Treviso, but by 1250 it was declining and possessed only 100 Perfects. Farther south was the church of Tuscany, the *Florentina*. Florence in the twelfth century had been a great heretic centre. Peter, first bishop of the Church of Concoresso, had been a Florentine, and in 1173 the heretics caused a revolution in the town.[2] We have the list of the Florentine bishops during the first half of the thirteenth century. Bishop Paternonus, from 1212 to 1227, brought it to a high pitch of prosperity, but under his successors its adherents dwindled. By 1250 it only could claim 100 Perfects in conjunction with the southernmost church, *de Valle Spoletina*, whose range included Rome but which never seems to have enjoyed much prosperity. In Orvieto, on the other hand, the Cathars had been very powerful in the twelfth century, but they were already declining in the thirteenth.[3] In Rome itself would-be heretics tended rather to follow Arnold of Brescia's Waldensianism. In the South of the peninsula and in Sicily, though occasional groups of heretics were noted, they seem never to have assumed serious proportions.

The list of Cathar churches, provided by the renegade Cathar, Rainier Sacchoni, cannot, however, tell us of the state of the Cathar churches at the height of their prosperity. By 1250 the authorities

---

[1] John Lugio, heretic bishop of Bergamo in the XIIIth century, wrote a treatise, the *Liber de Duobus Principiis*, attacking the Church of Concoresso and its adherents, whom he called 'Garatenses' for their Monarchianism. He preached unqualified Dualism.

[2] Lami, *Della Eresia dei Paterini in Firenze, passim.*

[3] *Vita S. Parentii*, in *Acta Sanctorum*, May, vol. v, p. 86.

at Rome had evolved the means for combating heresy and had begun on their task. The numbers of heretics must therefore have been diminishing. On the other hand the Italian Cathars never seem to have been persecuted so severely as those of France; and many refugees from France came in the course of the years that followed the Albigensian Crusade to find safety in Italy.[1]

This gentler treatment was due in part to the influence of St Francis and his disciples. But another reason was that in Italy the Cathars never were a great political danger. They might be very numerous, but in view of the teeming population of Lombardy the proportion was not so portentous. Nor were they the only heretical school there. The Waldenses too had their communities in Italy. Moreover the Italian Cathar churches remained purely popular. There is no evidence that the local nobility ever adhered to them or, except for Ezzelino of Treviso,[2] ever gave them much protection. The Lombard noble had no need of their help. If he were jealous of the local bishop or abbot, the perpetual wars of the Emperors against the Pope and the Communes gave him ample opportunities to annex his neighbours' lands without endangering his immortal soul for ever. Nor does it seem that the Cathars, despite various riots, ever as in France captured the municipal government of the towns. But on the other hand if the humble rank of its supporters absolved Italian Catharism from too much publicity, it also deprived it of any material resources with which to combat the steady labours of the missionaries of the Church, of the Franciscans and the Dominicans who had learnt the lessons of humility and poverty and worked amongst the poor as the Cathar missionaries had worked, but with the whole force and wealth of the Church behind them. The story of the decline and fall of the Cathars in Italy is obscure because it was slow and on the whole bloodless, lacking in sensational qualities. Occasionally, as at Verona in 1233[3] or at Pisa or at Milan in 1240,[4]

[1] For example, Sacchoni says that 150 Perfects from the Church of France were in refuge in Lombardy in his time.
[2] Ezzelino "persecutor of the Faith and favourer of heretics"—letter of Innocent IV in Ripoll, *Bullarium Ordinis Fratrum Praedicatorum*, vol. I, p. 135.
[3] The work of the Dominican Robert, an ex-heretic, surnamed therefore the Bougre (Matthew Paris, III, p. 361).
[4] At Pisa two Perfects were burnt: Lami, *Lezioni di Antichità Toscana*, vol. II,

large numbers of heretics were burnt at the stake. Occasionally the Cathars attracted force against themselves, as when in 1225 they burnt Catholic churches at Brescia[1] or in 1235 murdered the Catholic bishop of Mantua.[2] In Florence in 1240 large numbers were arrested but apparently were unpunished.[3] But on the whole the success of the Catholic missionaries was steady, though very slow; and occasionally there would be some encouraging triumph, as when the preaching of Antony of Padua in Rimini in 1225 brought back to the fold the arch-heretic Bonivillus who for thirty years had led the local opposition to orthodoxy.[4] By the middle of the fourteenth century it was all over. The only trace of Cathar doctrine was now to be found in certain of St Francis's own teachings. Consciously or unconsciously he had absorbed something of their ideas of the evil of matter and of the identity of the human with the animal soul.

The County of Provence formed the geographical link between Italy and Languedoc. Heresy spread early there, both from across the passes of the Maritime Alps and through the trading cities on the coast. But the history of its spread is as obscure as that of its spread in Italy. By the close of the twelfth century both Marseille and Avignon were heretic centres; and the nobles of Provence, unlike those of Italy, were beginning to toy with heresy. Probably this was a later development. In the twelfth century Provence was kept unsettled by the various attempts of the Emperor to make effective his rights as King of Burgundy and the quarrels of the rivals to the County of Provence, the Counts of Toulouse and Barcelona. The local nobility thus suffered few restraints and could even rob the estates of the Church at their pleasure. But with the aggression from the North represented by the Albigensian Crusade,

---

pp. 537 ff. At Milan it was the work of the Podestà Oldrado of Tresseno, of whom therefore an equestrian statue was erected with the inscription "Catharos ut debuit ussit". Muratori, *Antiquitates Italicae*, vol. v, p. 90.

[1] Baronius, *Continuatio Annalium*, vol. XIII, p. 323, no. 47.

[2] Baronius, *op. cit.* vol. XIII, p. 425, no. 16.

[3] Lami, *op. cit.* vol. II, *loc. cit.*

[4] Wadding, *Annales Minorum*, vol. II, p. 166. The conversion of such men as Rainier Sacchoni is a tribute to the success of the Friar's preaching.

and then the marriage of the ultimate heiress of Provence, Beatrix of
Barcelona, to Charles, the French King's brother, the nobility began
to seek the alliance of the heretic nobles across the Rhône and to
favour their own heretic populace. Even Beatrix's father, Raymond
Berenger, was at one moment suspect; and in later lists of the
heretics and their patrons are found a Lord of Montélimar, co-
Viscount of Marseille, a Lord of Cavaillon, a Count of Die and a
Seigneur of Lambesc.[1] The great and pious family of Les Baux
that traced its descent from the Magus Balthasar had not an entirely
clear record, though the martyrdom of William des Baux, Count of
Orange, at the hands of the heretics of Avignon in 1218 to some
extent cleansed the family name.[2]

But the Provençal nobles were ineffective and too late. Local
Catharism was stamped out. When in 1250 Rainier Sacchoni
described the various Cathar churches he never mentioned Provence.
The Alpine valleys where heretics could find refuge were by now
given over to the Waldensian sects. The rest of the County was
groaning under the iron hand of Charles of Anjou. Allied to him
and his saintly brother King Louis, the Catholic Church was once
again triumphant.

II

In Languedoc, also, across the Rhône, the Church had recovered
herself by 1250. But there the fight had been desperate. The heretics
had been defeated only by the genius of St Dominic and still more
by the swords of fierce rapacious warriors from the North. For
over half a century Languedoc was dominated by the Cathars and
seemed to be lost to Rome for ever. And, though they were to be
stamped out utterly, the epic tales of their conquest and the subtle
interrogatories of the Dominicans of the Inquisition were to paint
for posterity a vivid picture of the flowering of the Gnostic-
Manichaean faith in the hours of its final glory.

[1] Vaissète-Molinier, *Histoire de Languedoc*, vol. VI, p. 608.
[2] *Chanson de la Croisade*, verses 4240 and 4390 ff., ed. Meyer, I, pp. 185, 191.

The Cathar Council of Saint-Félix-de-Caraman may be taken to be the beginning of heretic domination in Languedoc. Henceforward the Cathars made no attempt to hide themselves. Sure of popular support their leaders could defy the authorities, the more so as the most powerful local authorities, the nobles, were beginning to join their ranks. The circumstances were ideal. For long the nobles had been jealous of the vast ecclesiastical estates of the South. The Archbishops of Arles, Narbonne and Auch, the Bishops of Béziers, Carcassonne and Toulouse and the other great churchmen were now at last vulnerable to attack. No help could come from outside the country. The Pope was distracted by his conflict with the Emperor Frederick Barbarossa; the Kings of France and England watched each other's movements too jealously for either to take action; the Spanish Kings could never forget the Moors. And so the nobles of Languedoc, if they could win by a timely apostasy the support of the increasingly heretic populace, were able to despoil the Church in comfort. And the more the nobles favoured heresy the more rapidly the numbers of heretics increased.

How far there were genuine converts amongst the nobles it is difficult to assess. Many of the lesser nobility can have had little opportunity of enriching themselves at the expense of the Church and yet were to be found in the ranks of the heretics. They must be presumed to have crossed over in all sincerity. But the greater nobles, such as the Counts of Toulouse or of Foix, usually took care to die reconciled to the Church. Catholic writers called them not *heretici* but *hereticales*. On the other hand their womenfolk were usually amongst the most fervent heretics. Count Raymond-Roger of Foix might remain only a *hereticalis* and die a Catholic, but his Countess left him with his consent to take the strictest vows of a Perfect and his sister Esclarmonde was for many years recognized as the most holy of all the Cathar women.[1] Indeed one of the most spectacular aspects of the Cathar movement in Southern France was the enthusiasm with which it was supported by the great ladies of the country.

[1] Doat, *Registres de l'Inquisition*, vol. XXIV, pp. 40, 240, 250, 251: Vaissète-Molinier, *Histoire de Languedoc*, vol. VIII, p. 224.

We cannot tell when and how the lesser nobility joined the movement. Among the greater nobles the first to give it open patronage was Roger II, Viscount of Béziers and Carcassonne, and ruler of the Narbonnais. In 1174 he flatly refused the request of the Church authorities that he should end his protection of the heretics, and in 1178 he was excommunicated for his alliance with them.[1] Count Raymond V of Toulouse always professed his disapproval of them, though he avoided taking active measures. But his son Raymond VI, who succeeded him in 1195, was their avowed friend.[2] Raymond-Roger of Foix by 1200 had brought his great family influence to their support; and by the beginning of the thirteenth century they could number in their ranks the noble families of Niort, of Cabaret, of Termes, of Saissac and many others besides.[3] In 1193 the Lady Cavaers of Fanjeaux placed a house in her prosperous town at their disposal.[4] A few years later the Lady Furneria of Mirepoix was in charge of three communities of Perfect women.[5] When in 1205 Esclarmonde of Foix received the Consolamentum the ceremony was attended not only by her brother the Count but also by most of the nobility of the County.[6] A little later in the thirteenth century we have the records of the Inquisition and the royal lists of heretic nobles whose lands were confiscated after the wars. From them it seems that there was no district between the Rhône and Gascony that was not largely or wholly devoted to heresy.

For Catharism, despite its gnosis, was essentially a popular religion. If the nobles were Cathars then the populace must already have been converted. It was this combination of popular fervour with the swords of the nobility that made the heresy so formidable to the Church. The agents through whom the nobles were converted

[1] Vaissète-Molinier, *Histoire de Languedoc*, vol. VI, p. 85.

[2] Pierre de Vaux-Cernay, *Hystoria Albigensis*, ed. Société de France, vol. I, pp. 31–41.

[3] See Guiraud, *Histoire de l'Inquisition*, vol. I, chaps. X and XI.

[4] For Cavaers, see Guiraud, *ibid.* p. 291. Helis de Mazeroles testified in 1243 that there had been a convent in Fanjeaux for fifty years. Doat, *Registres*, vol. XXIII, p. 162.

[5] Doat, *Registres*, vol. XXII, p. 111.

[6] Doat, *Registres*, vol. XXIV, pp. 240, 250–1: Vaissète-Molinier, *Histoire de Languedoc*, preuves, no. 263.

seem to have been heretic cloth-merchants and doctors of medicine. The cloth-merchant, particularly the travelling draper with goods from the East, was always welcomed in noble houses: noble ladies naturally wanted to see his wares and would even visit his shops. But his business connections kept him in close touch with Lombardy and with Constantinople. It was probably through the cloth trade that heretic communications travelled across Europe and could be brought into the inner apartments of noble castles. Similarly heretic doctors could always penetrate easily into the intimate life of the nobility. The Cathars encouraged the study of medicine, for all their contempt for the body; but their medical theories were probably very similar to those of the Christian Scientist healers of to-day. Faith healing played a large and effective part in their cures and gave them great renown: which they used the better to disseminate heresy.[1]

By the close of the twelfth century the Church was thoroughly alarmed. The decrees of the Council of Tours were abortive. The local bishops' synods had achieved nothing. Louis VII, for all his piety, was prevented by his fear of the Angevins from giving the help of the secular arm. But at his request Pope Alexander III took action again in 1178, sending a special mission to Toulouse headed by a learned Cistercian, Peter, Cardinal of St Chrysogonus, with whom were the Archbishop of Bourges, the Bishop of Poitiers, Henry, Abbot of Clairvaux and Reginald, Abbot of Bath. This distinguished mission was eagerly welcomed by Count Raymond V of Toulouse; but his people did not share his enthusiasm. The Cardinal was booed in the streets of the city. Nevertheless an inquiry was set up. As an example a rich heretic of Toulouse, called Maurand, was interrogated and sentenced to the confiscation of his goods and the destruction of his houses. He himself escaped by a timely recantation and by promising to perform the canonical penances. Even his goods were returned to him after the Count had extracted a fine. But Maurand's repentance was all that the Cardinal achieved. Except for Raymond V no lay authority would support him, while

[1] See Guiraud, *op. cit.* vol. I, pp. 350–7.

the powerful Viscount of Béziers was openly hostile, and indifferent even when the Cardinal excommunicated him.[1]

In 1179 at the Lateran Council Alexander III repeated previous condemnations of heresy, complaining bitterly of the open practices of the "Cathars, Paterins and Publicans".[2] A new mission was sent to Southern France under Henry of Clairvaux, who had now risen to be Cardinal-Bishop of Albano. Henry worked for several years in Languedoc, preaching, reforming the Church and even leading armed forces against the obstinate Viscount of Béziers. But it was all in vain. Henry's work was sufficiently appreciated for him to be sent on similar missions in the North and in Germany (where he was more successful, for the heretics there were few and ill-supported): but it had no lasting results.[3] In 1195 Raymond V died. His successor Raymond VI was the acknowledged friend of heresy. The Church had no lay supporter left in the South.

In 1198, when Innocent III succeeded to the Papacy, Languedoc seemed utterly lost to Rome. In many ways the Church had herself to blame. The corruption and incompetence of many of her hierarchs were notorious. In 1181 Henry of Albano had deposed Archbishop Pons of Narbonne because of the weakness and utter inefficiency of his actions against the heretics.[4] But Pons was admirable compared to the subsequent Archbishop Bérenger, the bastard son of the Count of Barcelona, who was appointed to the see in 1191. Despite his repeated condemnation for simony and for negligence, Bérenger refused to be deposed. It was not till 1212 that Innocent was able, with the help of the Crusaders, to get rid of him.[5] Bernard de la Barthe, Archbishop of Auch, was an intimate friend of the heretics' patron, Raymond VI of Toulouse;[6] William de Roquesel, Bishop of

---

[1] Vaissète-Molinier, *Histoire de Languedoc*, vol. VI, pp. 79–85.

[2] Mansi, *Concilia*, vol. XXII, pp. 231–2.

[3] Gaufredus, *Chronicon*, in Bouquet, *Recueil des Historiens de France*, vol. XII, p. 448.

[4] Albanes, *Gallia Christiana*, vol. VI, col. 56.

[5] Innocent III, *Epistolae*, VII, no. 79, X, no. 69, XIV, no. 34 in *M.P.L.* vol. CCXV, coll. 361–2, 1166–8, vol. CCXVI, col. 410: Vaissète-Molinier, *Histoire de Languedoc*, vol. VII, p. 218: Albanes, *op. cit.* coll. 60–61.

[6] Pierre de Vaux-Cernay, *Hystoria Albigensis*, vol. I, pp. 67–8.

Béziers, died suspended of his functions because he refused ever to take steps against heretic noblemen.[1] Raymond de Rabastens who intrigued himself into the see of Toulouse in 1202 probably himself had heretic leanings.[2] The bishops of Carcassonne had for some generations been useless. Bishop Otho, who resigned his functions, probably not altogether willingly, in 1198, was self-admittedly too old to indulge in any activity against the heretics; while his successor Bishop Bérenger found that such activity merely resulted in his enforced departure from the city. The next bishop Bernard-Raymond de Roquefort belonged to a heretic family and acted accordingly.[3] From 1168 to 1195 the diocese of Maguelonne, under John de Montlaur, had been an arch-example of corruption and cynical secularization. Even the ordinary rules of the Church, such as clerical celibacy and tonsure, had been cheerfully ignored.[4]

The abbeys could show no better record than the bishoprics. The abbots in the diocese of Maguelonne followed their bishop's example.[5] The vices of the Abbot of Fos and his inordinate passion for hunting reached the ears of the Pope himself.[6] The Abbatial election at Alet in 1197 scandalized all Christendom. Bertrand of Saissac, regent of Foix, forced the monks, at a council over which the exhumed corpse of their previous abbot was set to preside, to cancel the election of their appointed candidate in favour of his nominee, the monk Boso: who within a year had ruined the abbey by selling off all its property to pay his debts to his patrons.[7] Other abbeys, disgusted no doubt with the Church, were on the friendliest terms with the heretics. It is impossible to say that any of them were actually won over to the heresy; but certain abbots, for example the Abbots of Saint-Volusien de Foix or of Saint-Papoul,

[1] Innocent III, *Epistolae*, VII, no. 242 in *M.P.L.* vol. CCXV, coll. 272–3.
[2] Vaissète-Molinier, *Histoire de Languedoc*, vol. VII, p. 602.
[3] Innocent III, *Epistolae*, I, no. 165 in *M.P.L.* vol. CCXIV, coll. 142–3: Vaissète-Molinier, *Histoire de Languedoc*, vol. VI, pp. 342, 349, 614.
[4] Alexander III, *Epistolae*, no. 2, IV, 1165, in *M.P.L.* vol. CC, col. 1165: Baluze, *Concilia Galliae Narbonensis*, pp. 34–7.
[5] Baluze, *loc. cit.*
[6] Albanes, *op. cit.* coll. 309, 315.
[7] Vaissète-Molinier, *Histoire de Languedoc*, vol. VI, p. 418.

belonged to heretic families, while the Abbey of Saint-Hilaire, specially favoured by the heretic Roger II of Béziers, rose and fell with the heretic cause.[1]

The parish priests, faced with such examples, either followed suit or sank into despondent apathy. Some, like the chaplain of Saint-Michel de Lanes, who would not interrupt his gaming even to celebrate the Sacraments, were as worldly as any of their superiors.[2] Others were frankly immoral, like the chaplain of Rieux-en-Val, who lived in sin with the lady of the village, after she had murdered her husband.[3] Others again, to save trouble, maintained the friendliest relations with the heretics and even were present at their ceremonies.[4] None of them could command a fraction of the respect given to the heretic leaders either for the purity of their lives or for the force and efficiency of their preaching.[5]

This was the situation that Pope Innocent III had to face on his accession—the Cathar heresy widespread throughout Northern Italy and Southern France and dominant in Languedoc, where all classes of the populace seemed to find in it an answer to their spiritual needs and where the nobles gave to it the backing of their material power; and his own hierarchy, in its corruption and apathy, was unable to check its growth. Innocent's first care was to provide efficient preachers for Languedoc. In 1199 a Cistercian mission was despatched there, its head, the monk Rainier, becoming Papal legate in the province. Peter de Castelnau, formerly Archdeacon of Maguelonne and now likewise a Cistercian, was sent to help him. In 1200 there was a new legate, John de Saint Paul, Cardinal of St Prisca. In 1203 Peter de Castelnau was definitely chief Papal representative, but next year the Abbot of Cîteaux himself, Arnald-Amaury, was summoned to give assistance. The Cistercians were accompanied by Papal letters ordering all the lay princes to rally to

[1] Vaissète-Molinier, *Histoire de Languedoc*, vol. VI, pp. 153, 154.
[2] MS. in Library of Toulouse, quoted by Guiraud, *Histoire de l'Inquisition*, vol. I, p. 347.
[3] Vaissète-Molinier, *Histoire de Languedoc*, vol. VII, p. 368.
[4] Guiraud, *op. cit.* pp. 346–9, gives further examples.
[5] Guillaume of Puylaurens, *Historia Albigensis*, in Bouquet, *Recueil des Historiens de France*, vol. XIX, p. 194.

their support; and they themselves had orders to preach as widely as possible and to set up enquiries wherever they could. In the meantime they were to reform the official clergy.

Under Peter de Castelnau and Arnald-Amaury the Cistercian mission did well. Late in 1203 the city of Toulouse was induced to promise to persecute heresy, and next year Count Raymond VI agreed to sever his connections with the heretics. After a debate at Carcassonne in 1204 between the Cistercians and the heretics, King Peter of Aragon was convinced of the sins of heresy and gave full co-operation to the mission. Meanwhile action was taken against the more scandalous of the local clergy, such as the Archbishop of Narbonne. But these successes were short-lived and empty. The local clergy resented the reforms and opposed the Cistercians. Raymond of Toulouse soon relapsed into his heretical friendships. The nobility and the people alike ignored the fulminations of Rome. By 1205 the situation was as bad as it ever had been.[1]

Innocent did not despair. His diplomacy lately had been elsewhere bearing fruit. Negotiations with the King of Bulgaria were inducing that monarch to take stern measures against the Dualist heresy in the land of its origin in Europe. In 1203 the Dualist King of Bosnia, Kulin, with all his courtiers returned to the fold of Rome. In 1204 the Knights of the Fourth Crusade atoned in Papal eyes for their strange lack of scruples and for the blood of fellow-Christians that they shed by bringing the whole Church of Constantinople under Papal domination. After such triumphs Languedoc could not be allowed to defy him.[2]

In December 1205 the Cistercian missionaries were joined at Castelnau by two Spaniards, Didacus Bishop of Osma and his prior Dominic de Guzman. They had passed through the country in 1203 and sadly noted its condition; and now their conviction, backed almost certainly by Papal approval, was that only by adopting complete poverty could the missionaries hope to counter the influence of the Cathar preachers. They must show equal austerity and purity of life. Then their arguments would stand a chance of being heard. With

[1] Vaissète-Molinier, *Histoire de Languedoc*, vol. VI, pp. 222 ff.: Guiraud, *Histoire de l'Inquisition*, vol. I, pp. 375–81.   [2] See above, pp. 104–5.

some reluctance the Cistercians adopted the Spaniards' ideas, and a new stage in preaching began.[1]

But even this preaching, by men who combined learning with utter poverty and who ultimately formed the Dominican Order, though the poor listened more attentively than before, produced at first negligible results. The nobles were unimpressed and resentful, and so long as they held back their vassals would not give up their heresy. The missionaries encouraged public debates, confident that they could defeat in argument the most learned of the heretics; knights and townsfolk would be chosen to act as arbiters. But though the Catholics never doubted who were the victors in each discussion, the arbiters would seldom commit themselves to a decision—to avoid, the Catholics said, having to pronounce against the heretics.[2] Neither the Cistercians nor Didacus and Dominic themselves could make any headway.

At last, in 1208, matters reached a climax. Raymond of Toulouse had once again submitted to Rome in 1205, and Peter de Castelnau as Papal legate had tried a policy of extreme friendliness with him, helping him to recover some of the territory on the Rhône that he claimed as Marquis of Provence. But Raymond was incorrigible. In 1207 Peter excommunicated him; and the Pope confirmed the sentence. In January 1208 Raymond pretended to submit, and asked Peter to visit him at his residence of Saint-Gilles. The legate came with his friend, Navar, Bishop of Conserans. But the interview was stormy. Peter determined to leave at once for Provence, and the Count shouted after him: "Wherever you go, by land or by sea, take care! I shall have my eye on you." The Abbot of Saint-Gilles tried to calm Raymond and offered Peter an escort. But on January 15, as Peter prepared to cross the Rhône, a horseman came up and struck him dead.[3]

With the murder of his legate, Innocent III felt himself justified in

[1] Pierre de Vaux-Cernay, *Hystoria Albigensis*, vol. I, pp. 20–3: Bennett, *The Early Dominicans*.
[2] Pierre de Vaux-Cernay, *Hystoria Albigensis*, vol. I, pp. 24–6.
[3] Innocent III, *Epistolae*, x, no. 149 in *M.P.L.* vol. ccxv, coll. 1246–7: Pierre de Vaux-Cernay, *op. cit.* pp. 65 ff.: Luchaire, *Innocent III: La Croisade des Albigeois*, pp. 76 ff.

calling in secular help against these recalcitrant heretics. Raymond of Toulouse was too heavily implicated, and nothing but force would cow him. The preaching of the White Brothers might bring the heretic poor back to orthodoxy; but they would never succeed till the heretic nobles' power was destroyed for ever. The Northern nobility must be called in to crush the Southern. It was time for the Crusade.

Already in 1204 and 1205 Innocent III had appealed to King Philip Augustus, reminding him that he was entitled by the decree *Ad Abolendam* to deprive of their fiefs vassals who protected heretics.[1] But Philip Augustus needed what support he could get from his vassals in his wars against the Plantagenets. He would not commit himself to a policy that would stir up fresh enmities. He answered politely and did nothing. In November 1207 Innocent addressed himself to the main feudatories of the North, the Duke of Burgundy, the Counts of Bar, of Dreux, of Nevers, of Champagne and of Blois. Here for the first time the idea of a Crusade appears. Innocent begged for the help of these Northern lords, saying that the secular arm was necessary to suppress these incorrigible heretics and that the miseries of war must bring them back to the truth. He offered the same indulgences to anyone who went on such a war as were given to Crusaders going to the East.[2] The Northerners listened. The Eastern Crusades had taught them how satisfactorily the acquisition of spiritual merit could be combined with that of rich territories. But Philip Augustus again insisted on prudence. He gave permission only to five hundred knights from Burgundy and the Nivernais to go off to the South. The number, he told his vassals, must be strictly limited.[3]

The murder of Peter of Castelnau altered the situation. Moral indignation all over France supported the Pope. Philip Augustus might content himself with writing sympathetically to the Pope, saying that he too had reason to be displeased with the Count of Toulouse, whose conduct during the English Wars was far from

[1] Innocent III, *Epistolae*, XI, no. 229, in *M.P.L.* vol. CCXV, col. 1545.
[2] Pierre de Vaux-Cernay, *Hystoria Albigensis*, vol. I, pp. 72–4; Innocent III, *Epistolae*, XI, nos. 230–2, in *M.P.L.* vol. CCXV, coll. 1246–7.
[3] Pierre de Vaux-Cernay, *ibid.*, *loc. cit.*

satisfactory, but reminding him that the Count could not be deprived of his lands (which he held from the French King), unless heresy was definitely proved. The Pope's Crusade was, in fact, an infringement of the King's sovereignty.[1] But the nobles of the North would no longer be restrained. They found their leader, rather surprisingly, in a petty noble of the Ile de France, Simon de Montfort, who had become Earl of Leicester as the husband of a great English heiress. Under his guidance, and inspired by the ceaseless preaching of the Pope's new legate, Arnald of Cîteaux, the Crusaders gathered together in the course of 1208, and in the autumn marched southwards. A series of wars was begun that would end at last in the suppression of heresy.

But the first war took twenty years; and even so the heretics' resistance was not over. They on their side had considerable material resources. Great nobles like Raymond of Toulouse or Raymond-Roger of Foix might only be *hereticales* and unreliable; but they would obviously oppose to their utmost the barbarians from the North. Other nobles, such as the Viscount of Béziers, and almost all the nobility of the second rank, were devoted to heresy. There were towns, such as Fanjeaux, Béziers, Duns, or Laurac, where, whatever the overlord might think, the population was so wholly heretic that they might count as heretic fortresses. There were castles that were admittedly heretic fortresses, for example Servian, by Béziers, or Minerve, above Narbonne. Above all, there was the impregnable city of Montségur, the Mountain of Safety, the Mount Thabor of the Cathars. This great castle stood on the territory of the Counts of Foix, and was, it seems, part of the dowry of the heretic princess Esclarmonde of Foix, from whom it was held by Raymond of Perelle. He was a fervent heretic and in effect handed the whole fortress over to the unrestricted use of the Cathar Church. Here the heretics found a safe asylum during their troubles, and here they kept up their best establishments of Perfects, over one of which Esclarmonde herself presided.[2]

---

[1] See Luchaire, *op. cit.* pp. 127 ff.
[2] Doat, *Registres*, vol. XXIV, pp. 44–62. Montségur is continually referred to throughout Cathar depositions. See also Guiraud, *op. cit.* vol. II, chap. V.

The story of the war known as the Albigensian Crusade is long and intricate.[1] The religious issue became blurred in the territorial issue. Pope Innocent III and the Dominican Brothers were above all eager to extirpate heresy as quickly and efficiently as possible, by force and fire if need be but preferably by preaching and willing repentance. But their allies, the Northern barons under Simon de Montfort, though many of them were sincerely religious, were all of them anxious to enrich themselves at the expense of the wealthy Southern lords; and they were encouraged by the Papal legate, Arnald-Amaury of Cîteaux, and by the French bishops who saw in Raymond of Toulouse and his peers slippery renegades, the murderers of Peter of Castelnau, men whose power must be broken for ever if heresy was to be eliminated. The Southern barons were in a difficult position. Many like Raymond himself were anxious to reconcile themselves with the Church, but they were temperamentally easy-going and they could not afford to persecute a sect that included half their subjects; and they naturally wished to retain their lands. Others, like Raymond-Roger of Béziers, felt that the best policy was an open support of heresy. Others again, like King Peter of Aragon, were steadfastly Catholic but deeply resented this Northern invasion into territory over parts of which (such as Carcassonne) he was suzerain. But, for all their hatred of the Northerners, the Southern lords would not join together. Raymond of Toulouse in vain approached Raymond-Roger, who was his nephew; in vain Raymond-Roger sought help from King Peter, who was his suzerain. Raymond of Toulouse made his submission to the Church and performed a humiliating penance at Saint-Gilles and for a campaign joined the Crusaders, and a little later went with his son on a weary journey to Rome to interview the Pope himself. Meanwhile Simon de Montfort, urged on by the Abbot of Cîteaux, annexed his lands and his titles. Raymond-Roger equally tried to submit in time; but his was the first territory to be attacked. The

---

[1] For the war, see Luchaire, *op. cit.* (who unfortunately gives no references) and Schmidt, *Histoire des Cathares*, vol. i, pp. 222 ff. The fullest contemporary texts are Pierre de Vaux-Cernay's *Hystoria Albigensis* and the *Chanson de la Croisade*.

holocaust and massacres at Béziers in July 1209 were a foretaste of what the South might expect. After the capture of Carcassonne later in the year Raymond-Roger was declared to have forfeited his territory, which was annexed by Simon de Montfort. Atrocities grew in number, encouraged by the legate despite Innocent's disavowal. At the capitulation of Minerve in July 1210, when the heretics' lives were to be saved by the terms of the surrender, de Montfort's troops butchered them at his orders, and the legate did not interfere. Finally at the Council of Montpellier in 1211 Innocent III yielded to the extremist party; the Northern barons were established in the South with the fullest right and intention of persecution.

Then came the reaction. The Count of Toulouse returned from Rome and was welcomed as a deliverer. The King of Aragon came out openly against the Northerners, after the failure of his attempt to stop the Crusade with Innocent's help. Innocent's hand was forced again by his extremists; and Peter of Aragon joined his forces to those of Raymond of Toulouse, Raymond-Roger of Foix and the Count of Comminges. With the reaction, the heretics came out of hiding again, and preached openly in the Toulousain and Foix. But their revival was short-lived; the Southern lords met disaster by the castle of Muret in 1213. Their army was scattered by the knights of Simon de Montfort. The Counts of Toulouse and Foix fled to English territory, and Peter of Aragon lay dead on the battlefield.

The disaster at Muret was not so fatal as might have been expected. Innocent preached moderation and grudged Simon de Montfort the fruits of victory; and King Philip Augustus sent his son Louis to the South to see what was happening. At the Lateran Council of 1215 the Southern lords were reconciled again with the Church, promising again to persecute heresy. They returned to their battered lands; and Simon de Montfort's attempt to dislodge them once more was closed by his death before the walls of Toulouse in June 1218. The South was secure for a while, and by 1220 the heretics again worshipped freely. The Albigensian Crusade seemed to be over, having achieved nothing but material destruction. Heresy still was rampant.

Innocent III was dead by now, and Honorius III had committed the Church to Simon's support. With Simon's death his cause crumbled. His heirs and the Pope saved it by handing his rights over to the new King of France, Louis VIII. Raymond VI died in 1222. Raymond VII, his son, had a better record of orthodoxy. But it did not avail him. In 1226, after a comparatively peaceful interlude, too short for the country's recovery, Languedoc again was invaded by the enemy, a great army of Northern barons under King Louis VIII himself. In three years the royal army achieved its ends. Raymond VII was reduced to sign the treaty of Meaux in April 1227 with the young King Louis IX and his mother the Regent Blanche— Louis VIII had died in the previous year. Raymond performed a humiliating penance, agreed to pay an indemnity and a heavy tribute for five years, married his daughter and heiress Jeanne to the King's brother Alphonse, and undertook to persecute heresy. His allies, the Counts of Foix and of Comminges and the Viscounts of Béziers and Béarn, joined in the treaty, giving up castles as guarantees but refusing to promise a thorough repression of the Cathars.

For ten years an uneasy peace reigned in Languedoc. Raymond periodically tried to carry out his side of the bargain. The Dominicans were allowed to set up their Inquisition at Toulouse, at Albi and at Narbonne; large numbers of heretics were arrested and examined and the majority of them were burnt. But the town authorities, the Consuls and the *Capitouls*, resented the Inquisition as much as an infringement of their rights as from love of heresy. Many of the nobles, in particular the Count of Foix and the Viscount of Béziers, still openly gave the heretics protection. The heretic preachers again wandered through the countryside, avoiding now the bigger towns but preaching freely in many of the castles of the nobility; in the smaller towns communities of the Perfect were maintained undisguised. But they were nervous. In 1232 the heretic leaders negotiated with the Lord of Perelle to have his guarantee that Montségur should continue to be their asylum. He agreed, and henceforward it became the recognized centre of their power.[1] Raymond of Perelle's alliance with the heresy was to be cemented

[1] Doat, *Registres*, vol. XXIV, pp. 43, 68, 201, 202.

in the blood of his daughter Esclarmonde. Periodically a concentrated attack of the Inquisitors would destroy for the time being a Cathar community; for example at Moissac in 1234 the leading Cathars were burnt or forced to flee for refuge, some to Lombardy and some to Montségur. But so long as the native nobility survived, the heretics could still be hopeful.

For the native nobility, however, the situation was difficult. Pressed by the Church and by the French King, Raymond of Toulouse found himself steadily shorn of his power and unable to give legitimate protection to his subjects. Raymond Trencavel, Viscount of Béziers, belonging to a family long suspected by the Church, with his town of Carcassonne forfeited, felt even more desperate. In 1239 the two of them tried to recapture their freedom. But Raymond Trencavel's attempt was crushed before Carcassonne; and in two years Raymond of Toulouse was reduced to submission by the royal troops of France. Raymond Trencavel retired broken to his estates in Catalonia. The Count of Toulouse became once more a dutiful son of the Church.

His first duty was to deal with the castle of Montségur. So long as the Cathars had their City of Refuge, it would be impossible to stamp them out. But he was unwilling to act, till the heretics themselves gave provocation. They had had great hopes of the 1239 rising; and its failure had been a shock to them. Moreover in 1241 their friend Roger-Bernard of Foix died, reconciled on his deathbed to the Church. His son Roger IV was more anxious to preserve his lands than to protect his father's friends. In 1242 a band of desperate heretics from Montségur joined with the heretics of Avignonet to ambush the party of Inquisitors that was on its way to visit the latter town and massacred them all. The crime was disastrous in its effects. Public opinion, remembering the murder of Peter of Castelnau in his father's day, at once suspected Raymond of Toulouse. He, to disassociate himself from it, wrote letters of humble submission to the Queen-Regent Blanche and vowed vengeance on the murderers. His officers hastened to hand over large numbers of heretics to the Inquisitors. Throughout 1243 and 1244 the fires of the Inquisition burnt merrily. Many of the nobility perished in the flames: Peter

Robert of Mirepoix, Arnalda of Massa, Peter of Navidals, the Dowager Lady of Fanjaux, and the young Esclarmonde of Perelle. The heretics fled to the mountain valleys of the Pyrenees or away to Lombardy or to Bosnia; their leaders congregated in Montségur. There on their mountain-top where no Catholic had set foot for a generation they carried on their rites and defied the Catholic world. Raymond saw clearly that to fulfil his obligations to the Church Montségur must be destroyed.

At Montségur the heretics prepared their resistance. They appealed to their overlord, the young Count of Foix, but he disowned them and left them to their fate. In 1238 they had easily withstood a siege attempted by Raymond; but Raymond had been only half-hearted then. This time he was in earnest with the royal troops backing him; and they had less hope. Men and women alike took part in the defence, led by the Lord of Perelle and by Guillebert of Castres, the most venerated of the Cathar bishops. But, hopelessly outnumbered, they could not for all their courage hold the fortress for ever. When the end seemed near, the greater part of the defenders received the Consolamentum, the final rite of their church, although by so becoming Perfects they condemned themselves to the fires of the Inquisitors. Then, one dark March night, four of the Perfect crept from the castle with the holiest books and the treasure of the Cathars, to carry them through to the Cathar communities in the high Pyrenees. Next day Montségur surrendered to the Court of Toulouse.

The fortress was destroyed. The Perfect, to the number of about two hundred, were burnt without trial. The rest of the defenders were imprisoned, to be released some months later on the payment of fines and penances.

The fall of their citadel was a blow from which the Cathars never recovered. They became an underground sect, without a centre, without a storehouse for their treasure and their lore. The Perfect with the holy books from Montségur reached the Pyrenean castle of So, but they could not stay in peace there. Wherever they rested, soon they had to move on; and their treasure and their writings gradually were scattered in the wandering. But still large Cathar communities remained. For another half-century the Inquisitors were fully occupied, perpetually discovering nests of heretics and destroying them. During these years there was a steady migration of the Cathars to the comparative safety of Lombardy; some went farther to the greater safety of Bosnia.[1]

In 1249 after the death of Raymond VII, his successor, his son-in-law Alphonse of France, attempted an act of clemency, promising to restore confiscated goods to the repentant children of heretics. The Church forbade him. In the discouragement that followed, the native dynasty now extinct, the leading Cathars of Toulouse fled to Lombardy. About the same time St Louis destroyed the Cathar church of Languedoïl; and its remnants also fled across the Alps. By 1274 there were said to be no more Cathar bishops in the French King's lands. The heretic that wished to become a Perfect had to come to Italy to his old bishops that were settled there to receive the rite. In France the Consolamentum was administered only to the dying.[2]

In 1277 and 1278 we find the Inquisition indulging in fresh activities. By 1290 its fierceness seems to have provoked a popular recrudescence of sympathy towards the Cathars. At Béziers and at Carcassonne in 1296 Inquisitors were driven out by the people and by the municipal authorities. Cathar bishops came back from Lombardy and held assemblies again in Languedoc.[3] But it was not for long. The great persecutions of Philip IV's reign, from 1304 to 1312, destroyed the new enthusiasm; and persecution went steadily on throughout the next decades. By 1330 it seems that the Cathar church in France was effectively crushed; henceforward it was negligible.[4]

---

[1] Gervasius Premonstratensis, *Epistolae*, no. 129 in Hugo, *Sacrae Antiquitatis Monumenta*, p. 116—a letter from the legate Conrad of Porto which says that the Bosnian bishop had written to the French heretics to offer them shelter.

[2] Doat, *Registres*, vol. xxv, pp. 68, 243 ff., 248 ff.

[3] *Ibid.* vol. xxxii, pp. 264 ff.

[4] The last burning of heretics (including one Perfect) seems to have taken place in 1330, Doat, *op. cit.* vol. xxvii, pp. 179 ff.: Limborch, *Historia Inquisitionis*, quotes from the Toulouse register the accounts of the last persecutions (pp. 183 ff., 277 ff., 282 ff., 334 ff.).

Once the Cathars lost the support of the nobility their fate was inevitable. The Albigensian crusade and the defeat of the Southern lords by the Northern barons and the French King destroyed the whole foundation of their success. Their religion, for all its severity, suited the people of Languedoc, just as they were later to welcome the stern doctrine of Calvin, and fitted in well with the melancholy gaiety of the troubadours. But it owed its ephemeral success to the fact that it provided the Southern barons not only with an excuse to rob a Church of which they were desperately jealous but also with a nationalist creed with which to oppose the Capetians, the Plantagenets and the internationally-minded prelates of Italy. When the particular nationalism perished the creed perished also.

III

Historians must be grateful to the Inquisition. Of the Paulicians we have only vague hostile accounts. We are slightly better informed about the Bogomils, for we have details of the creed of one particular Bogomil, Basil, whom the Emperor Alexius questioned. But thanks to the Inquisition the French and Italian Cathars' creed is far more fully ascertainable. The Inquisitors questioned large numbers of heretics and recorded their replies. Thus their records, despite their hostile intention, give us a fair idea of what the Cathars believed.

A large selection of evidence is the more necessary in that Cathar theology was not fully worked out. One finds several variations in their fundamental dogmas. The chief of these concerns the eternity of the Devil. The Cathars, following the Bogomils, had their two schools of thought, the strictly Dualist or Manichaean, that believed in two principles, and the Monarchian, according to which the Evil God was a fallen angel.[1] These two views necessarily differed in their eschatology. To the Dualist evil would last on into eternity; to the Monarchians it would be destroyed at the end of the material world. For the question why Lucifer fell the Monarchians had the same hesitating answers as the Early Church. Some said from

[1] Sacchoni, *Summa*, pp. 1768 ff.

concupiscence,[1] others from pride[2] and others from envy.[3] Dualists and Monarchians alike were agreed that it was from envy of God's dominion over the celestial world that the Devil created the terrestrial world.[4]

The Creation equally brought up divergent views. Some said that the whole creation of the material world was the Devil's work, others that the Devil made the world out of material elements already existing.[5] This latter was probably the usual Monarchian view; some Monarchians even allowed that the Devil had God's permission for his work.[6] That in some eyes explained the reason why the Devil was able to imprison souls in his creation. Others held that the Devil imprisoned a fallen angel in the body of a man and thus created Adam. Eve was similarly created, and their children inherited the spark of angelic divinity.[7] The Dualists mostly believed that the Devil had invaded Heaven successfully enough to capture a third of the celestial spirits, and since then in every man or woman that he created he imprisoned one of them.[8] But such clear-cut declarations of doctrine were rare. For the most part Cathar preachers seem to have used symbolic legends to explain their beliefs.

The Cathar doctrine of Christ and of the Holy Ghost puzzled the Inquisitors. The *Summa Auctoritatis* maintained that the Cathars alone of heretics denied the divinity of Christ, and stated positively that Christ was not God.[9] On the other hand depositions often

---

[1] Legend in Döllinger, *Dokumente für Geschichte der Valdesier und Katharer*, pp. 149–51 Cf. also Doat, *Registres*, vol. xxxiv, p. 95.

[2] Moneta, *Summa*, pp. 4, 36, 39.

[3] *Summa Auctoritatis*, ed. Douais.

[4] E.g. the opinion of the heretic Peter Garsias, who said: "God is very good and nothing in this visible world is good. Therefore He cannot have made the visible world." Deposition in Douais, *Documents de l'Histoire de l'Inquisition*, vol. ii, p. 92.

[5] *Summa Auctoritatis*, p. 123.

[6] MS. quoted by Guiraud, *op. cit.* p. 49, n. 1.

[7] Döllinger, *op. cit.* p. 60—extract from the book known as the *Suprastella* written in 1235 by the heretic Salvi Burcé: Moneta, *op. cit.* p. 110.

[8] Sacchoni, *Summa*, p. 1768. This was the view of Balasinansa, Cathar bishop of Verona.

[9] *Summa Auctoritatis*, p. 130.

mentioned "God who was placed on the Cross";[1] and in Cathar ceremonies the Trinity, Father, Son and Holy Ghost, were frequently cited.[2] Pierre de Vaux-Cernay believed them to have two Christs.[3] Probably there was not so much divergence here as the Inquisitors thought. The Cathars were essentially believers in pantheism throughout the celestial realm. That is to say, good to them was God. They built up a sequence of *eons* between God Himself and the material world, all of which were filled with divinity. The Holy Ghost emanated from God as a sort of instrument by means of which divinity could be instilled into creatures. The Son, or Christ, was chief of these *eons* and as such was sent in a mortal casing to earth to combat the Devil and rescue the captive sparks of divinity. On the whole the Cathars tended to be docetist. It was simpler to believe that this Christ-eon being divine only seemed to assume human form and only seemed to be crucified; for if matter is wholly bad then a divine Being cannot be clothed in it. But docetism was not invariable. It would be possible (particularly in the eyes of those Monarchians who believed that God somehow had a hand in the creation, at least of the elements) for a divine Being to enter into matter if he so wished to dupe the Devil and rescue good. But the Cathars could not allow Christ actually to be in any way human. That would be an impossibility. The Redemption therefore was an untenable doctrine. Christ taught by His example; He showed the Way—like a Buddha rather than the Christ of Orthodox Christianity.[4]

This doctrine made the Virgin Mary a figure of little importance, about whom various views were held. To some she was a symbol of the Church,[5] to others an *eon* through whom the Christ-eon passed on its downward path,[6] to others a mere woman whom the Christ-eon used for its entrance into the material world. Many of the

---

[1] Doat, *Registres*, vol. XXII, pp. 21, 89.
[2] See below, p. 156, n. 3.
[3] Pierre de Vaux-Cernay, *Hystoria Albigensis*, vol. I, pp. 11–12. He says (p. 12) that some say that God the Father had two sons Satan and Christ. This is the doctrine of the Bogomils of Constantinople. See above, p. 75.
[4] See Guiraud, *Histoire de l'Inquisition*, pp. 67–70 and notes.
[5] Bernard Gui, *Practica Inquisitionis*, p. 238.
[6] *Summa Auctoritatis*, p. 130.

Cathars accepted the Bogomil belief that Christ entered Mary through her ear (a theory well known to the Early Christians) and, they said, having assumed flesh from her, left by the same door.[1]

The Cathars could believe neither in Hell nor in Purgatory. The Devil's domain was this world, and the material part of man must remain in this world, whereas the soul when ultimately detached from matter will ascend again to the celestial world. But the soul could only so free itself, if its human wearer lived a life as remote as possible from matter. It must go through its purification—its Purgatory—in this world. If its human wearer lived too material a life, then the soul would be too badly entangled with matter, too earth-bound to escape, and would have to enter again into some other living material body. This doctrine of Metempsychosis was somewhat vague. Probably the migration of the soul was not in any way a personal affair; rather, the mass of earthbound soul was perpetually divided up between living creatures; but it was hoped, when lives were pure the fragments of soul attached to them were able to catch on to the divine spirit which descended on to such perfected persons and thus won release. Thus if all the world became Cathar the amount of earthbound soul would rapidly diminish. But unfortunately the creation of new life somehow embedded it further into matter. For that reason, far more than because it meant the indulgence of the material sexual appetite, marriage was firmly to be deplored.[2]

The Cathars followed Gnostic tradition in distrusting the Old Testament and in identifying Jehovah and Satan. The heroes of the Old Testament, even Abraham and Moses, were inspired by the Devil. They were even said to call Jehovah a murderer, because He destroyed Pharaoh and his hosts, and Sodom and Gomorrah.[3] But they were inclined to admit the books of the Prophets, the Psalms

[1] *The Secret Book*, quoted in Ivanov, *Bogomil Books and Legends* (in Bulgarian), p. 82. "Ego autem descendens intravi per auditum et exivi per auditum" (Carcassonne MS.), see above, p. 76 and n. 4.

[2] Doat, *Registres*, vol. XXII, p. 99: Alain de Lille, *Contra Hereticos*, I, § 63, in *M.P.L.*, vol. CCX, coll. 365–6: MS. in Toulouse Library quoted in Guiraud, *Histoire de l'Inquisition*, vol. I. p. 60, n. 3.

[3] Pierre de Vaux-Cernay, *Hystoria Albigensis*, vol. I, p. 10.

and the five books of Solomon, as the New Testament so often referred back to them.[1] They knew the New Testament intimately, but they did not accept all the usual New Testament saints. John the Baptist was a false prophet, for he baptized by water and not by the spirit.[2] On this point they felt strongly; and though they quoted the words of Christ mentioning baptism by water they interpreted them in a strictly symbolical sense.[3] Some indeed felt kindlier about John the Baptist, regarding him as an angel and symbolizing his baptisms.[4]

They were necessarily intolerant of all creeds that did not accept the wickedness of matter, regarding any such believer as an adherent of Satan and inevitably damned. But they were prepared themselves to go very far in outward conformity if by so doing they could benefit their faith.[5]

Had it been possible the Cathars would have desired race-suicide, either immediate or by the non-procreation of children. The ideal believer would live a life of perfect chastity, eating only a minimum of food and denying himself all physical pleasure or comfort. All this was directed towards the freeing of the soul from the body. The Inquisitor Alain of Lille remarked that while the Catholics abstained from meat on Fridays because meat encouraged concupiscence, the Cathar adepts abstained from meat because of their doctrine of metempsychosis. The meat might contain a fragment of

---

[1] Doat, *Registres*, vol. XXII, pp. 89, 92: *Summa Auctoritatis*, pp. 126 ff. The good precepts which existed in the Old Testament were inserted by Satan, the better to deceive us (*Summa Auctoritatis*, p. 126).

[2] "Johannes Baptista fuit unus de majoribus diabolis qui unquam fuissent." Garsias's deposition in Douais, *Documents de l'Histoire de l'Inquisition*, vol. II, pp. 93, 103, 112: Rainier Sacchoni, *Summa*, p. 1773: Pierre de Vaux-Cernay, *Hystoria Albigensis*, p. 10. In the *Secret Book* he is identified with the false Prophet Elijah (Ivanov, *op. cit.* p. 82).

[3] In the Consolamentum ceremony (Lyons ritual) they quote St John's Gospel, iii, 5, which definitely mentions water.

[4] The *Liber de Duobus Principiis*, a work written probably by John of Lugio, heretic Bishop of Bergamo, accepts the whole Bible, while Rainier Sacchoni confirms (*Summa,* p. 1772) that John of Lugio considered John the Baptist and the Patriarchs to have been servants of God. He adds that the Church of Concoresso, which John of Lugio opposed, contained adherents who thought well of John the Baptist—a new doctrine, he says (*ibid.* p. 1773).   [5] Bernard Gui, *Practica Inquisitionis*, p. 238.

earthbound soul which would thus become more earthbound by metabolism.[1] Indeed to the Catholics it seemed that the Cathars cared far too little for chastity as bodily discipline. So long as it did not lead to the conception of children they positively seemed to encourage sexual intercourse or at least not to discourage it—a complete reversal of the Catholic view. They were in consequence suspected of all forms of unnatural orgies.[2] The Catholics' disapproval was justified in that the Cathars frankly admitted that they preferred casual debauchery to marriage, because marriage was a more serious affair, an official regularization of a wicked thing; and if its bonds are perpetual then the married person cannot ever hope to achieve the negation of the body necessary for perfection.[3]

The reason for this apparent carelessness about the sexual life of the ordinary Cathar was that the Cathar authorities realized a life of complete negation of matter to be beyond the reach of the average mortal. Consequently, again in the Gnostic-Manichaean tradition, their society was divided up into grades, the Believers and the Perfect. Nor was every heretic even a believer. Before the rite of entry into the sect, the ceremony of the Convenenza (Convenientia), could be performed, the would-be believer had to be adjudged a suitable recipient. Large numbers of persons who certainly sympathized with and even believed in the heresy never went through the ceremony. It was only when they were already besieged in Montségur in 1244 that the soldiers who were fighting for Catharism all celebrated the Convenenza. Till then they had not strictly been members of the sect.[4]

At the ceremony of the Convenenza the celebrant made one promise, to honour the superior caste in the sect, the Perfects, and to

---

[1] Alain de Lille, *Contra Hereticos*, I, § 74, *M.P.L.*, vol. ccx, col. 376: Sacchoni, *Summa*, p. 1762.

[2] As is shown by the subsequent history of the word "Bougre" or Bulgarian, given freely to them. Pierre de Vaux-Cernay declares that they believed it to be impossible to sin with any part of the body below the navel (*Hystoria Albigensis*, vol. I, p. 17).

[3] See the discussion in Guiraud, *Histoire de l'Inquisition*, vol. I, pp. 96–9.

[4] Bernard Gui, *Practica Inquisitionis*, p. 240: Doat, *Registres*, vol. xxii, pp. 107, 140, 210, 241, 281.

hold himself at their disposal whenever they should need him. In return he was promised that he should have the second initiatory rite, the Consolamentum, that would make him a Perfect, administered to him on his deathbed, or sooner if he so desired.[1] In the latter case the initiation was very stringent. The novitiate might last for a year or more, and the candidate would be very carefully examined to be sure that he could stand the rigours of a Perfect's life. William Tardieu told the Inquisitors that for a year he was kept as a novice under the charge of a Perfect; but because he fell very ill he was given the Consolamentum sooner than at first was intended, as his death seemed probable.[2] Dulcia of Villeneuve-la-Comtal was kept as a novice for three years in various establishments of Perfect women and then it was decided that she was still too young and her vocation was not clear enough. Raymonde Jougla of Saint-Martin de Lande, a candidate who for a year was being prepared at a community of Perfect women, was left behind by them when they fled for safety to Montségur, as they did not think her nearly ready—she was not firm enough in the faith.[3] The period of preparation, the *Abstinentia*, lasted for a year at least; and during that time the candidate had to live a life of the utmost austerity and strictness, under the care of some Perfect. The various churches seem to have followed with singularly little variation the same ritual for their great distinctive ceremony of the Consolamentum.[4] The Consolamentum could not be compared with any contemporary Catholic sacrament. It combined Baptism, or perhaps more exactly Confirmation, and Ordination into a priestly caste, with Confession, Penitence and Absolution, and, sometimes in extension of the latter, Supreme Unction for the dying. We are fortunate in possessing both from Catholic and heretic sources a full account of its ritual. Not only did the Inquisition unearth considerable evidence, and Catholic writers such as Bernard Gui and still more Moneta and the ex-Perfect Rainier

---

[1] Bernard Gui, *loc. cit.*   [2] Doat, *Registres*, vol. XXIII, pp. 201 ff.
[3] Examples quoted from MSS. by Guiraud, *Histoire de l'Inquisition*, vol. I, pp. 111-12.
[4] For the Consolamentum see the important chapter in Guiraud, *Histoire de l'Inquisition*, vol. I, pp. 107-42.

Sacchoni give a coherent account, but there survives in Lyons a handbook to the ritual compiled by the Cathars themselves.[1]

But the ritual of the Consolamentum provides strangely little evidence about Cathar beliefs. The candidate for admission had been prepared by the asceticism of the Abstinentia, a course demanding a renunciation of matter stricter than even the most extreme orthodox orders suggested. But the ceremony itself was conducted in words and actions that almost all might have been written by Catholics for Catholics.[2] Almost the only formula that would at once strike a Catholic as strange was the substitution in the Lord's Prayer of "supersubstantial bread" for "daily bread".[3]

The Consolamentum took place in the room of some sympathizer's house. The Senior Perfect would conduct it, but others would be present, both Perfect and believers. First came the Servitium, the General Confession made by the whole congregation, while the Senior, or conducting Perfect, held a copy of the Gospels opened before him. The Servitium was apparently recited in the vernacular. It contains no heretical statement. Only the stress that it laid upon the sins of the flesh and the phrase "Have no mercy on the flesh born in corruption but have mercy on the spirit held in prison" indicate the dualist nature of its reciters.

The Servitium was followed by the ceremony of the candidate's Reception of the Lord's Prayer. The whole congregation washed its hands. Then, with three reverences repeated between each action, the Perfect next in rank to the Senior prepared a table, covered it with a napkin and placed a book on it. The Catechumen performed his Melioramentum, saying with prostrations before the Senior, "Bless me"; and the Senior would reply with the formula "May God bless you" Finally the Catechumen would say: "Lord, pray God for me, a sinner, that He may bring me to a good end", and the Senior replied, "May God bless you and make of you a Good Christian and bring you to a good end." The Senior then handed

---

[1] Sacchoni, *Summa*, p. 1762: Moneta, *Summa*, pp. 277–8: the Cathar ritual is published by Clédat, in *Le Nouveau Testament traduit au XIIIe Siècle en Langue Provençale, suivi d'un Rituel Cathare*.

[2] See Guiraud, *loc. cit.* for a discussion of the question. [3] See below, p. 166.

him the book, admonishing him in a long address, again in the
vernacular. Here again nothing is said that is heterodox. The
admonition consists mostly of quotations from the Gospels and the
Epistles of St Paul, stressing the dogma that wherever the Church is,
there is God—passages that would appeal to a body that disliked
ecclesiastical buildings, but that are theologically unexceptionable.
The Catechumen is thus reminded that he is before God. The one
non-Catholic sign is that he was addressed by the ritual name of
Peter.[1] The homily finished, the Senior repeated the Lord's Prayer
with the Catechumen following him. The Senior then gave a final
admonition, telling him to repeat the Prayer constantly throughout
his life and never to eat nor drink without saying it first, and to bear
penance for any omission to do so. The Catechumen replied saying:
"I receive it from God and from you and from the Church". This
stage was closed by the Catechumen making once more his Melioramentum and joining with the Perfect in performing a "double"[2]
and a "*venia*", or penitential prostration.

The Consolamentum itself could, and usually did, follow im-
mediately after the Reception of the Prayer. Indeed, when it was
administered to the dying no delay could be risked. The full Consolamentum began with a dialogue between the Senior and the
Catechumen. The latter was asked if he were willing to renounce
the eating of flesh and of eggs, lying and swearing, and all luxuries,
and solitude, and to promise that not even the fear of death would
make him desert the faith. He would promise, repeating the
Melioramentum.

It was probably during this dialogue that the Catechumen was
required to renounce the Church of Rome and the Cross made by
the Roman priest at his baptism, and the oil and the chrism used by
the Romans.[3]

---

[1] The text in the Lyons ritual runs: "E sil crezent a nom Piere, diza enaissi:
En Piere, vos devez entendre...", i.e. "*If* the believer is called Peter...".
This must either be a copyist's error, or rather, I am inclined to think, a
deliberate attempt to make the formula seem harmless in the eyes of Inquisitors.
[2] A "double" was, according to the Lyons ritual, a repetition of the Lord's
Prayer sixteen times, a "single" being its repetition eight times.
[3] This passage is left out of the Lyons ritual, again perhaps for prudence's sake.

Once again the Senior delivered a long homily, addressing the candidate as Peter. Again the sermon consisted mostly of quotations from the New Testament, from passages that stressed Christ's baptism as baptism with the spirit and that gave the power to bind and loose to all Christ's disciples; and the Catechumen was ordered to keep all Christ's commandments to hate the world and all its works. But again there was nothing heterodox in the whole allocution; indeed it included the passage "No one shall enter the Kingdom of God unless he be reborn of water and of the Holy Spirit", a strange text for a sect so strictly opposed to baptism by water to choose.[1]

The Catechumen accepted this homily, and again performed the Melioramentum together with one of the Perfect who acted apparently as his sponsor. Having made his confession he knelt before the Senior, who placed an open Gospel on his head; and all the other Perfects present placed their right hands upon it, and said three *parcias*[2] and three *adoremus*[3] and then, in Latin, "Holy Father, take Thy servant in Thy justice and send Thy grace and holy spirit over him". The Senior murmured the "sixtene"[4] over him, then, aloud, three *adoremus*, the Lord's Prayer and the Gospel which was always, it seems, the first seventeen verses of St John's Gospel, read in Latin.[5] The congregation then repeated the *adoremus* thrice and the *gratia*[6] and three *parcias*. Then everyone performed the "peace" or ceremonial kiss with each other and with the Gospel and the ceremony terminated with another "double" and with *veniae*.

The ceremony was alike whatever the sex of the Catechumen,

---

[1] Presumably the "water" was understood symbolically.

[2] The *Parcia* was the formula "Benedicite, parcite nobis, Amen". Possibly a *Parcia* included also the following three sentences in the text.

[3] The *Adoremus* was the formula, "Adhoremus patrem et filium et spiritum sanctum".

[4] The *Sixtene* or *Sixaine* was probably a sixfold repetition of the Paternoster. It is not possible to identify it clearly. See Clédat, *Le Nouveau Testament*, p. xxvi, n. 2.

[5] Sacchoni (p. 1776). The Lyons ritual begins with a *Parcia*, an *Adoremus* and this passage, obviously in explanation of the terms.

[6] The *Gratia* was the formula "Gratia domini nostri Ihesu Christi sit cum omnibus vobis."

except for one or two necessary verbal changes;[1] and if the recipient were a woman the male Perfects would be careful never actually to touch her, holding their hands slightly above her, nor would female Perfects touch a male catechumen.[2] In the case of the dying, however, it was considerably curtailed. Every dying believer wished to receive the Consolamentum but naturally few had prepared themselves by the Abstinentia. But by making a private confession, and a money payment, if he owed any obligation to the Church, and by promising to keep to the rules of the Abstinentia if he survived, he could arrive at the requisite state. For the Reception of the Prayer he was partially dressed and held up in bed; and the bed was used as the table. The Senior could shorten or omit his homily if the recipient seemed dangerously close to death. For the Consolamentum itself the actual dialogue and repetitions of the *partia* and the *adoremus* seem not to have varied, but the dying man could not be expected to perform the Melioramentum nor the ritual gestures of the *venia*; and again the Senior could shorten or omit his homily at his discretion. It was apparently necessary for the Catechumen to be able to speak his answers himself. The ceremony had therefore to take place before he lapsed into unconsciousness. Moreover if he survived he was expected to undergo the ceremony again, after a suitable Abstinentia, of his own free will and not under the constraining shadow of death.[3]

The ordinary religious ceremonies of the Cathars were conducted by the Perfect. These consisted of the Ritual Feast, where a Perfect blessed bread and broke it, and the congregation partook of it, saying "Benedicite", to which the Perfect replied: "Deus vos benedicat"; and of the Melioramentum, where the Perfect was adored by Believers, who promised to die a good death in the Cathar fold, as opposed to a bad death as a Catholic;[4] and of the Apparelliamentum. The Ritual Feast and the Melioramentum took

[1] I.e. "suspice ancillam tuam" for a woman and "suspice servum tuum" for a man.
[2] Doat, *Registres*, vol. XXIII, pp. 58, 128.
[3] Guiraud, *op. cit.* pp. 134–40: Doat, *Registres*, vol. XXIII, pp. 19, 109, vol. XXIV, p. 86 are examples.
[4] Guiraud, *op. cit.* pp. 178–84.

place whenever circumstances allowed. The latter, being a denial of the Catholic church, was performed particularly whenever the believer had been exposed to Catholic influences. The Lady Fizas of Saint Michel, in waiting on the Countess Eleanor of Toulouse, took a Perfect with her to Rome to worship him in the very chapel of the Pope.[1] The Apparelliamentum was the monthly service of the Cathars. This ceremony consisted in a general confession and examination of conscience, made according to a regular formula before a Perfect. The Believers announced that "We are come before God and before you and before the rule of the Holy Church to receive service, pardon and penitence for all our sins that we have made or said or thought or acted from the time of our birth up to now, and we ask for pity of God and of you that you pray for us to the Holy Father of pity that He pardon us". They then recited a Confiteor, worded in all-embracing terms, and finally demanded a pardon and penitence. The Perfect would then order three days of fasting and a hundred genuflexions, or *veniae*. Probably also the "apparelled" Believers would have to recite a certain number of prayers.[2] Attendance at sermons was probably always obligatory on any Believer who was given the chance to be present. Every Perfect had to preach as often as he had the opportunity.

There was one other ceremony or rather practice in which the Perfect indulged, though its importance and frequency has probably been exaggerated by horrified orthodox writers. This was the Endura. Certain of the Perfect carried out their doctrines to their logical end and deliberately committed suicide by self-starvation. The whole process was undertaken with the observance of a ritual, and the actual deathbed was the scene of rejoicing amongst the sectaries, the dying man or woman being regarded with deep reverential admiration. There were certainly cases of the Endura, though perhaps the Cathar Church did not approve of such over-enthusiasm.[3] On the other hand, for all their disapproval of slaughter,

[1] Doat. *Registres*, vol. XXIII, pp. 91–2.
[2] Guiraud, *op. cit.* pp. 185–91.
[3] Döllinger, *Dokumente*, pp. 19 and 25, gives two instances. There are several others in the records.

the taking of life by passive means did not distress the heretics; and the Perfect were suspected of hastening on the death of invalids who had received the Consolamentum and now showed signs of recovery. The risk of their sinning again and thus annulling the ceremony was to be avoided at all costs.[1] Sometimes the suicide was performed by more rapid means, by poison or the opening of veins.[2]

All Cathar ceremonies ended with the "Peace", the ceremonial kiss exchanged between all that attended. The Perfects first kissed each other on both cheeks, then kissed the Believers, who afterwards kissed each other. But the kiss was modified to prevent any Perfect from having to touch anyone of the other sex. On such occasions a male Perfect would kiss the Gospel. and hand it to the woman-Perfect or Believer to kiss, and a woman-Perfect would act similarly with a male Believer.[3]

All this illustrates how great was the role played by the Perfect. He (or she) was in a state superior to that of any priest in an orthodox Church; filled with the Holy Spirit he was to some extent God Himself; and as God he was worshipped by the ordinary believer. He had no home. Either he lived a strictly communal life in some establishment, which the fear of persecution prevented from staying too long in any one place; or else he wandered preaching and administering the Consolamentum to the dying all over the countryside. The women Perfects seem always to have lived in communities, though they did not remain immured in them. The arch-heretic princess, Esclarmonde of Foix, used to appear at her brother's court in the interests of her faith or go to debates between the heretics and Catholic preachers.[4] Every Perfect had a Believer attached to his

---

[1] Guiraud (*op. cit.* vol. I, pp. 81–2) quotes from a MS. in the Library of Toulouse (no. 609) an undoubted case of what was really a condemnation to death of a Consoled invalid woman.

[2] Guiraud, *loc. cit.* quotes instances. For the question see Molinier, *L'Endura*.

[3] Clédat, *Le Nouveau Testament*, p. xxv; Bernard Gui, *Practica Inquisitionis*, p. 241.

[4] Her insistence in taking part in the debates was considered very unseemly by the Catholics. At a debate in her brother's castle of Pamiers her intervention was cut short by a monk who told her: "Go, Madame, spin at your distaff. You know nothing of such matters." Vaissète-Molinier, *Histoire du Languedoc*, vol. VIII, p. 224.

(or her) person, to deal with his bodily wants, to prepare his food, to handle the money that he might need. This Believer was probably a candidate for the Consolamentum and in return for his services received instruction.[1]

As befitted one who was almost pure spirit, the Perfect led a life of extreme severity. He or she wore a special costume, black, with apparently a distinctive girdle, and a leather bag in which a New Testament was kept. When the Inquisition became severe the distinctive dress was abandoned; but the Perfect continued to wear the girdle underneath their outer garments.[2] Their communities had no private property. The houses themselves were the gifts of wealthier believers, and the charity of the believers supplied also their simple daily wants. It was only after years of persecution that the leaders of the heresy began to realize the need for permanent resources to safeguard its future.[3] The Perfect ate no meat and drank no wine. Vegetables, bread and a little fish were all that was permitted to them.

In addition they observed three long fasts in the year. The first lasted from Quinquagesima Sunday to Easter Day, the second from Whitsunday to St Peter and St Paul's Day, the third from St Brice's Day (November 23) to Christmas. During the first and last week of each of these periods nothing might be consumed but bread and water. During the remainder of the fasts and likewise throughout the whole year this diet had to be followed for three days in the week, the fasts being only distinguished as times of particular self-control. No indulgences from this rule were ever granted. It is probable that the ordinary believer kept to a stricter régime during the fasts than that which he usually followed.[4]

[1] For the lives of the Perfects, see Guiraud, *op. cit.* vol. I, pp. 143–76: Schmidt, *Histoire des Cathares*, vol. II, pp. 91–7.

[2] Doat, *Registres*, vol. XXIII, p. 96, vol. XXV, p. 60: Pierre de Vaux-Cernay, *Hystoria Albigensis*, vol. I, p. 14.

[3] See discussion in Guiraud, *op. cit.* vol. I, pp. 147–52: see also Schmidt, *op. cit.* vol. II, p. 93, n. 1.

[4] *Archives de l'Inquisition de Carcassonne* in Limborch, *Historia Inquisitionis*, p. 1305: Doat, *Registres*, vol. XXXIV, p. 101: Eymericus, *Directorium Inquisitionis*, p. 440.

The organization of the Cathar church is not exactly known. For religious and ritual purposes the Perfect were the supreme caste; but there were also bishops and deacons. Their functions were probably purely administrative. Each diocese or church had its bishop, and each bishop had a *filius major* and a *filius minor*, who were, in modern terms, the suffragans of his diocese. Some of the larger churches, such as the Albanensis in Italy, were apparently divided into two dioceses.[1] Both the *filius major* and the *filius minor* were often commonly called bishops. When the bishop died, his *filius major* automatically became bishop in his stead and was ordained as such by the *filius minor*, who became *filius major*; and a new *filius minor* was appointed, probably by the bishop. It seems that certain youths were definitely brought up to be bishops and it was from them that the *filius minor* was chosen.[2] The bishop was responsible for the organization and administration of the diocese. He was further aided by the deacons, of whom there were a considerable number. The diocese of Toulouse, in the days of its prosperity, possessed about fifty deacons whose names we know.[3] Most of them must have held their posts simultaneously. The deacons were the local agents of the administration. Each deacon had the equivalent of a parish where he was pastor rather than preacher, seeing to the material welfare and order of his flock. He was also the responsible authority in charge of the communities of the Perfect in his area. It is possible that there were also deaconesses, but there is no direct evidence of it. Each deacon was necessarily one of the Perfect and had apparently to undergo, on his appointment by the bishop, a special *consolamentum* ceremony. But it is doubtful if that in any way enhanced his spiritual prestige. Many of the most influential leaders of the sect, such as Esclarmonde of Foix or the preachers Raymond Gros and Martin Rotland, held no administrative position. Preaching could also be combined with an administrative post. Guillebert of Castres and Bertrand Marty, perhaps the most celebrated preachers of the whole

[1] Sacchoni, *Summa*, p. 1768.
[2] Sacchoni, *Summa*, pp. 1765–6; Moneta, pp. 278, 313.
[3] Guiraud, *Histoire de l'Inquisition*, vol. I, pp. 212 ff. gives their names; see Doat, *Registres*, vol. XXXII, p. 76.

Cathar church, continued their preaching work unimpaired even after their ordinations as bishops of Toulouse and Carcassonne.[1]

Rumour amongst the Catholics told of a Black Pope, the supreme ruler of the heretical church. Ever since 1030, when the Cathars of Monteforte in Italy declared that their head was not the Roman pontiff but another, meaning God himself, an Arch-heretic figured in Catholic imaginations.[2] In 1226 the Cardinal Conrad, Papal legate in France, wrote that the heretic Pope lived in Bulgaria and had a certain Bartholomew as his vicar in Languedoc.[3] The confusion here arose out of the word Pope. The Greek word *Papa* and the Slavonic *Pop* was and is used to describe the ordinary parish priest. There were therefore numbers of heretic "popes" in Bulgaria. Moreover the word was occasionally used in this sense by the Western heretics. But it is probable, to judge from the occasions when it appears, that it was used as a title for priests coming from one of the Eastern heretic churches.[4] A somewhat loose use of the word *Apostolicus* added to the confusion.[5] Almost certainly the Cathar churches had no one head. Indeed the variations in dogma that existed amongst them made that impracticable. On the other hand they worked in friendly co-operation and were prepared to hold council with each other.

[1] For Esclarmonde, see above, pp. 131, 159; for Guillebert de Castres, see Doat, *Registres*, vol. XXIII, pp. 162, 270; vol. XXIV, p. 113. It was he who, in the name of all the heretics, negotiated with Raymond de Perelle for the fortress of Montségur, Doat, vol. XXII, p. 226; for Bertrand Marty, see Doat, *Registres*, vol. XXIII, pp. 91, 95–7, 173; vol. XXIV, p. 48. It is possible that Bertrand Marty for the bulk of his career was really only *filius major*.

[2] Landulphus, *Historia Mediolanensis*, p. 89.

[3] Letter in Gervasii Premonstratensis *Epistolae*, ep. 120, p. 116.

[4] E.g. Papa Niquinta (see above, p. 124, n. 1). There was a Gregorius Papa at Treves in 1231 (*Gesta Trevesensium Archiepiscoporum*, Martène et Durand, *Amplissima Collectio*, vol. IV, p. 244) and a Papa Johannes Beneventi (Baronius, *Continuatio Annalium*, vol. XIII, p. 424). The latter was almost certainly a Greek, and probably the former also.

[5] E.g. "Guilielmus Albigensium Apostolicus" (Albericus, *Chronicon*, ad ann. 1229, in *R.H.F.*, vol. XXI, p. 599, who was a distinguished heretic bishop.

IV

The close connection between the Cathars of France and Italy and the Bogomils of the Balkan Peninsula is a fact that no one need doubt. Both the Cathars themselves and their contemporary opponents bear full witness to it. There is a remarkable similarity between Bogomil and Cathar doctrines and habits. But we are more fully informed of those of the Cathars than of those of the Bogomils. Certain questions therefore arise: were the Churches so completely identical that we can attribute all Cathar habits to the Bogomils also? If not, were the divergences due to the development of varying local usages from one common source? or were they due to basic differences between the Churches that a superficial similarity glossed over?

The first troublesome piece of evidence of which to dispose is that provided by the ritual of the Consolamentum, with its strange lack of heterodoxy. But this inoffensiveness is probably more apparent than real. The Lyons ritual as it survives cannot depict the full ceremony. It leaves out the renunciation of the Roman Church and Roman baptism, which were certainly part of the ceremony, and it qualifies the use of the name Peter by the meaningless but tactful preamble "If the Believer's name be Peter...."[1] It is impossible to resist the suspicion that this written ritual has been edited for safety's sake, lest it should fall into the hands of the Inquisition. It would be difficult for an Inquisitor to lay his finger on any heretic doctrine in it; while a Cathar could, if he needed to use it, supply the omissions from his own memory. Nor was the apparent orthodoxy more than superficial. The texts chosen from the New Testament were those that would readily yield a "Manichaean" interpretation. The Trinity might be invoked, but always as three separate Persons, in conformity with Cathar views; while the ethical teaching was so general as to be of universal application.

Nevertheless the resemblance of the whole wording of the

---

[1] Cf. p. 155. We may note further the same choice of Holy Writ, and the same use of St John's Gospel in the Initiation ceremony.

ceremony tempted certain orthodox writers to see in it a travesty of Catholic Church ceremonies.[1] In this they entirely misunderstood the position. Any similarity between the ceremonies of the Cathars and those of the Catholic Church was due not to conscious mockery on the part of the former sect but to their common origin. The services of the Early Christian Church up to the fifth century show almost all the characteristics to be found in Cathar services. The Ritual Feast of the Cathars is, if we equate the Perfect with the Early Christian priest, exactly the same as the Early Christian Communion Feast. The Kiss of Peace terminated Early Christian services as it did those of the Cathars. The Apparelliamentum of the Cathars was couched in almost the same terms as the General Confession of the Early Christians, indeed as the Confiteor that still survives in the Catholic Church. The Consolamentum itself in its two aspects was closely akin to the adult baptism administered by the Early Church to the dying and to the ordination or initiation into its ministry. The very details of the service are similar. In the Early Church the catechumen was tested by a long and stern probationary period. His initiation ceremony began with his reception of the Symbol and the Pater Noster. They were recited to him with a homily by the Presbyter who conducted the service and he had to repeat them. The Melioramentum that followed was not unlike the Confessional ceremony held by the Early Christians on Holy Thursday or Good Friday. Finally, the actual ordination was identical, consisting of the laying of hands and of the Gospel upon the catechumen's head.[2]

Such similarity cannot be fortuitous. Obviously the Cathar Church had preserved, only slightly amended to suit its doctrines of the time, the services extant in the Christian Church during the first four centuries of its life. But were these services confined to the Western dualists? Was this a Western tradition that the Cathar church preserved?

The Greek theologians tended to regard heresy as a delightful opportunity for dialectical argument. Consequently they tell us less

[1] E.g. Bernard Gui, *Practica Inquisitionis*, p. 238.
[2] Guiraud, *Histoire de l'Inquisition*, chaps. VIII and X *passim*, brings this out very clearly.

about the practices of heretics than about their creed. So we know very little about the services of the Eastern Bogomils. Zigabenus's description of their initiation rites indicates two ceremonies with two periods of strict probation; at each ceremony the distinctive feature is the laying of the Gospel of St John on the catechumen's head. From this account one can assume that the initiation ceremonies of the Bogomils of Constantinople and the Cathars of Languedoc were basically the same. But we do not know anything of the words employed by the former in their ceremonies except for their frequent use of the Pater Noster; nor are any other ceremonies described.[1]

To argue from silence is dangerous, but it is just possible therefore that the other Cathar ceremonies and part of the Consolamentum itself were derived from Western traditions. The ceremony of the Reconciliation of the Penitent that Tertullian describes shows the Early Christian usages still firmly established in Rome in the fifth century;[2] and doubtless they lingered on in Italy and perhaps also in Gaul. The appearance of such a heretic as Felix of Urgel in the late eighth century suggests the existence of a tradition by now considered heretical.[3] It would be rash to deny this Western tradition any part in building up the Western Cathar Church and all its practices.

But such a part cannot have been large. The internal evidence of the Cathar ceremonies points strongly to an Eastern origin. First, the use of the name Peter and the citation of texts that apply the Petrine claims to all initiated Christians show Eastern ideas. The Bishops of Rome had arrogated the Petrine claims to themselves from a very early date, and the Western Church seems to have accepted this attribution without demur. But the Eastern Churches would not admit it. To them every apostle was a rock on which the Church was built. It was amongst certain Eastern Churches that Peter became a ritual name, probably amongst the Armenians. It appears as such in the Adoptionist handbook, *The Key of Truth*, that was taken over by the Thonraki heretics. Probably it was also used

[1] See above. pp. 74, 77.
[2] Tertullian, *De Pudicitia*, xiii, 7, in *M.P.L.* vol. ii, coll. 1023 ff.
[3] Felix of Urgel's Adoptionism was probably based on some primitive tradition.

by the Messalians. Either they or the Paulicians might have introduced it to the Bogomils and they to the Cathars.

A more certain sign of Eastern origin is to be found in the language of the quotations from Holy Writ used in the Cathar ceremonies. Moneta accuses the Cathars of falsifying the Pater Noster because they added to it the words "For Thine is the Kingdom, the Power and the Glory, for ever and ever".[1] These words do not exist in the Vulgate, either in St Matthew's or in St Luke's Gospel. But in the Greek version of St Matthew, the version accepted by the Orthodox Church, they occur, and they occur in all the Slavonic translations.[2] Moreover, where St Jerome in the Vulgate wrote "daily bread", the Cathars put "supersubstantial bread". This again is a permissible translation of the Greek and a literal translation of the so-called Nikolski gospel, the Slavonic gospel of the Bosnian heretics.[3] The Cathars must therefore have learnt the Pater Noster directly from Greek sources or through Slavonic intermediaries. When we read in Zigabenus and in Cosmas how fervently the Bogomils employed the Lord's Prayer, the affiliation seems certain.[4]

---

[1] Moneta, p. 445.

[2] Matthew vi, 13.

[3] The Greek word ἐπιούσιος, which is translated "Quotidianus" in the Vulgate and "daily" in the Authorised Version, is impossible to translate accurately. If we take it as ἐπὶ-οὐσιος, "supersubstantialis" is a literal translation, better, indeed, than "Quotidianus". The Slavonic Bibles regularly have the word насущный which is really a literal translation of ἐπὶ-οὐσιος but which has now acquired the sense of "daily" in this context. The Nikolski translation is иносущьны or иносоуштьны: see Danitchitch, *Nikolski Gospel* (in Serbian), pp. 8, 166.

[4] Pierre de Vaux-Cernay, *Hystoria Albigensis*, p. 11, accuses the Cathars of saying that the Good God had two wives, called Oolla and Ooliba. These are the two courtezans in Ezekiel xxiii, 4 who are the symbols of Samaria and Jerusalem. In the English Authorised Version they appear as Aholah and Aholibah; in the Vulgate as Oöla and Oöliba, in the Septuagint as Ὀόλὰ and Ὀθλιβά, in the Slavonic Bible of St Cyril as Ѡола and Ѡоліва. But in the less good MSS. of Pierre de Vaux-Cernay they are copied as Collam et Colibane or Collant et Collibant. Their Hebrew names begin with a gutteral א, which is as near to *K* as it is to *H*, while the termination *-ah* (ה) might be transliterated without much inaccuracy into the French *-ant*. It seems likely that the two courtezans reached the Cathars from a Hebrew source or more probably from a Greek or Slavonic source that itself was derived from the Hebrew. The good scribes would give them their proper Vulgate names, but

This affiliation brings up the whole question of the *Biblium Historiale*, the popular bibles in the vernacular that circulated round Western Europe in the Middle Ages.[1] It has long been a matter of stricture on the part of Protestant writers that the Medieval Church was too narrow and bigoted to permit the study of the Bible in the vernacular. But the bigotry becomes intelligible if we examine some of the vernacular Bibles that existed in the Middle Ages. The most respectable of these Bibles such as the *Historia Scholastica* of Peter Comestor, written about the year 1175, and the *Speculum* of Vincent of Beauvais, written about a century later, embody a large number of apocryphal legends, but none of them are definitely unorthodox.[2] There was, however, another group of Bibles, whose legendary additions are more startling. The French versified Bibles of the twelfth century, those of Herman of Valenciennes, of Geoffrey of Paris, of Macé de la Charité, or of Evrat, the dramatized version known as the *Mystère du Vieil Testament*, or the so-called *Romance Chronicle*, found in Provençal, Catalan and Béarnais, or certain of the German *Historien Bibeln*, such as the so-called *Chronicle of Rudolf*, all have characteristics that the Vulgate never contained and that Comestor lacked. Indeed certain of their compilers, such as Herman of Valenciennes, antedated Comestor.[3] They all contain the Legend of

careless scribes might use the popular names. Schmidt, *Histoire des Albigeois*, vol. II, p. 13, makes much of this point, but did not realize that the best MS. uses Oolla, etc. On the other hand I cannot agree with Guébin and Lyon in their edition of Pierre (from which I quote his text) that the evidence of bad MSS. is necessarily worthless.

[1] The relations of the *Biblium Historiale* with the Eastern bibles has not been yet fully worked out. The only comprehensive study of the question is in Gaster's rather out-of-date but still vitally important Appendix I to his lectures on *Greeko-Slavonic Literature*. The work can only be done by someone who, like Gaster, knows not only the Western European and the Slavonic languages intimately but also Hebrew.

[2] For Comestor and Vincent of Beauvais, see Bonnard, *op. cit.* below.

[3] Gaster, *op. cit.* pp. 198 ff. The French medieval translations are most fully described in Bonnard, *Traductions de la Bible en Vers Français au Moyen-Age*; but his comments are of very little value. See also, Rothschild, *Le Mystère du Vieil Testament*; Rohde, *Romanische Weltkronik*, in Suchier, *Denkmäler der Provenzalischen Literatur und Sprache*, vol. I, pp. 589 ff.; Merzdorf, *Historienbibel*. The Italian vernacular Bibles, such as the *Fioretti di Tutta la Biblia*, condemned at Trent, have not been, as far as I know, properly studied. They seem to belong to the same family of Bibles.

the Cross, and the name of Cain's sister and wife, Calomela, Calomena or Calmena; in several the days of Creation are transposed,
birds and animals being created on the Fifth Day;[1] in some appears
Jacob's blessing of Dan, connected to the story of Antichrist[2] and
the legends of the youth of Moses.[3] In almost all the comparison of
Joseph with Christ is made, Joseph being sold for thirty pieces of
silver, and not the twenty given in the Vulgate and the Septuagint.[4]

All these legends occur in the *Palea* in both its Greek and its
Slavonic forms, or in the *Prophecies of Pseudo-Methodius*.[5] They
do not occur in Western literature before the twelfth century. It
seems therefore fair to deduce that Western writers took them from
East European sources. Considering the Gnostic nature of most of
them, it is probable that they were originally part of the Bogomil
legacy to the Cathars. The heretics' love of the Vernacular Bible was
well known, and so was the Catholic Church's fear of it, a fear which
was increased when the Waldenses made Bible translations one of
the main planks of their programme, and which is easily understood
under the circumstances.

It is certain that separate biblical apocryphal legends were taken
by Cathar writers from the East. The chief example is the Cathar
Secret Book which was admittedly brought to them from Bulgaria,
and which partially exists in a Slavonic version.[6] The Latin version
of the *Vision of Isaiah* is an exact translation of the Slavonic.[7] It was
presumably possible for Cathar authors to have access to the whole
range of stories covered by the *Palea*.

This indicates that the Cathar heresy was itself derived from the
East, but it does not prove it. It is possible that the Western heretics,
when already established, found in Eastern heretical literature works
so sympathetic that they borrowed wholesale from them. But the
Eastern origin of the heresy can be given more definite proof. First,
the names are clearly indicative. The name Bulgar or Bougre, a

[1] E.g. Evrat and the *Mystère*.   [2] E.g. in Evrat.
[3] E.g. in Herman of Valenciennes.   [4] E.g. in Evrat and the *Mystère*.
[5] See Gaster, *op. cit.* pp. 161 ff.
[6] See above, p. 85.
[7] The two texts are printed side by side in Ivanov, *Bogomil Books and Legends*
(in Bulgarian), pp. 134–49.

word that later acquired an additional sinister meaning, was freely given to the heresy, but only in France and not before the thirteenth century.[1] By then there was undoubted connection between the Cathars of France and Bulgaria, but that proves nothing of an earlier connection. On the other hand, the name *Poplicani* altered in time to *Populicani* and inevitably to *Publicani*, can only be the word *Pauliciani*. The word may, it is just possible, have been heard at Constantinople by the Crusaders and brought back by them to describe their local heretics whose tenets were so similar. But at Constantinople the Crusaders would have heard as much of the Messalians as of the Paulicians and probably more of the Bogomils. If the name Paulician arrived in the West it probably arrived with persons who called themselves by it.[2] The name of "Weavers"[3] by which the Cathars were often called indicates the hold that the heresy had in the cloth industry. Many of the missionaries were itinerant cloth merchants, whose trade was the chief trade that linked Eastern and Western Europe. It was their function to carry the woven silks of Byzantium and the East to the eager markets of the West. They were therefore ideally placed to be the channels of an Eastern faith. From them the resident cloth merchants learnt the doctrine and spread it to the actual weavers. Clothiers' shops were well suited to be centres of the heresy, for it was perfectly natural for the women of the district to gather and gossip there.

But the heretics themselves supply the clearest information. Rainier Sacchoni wrote, it is true, in the thirteenth century, about the year 1230.[1] He may therefore have been ignorant of the early

---

[1] E.g. "Burguri, quia latibulum eorum speciale est in Burgaria" (Stephen of Bellavilla, *De Septem Donis*, in D'Argentré, *Collectio Juridica*, vol. I, pp. 86–90), or "Quos quidam vocant Bulgaros" (*Chronicle of St Médard*, in D'Achéry, *Spicilegium*, vol. II, p. 491), or "Les Bougres en Aubigeois" (*Vita Ludovici Sancti* by Queen Margaret's Confessor, in Bouquet, *Recueil des Historiens de France*, vol. XX, p. 63), to cite a few examples.

[2] See above, p. 122.

[3] E.g. "Textores" in letter of Geoffrey of Auxerre, in St Bernardi *Opera* (ed. Mabillon), vol. II, p. 1208.

[4] He was born at Piacenza in 1190 and died about 1258. On him, see Molinier, *Un Traité Inédit concernant les Sectes Albigeois*.

history of the Cathars. But he had been a Cathar himself and claimed to know their traditions; and his language is always moderate and convincing. Talking of the heretic Churches of Bulgaria and Dugunthia (that composite name of the Churches of Dragovitsa and Tragurium), he says that all the heretic churches have their origin from these two.[1] Further, the *Summa Auctoritatis* says of the Church of Concoresso that it "took its heresy from Slavonia and some others from Bulgaria",[2] and of certain French heretics it says "they have their error from Drugutia and are also called Albigensians".[3] The author of the *Summa* learnt from interrogated heretics, while Sacchoni had particularly good sources for his information. He was intimate before his conversion to the Catholic Church with the old Cathar bishop of Concoresso, Nazarius, who had been taught his heretical views in Bulgaria, sixty years before.[4] That is to say, in about 1160 Bulgaria was the school where heresy was learnt. If we add to this evidence the honour paid by the nascent Cathar church to such Eastern heresiarchs as Nicetas of Constantinople,[5] it seems unnecessary to attempt to find any other origin for the Cathar faith.

The Western Dualists may well have added variations and embroideries to the religion that they adopted, for in its greatest days their Church was more splendid and more prosperous than any of its Eastern fellow-churches. But it was of the same faith and tradition and represented its striking and spectacular climax.

[1] "...Ecclesia Burgaliae. Ecclesia Dugunthiae, et omnes habuerunt originem de duabus ultimis." Sacchoni, *Summa*, p. 1767.

[2] "Heretici de Concoreco, qui habent heresim suam de Sclavonia et quidam alii de Bulgaria." *Summa Auctoritatis*, p. 123.

[3] "Heretici qui habent errorem suum de Drugutia, qui et dicuntur Albigenses." *Ibid. loc. cit.*

[4] Sacchoni, *ibid.* pp. 1773-4.

[5] See above, p. 123.

CHAPTER VII

The Dualist Tradition

SO it was that one great confederate Dualist Church arose, stretching from the Black Sea to Biscay. In all the countries into which it spread, its successes were made sure by political conditions, by circumstances of racial politics, of class politics and of personal politics. But for the social condition of the peasants of Bulgaria, but for the diplomatic condition of Bosnia, midway between Eastern and Western Christendom, and but for the rapacity of certain great nobles of Languedoc, stimulated by the vulnerability of an inadequate Catholic hierarchy, the Dualists might have remained in obscurity. But the political impulse was not everything. Behind it there was a steady spiritual teaching, a definite religion, that developed and declined as most religions do, but that embodied a constant Tradition.

What was this Tradition? Where and when did it begin? Its birth lies far back in the days when man first consciously looked at the world and saw that it was bad; and he wondered how such evil should be, and why God, if there be a God, could permit it. "The earth is given into the hand of the wicked", cried Job: "He covereth the faces of the judges thereof; if not, where and who is He?" This is the problem behind the Tradition, a problem that every religious thinker must face and few can solve. At times it might be ignored. The Jews in the days of their prosperity, complacent at being the Chosen People, or the Greeks of the fifth century B.C., in love with the world around them, might forget its wickedness or despise the cause of it. But Greek philosophy in the later, wearier centuries wondered again about Evil. Stoics and Neoplatonists each in their way condemned the world of matter; and Jewish thinkers of Alexandria began to face the problem, influenced by the emphasis on spirit that they found in the Hermetic lore of Egypt. Over the frontiers in Persia Zoroaster had taught long ago of the permanent war between Good and Evil, spirit and matter. Farther away to the

East Gautama the Buddha told his followers that only by dissociation from the world could goodness be found, that peace came only with material annihilation. Such doctrines trickled through to the countries where Christianity was passing its childhood.

The Gnostics gathered together such tendencies and applied them to Christianity, adding Egyptian, Zoroastrian and even Buddhist ideas to the Greco-Judaic philosophy of the Christian Fathers. To distinguish precisely all these elements would be, after all these centuries, a hopeless task. It is possible that Hermetic usages were followed in the secret ceremonies of the Gnostics; it is certain that Buddhist tales and tales of Jewish origin were absorbed into Gnostic scripture. But Gnosticism, by admitting Jesus, the God that became Man, was a new religion. No older tradition could exist unaltered in it.

The characteristic doctrine of this new religion was Dualism. It taught that not God but Satan, the Demiurge, made the world and its wicked matter. Only Spirit was good and came from God. There is no need to seek the origin of this belief in any one age or any one place, for it is as old as mankind. But in amplifying it, sympathetic stories and practices would be borrowed from like-minded neighbours. To explain, for example, how it was that, if matter is bad, yet man is not altogether bad, for he can be conscious of good, unorthodox Jewish legends were borrowed, which told of the divine spark being somehow imprisoned in the bodies of material creatures. Gnosticism was a restatement of the Dualist position, made when religious opinion was excited by the growth of Christianity and seeking to use Christianity as the basis of the restatement.

The Gnostics included a large proportion of the Early Christian Church. But it could not be Christianity. To accept it, Christians must abandon their Jewish past. Jesus must come to destroy not to fulfil the promises of the Old Testament; nor could He atone by His death for the Fall of Man if man had always been bad and never fallen. Inevitably the vital importance of Jesus must fade in Gnostic cosmology, and Christianity loses its essential doctrine. Unless Christians were prepared to make this sacrifice of the Atonement, they must eject Gnosticism from the Church.

But the position was not clear to contemporaries from the outset.

The Atonement was an article of faith, the full implications of which were not fully thought out by every Early Christian. Such uncompromising thinkers as Irenaeus or Tertullian might point out the inconsistencies, but Gnostic clergy would continue to conduct their services with the same usages and the same ceremonies as their more orthodox fellows. And indeed, after Gnosticism had been definitely branded as unorthodoxy, it was the Gnostics that kept these ceremonies in their pure form; for the orthodox, with growing wealth and power, and, at last, with the patronage of Imperial Rome, began to enrich their services with pomp and splendour, till they lost their old simplicity. In the course of the centuries this led to a strange anomaly.

There is one characteristic quality in any Dualist church. Man, to escape from the vileness of his body, must seek to make himself spirit as far as may be. This is done by a gnosis, an experience that is usually won by an initiation ceremony. Thus a class of initiates arises, a spiritual aristocracy. Now to the Early Christians baptism, the reception into the Church, was a species of initiation ceremony. There were many sympathizers who might be called Christians but who had not been received into the Church and were not received into the Church till their death-beds—for example, the Emperor Constantine. It was only when the practice arose of giving baptism sooner in the Christian's life, in order that even dying infants should have the advantage of membership of the Church, that every Christian sympathizer became by his baptism as an infant an initiate; and gradually, with this cheapening of initiation, the ceremony of Confirmation rose in importance. By the end of the fifth century there was no spiritual aristocracy in Christendom, other than the official hierarchy of the Church. The Gnostic sects, however, by the stress that they laid on their gnosis, retained the older practice. Thus when polemical churchmen in the Middle Ages denounced the heretics for maintaining a class of the Elect or Perfect they were denouncing an Early Christian practice, and the heretic initiation service that they viewed with so much horror was almost word for word the ceremony with which Early Christians were admitted to the Church.

Nevertheless, though the Dualist tradition might retain antique Christian usages, it remained and must always have been a heresy.

Christianity could not compromise with a religion that denied God to be Creator and Man to have fallen. But we must remember that to themselves the Dualists of this Tradition were Christians, the only pure Christians. The attempts of modern writers to affiliate it to Buddhism would have filled them with horror, just as they rejected the name of Manichaean that it pleased the orthodox to bestow on them. Dualism is a creed that is easy to hold; there is no need to provide it with a complex ancestry. Even though the arrangement of Buddha's Church with its classes of adepts and simple adherents may be very similar to the Cathar arrangement of the Perfect and the Believers, yet such an arrangement is a natural outcome of any Church that has a gnosis. And the Buddhist characteristic of sympathy for all living things, a sympathy based on the doctrine of Metempsychosis—a sympathy that St Francis of Assisi learnt from the Cathars—is again a natural outcome of Dualist beliefs. Occasional Buddhist parables might buttress Dualist doctrines; but the Dualists of Bulgaria and of France were not Buddhists.[1]

We must seek for the origin of "Christian" Dualism in the same place and time as that in which orthodox Christianity was born. The ancestry of the former was more mixed and its theology less accurate, but it was inspired at the start by the same religious feeling. As time went on the differences became definite. The turning-point was probably Marcion's organization of a separate Gnostic Church. From that there could be no retreat. Soon after, when orthodox Christianity triumphed with the aid of Imperial Rome, the Gnostic churches lost touch, and divided into two main streams. The one, the more strictly Dualist or, if you will, the more Manichaean, lingered in Armenia and travelled with Armenian colonists to the Balkans. The other, the Monarchian stream, remained to a greater extent the repository of Gnostic tales and Early Christian usages, and, revitalized by an evangelical movement known as Messalianism, itself largely inspired by Montanism,[2] came also to Thrace and to the

[1] See Appendix IV.
[2] I think it is possible, indeed probable, that the Messalians derived their usages, but not their legends, from the Montanists rather than from any strictly Gnostic sect.

Balkans. There the two branches joined up again, though each retained its fundamental doctrine, and jointly they swept over Europe.

It is not remarkable that the spread of Dualism terrified not only right-thinking Churchmen but also many of the lay authorities. It was considered heresy, and correctly so considered. For Dualism, for all its claims, does not, any better than Orthodoxy, solve the problem of good and evil. The Orthodox might be unable to explain how God the Omnipotent should have permitted such a thing as evil to be and to enter into the world of His creation. But the Dualists only answered the question by raising a new difficulty. If Satan created the world, how and why did God allow any good to be imprisoned in it? For the Dualists had to admit that Man possesses the consciousness of good; otherwise there could be no such thing as religion at all. To solve this problem they had to invent innumerable stories to explain the presence of good in the world. But all of them involved a definite restriction of the sovereignty of God. The strictest Dualists might answer that God is not Omnipotent, and that He was defeated by Satan to that extent. This view is logically tenable, though still the mixture of good and evil in man needs much explanation, while Christ can only be either a peculiarly venerable member of the Initiate class or an angel who paid a brief visit to earth. His role shrinks to a mere triviality and the name of Christianity must be abandoned. There is no room for Christ in a truly Dualist religion.

Thus all good Christians must necessarily fight against Dualism. And the State will usually support them. For the doctrine of Dualism leads inevitably to the doctrine that race-suicide is desirable; and that is a doctrine that no lay authority can regard with approval. Moreover there was another reason why Church and State alike detested the Dualist Tradition. To their minds it was associated with orgiastic obscenity. It is possible to discount the horrible hints of orthodox writers as mere propaganda, but the regularity of the charges make some investigation necessary. Various of the Gnostic sects were said to be unashamedly vicious. The Messalians had a very bad name for orgiastic behaviour, both in their early days and in the days of Psellus. Anna Comnena refused from modesty to describe the frightful doings of the Bogomils. Again and again in France tales were told of the sexual promiscuity of the Cathars.

One thing is remarkable. There are no sincere accusations against the morals of the Paulicians, except for the obviously ignorant attack of John of Otzun, nor against the Bogomils of Cosmas's day. That implies that the orgiastic tradition was carried down by the Messalians. The horrified contempt meted out to the Messalians indicates a general contemporary belief in their immorality. That certain of the Gnostics indulged in organized orgies is undeniable. To this day theologians group such sects as the Carpocratians and the Cainites under the heading of the Licentious Gnostics. The Messalians probably inherited this tradition. But the accusations against the Messalians declare that the Messalian Initiate, after his strict three years' noviciate, was free to indulge in any excess that he pleased, for he was now God. On the other hand, even the most hostile depositions against the later Bogomils and Cathars declare that the Initiates led personally blameless lives, but that they associated with and seemed to encourage Believers who led lives of remarkable immorality. It is probable therefore that the charge should be withdrawn in so far as the Messalian Initiates are concerned. But it was probably justified if it were made against the Messalian Believer.[1]

Indeed, the accounts of Dualist orgies cannot be all entirely fictitious. Dualism necessarily disapproves of the propagation of the species. It therefore disapproves of marriage far more than of casual sexual intercourse, for the latter represents merely one isolated sin, while the former is a state of sin. Similarly sexual intercourse of an unnatural type, by removing any risk of procreating children, was preferable to normal intercourse between man and woman. Moreover till his initiation ceremony the Dualist Believer was merely

[1] Chastity was, even in the time of the Cathars, considered by the Orthodox to be evidence of heresy. See above, p. 121. But here again we see the tradition of the Early Church lingering on. Countless Early Christian inscriptions, particularly from those districts of Anatolia where Gnosticizing sects were popular, show that chastity even between married couples was regarded as holy and desirable.

a creation of the Devil's. To indulge his carnal appetites would make him no worse. It was only after his initiation that his actions mattered, and he must practise carnal self-restraint and live a life of unqualified asceticism. Bearing this in mind we can assess the accusations of immorality. As far as the adherents and Believers of the religion were concerned, they were not unjustified. Casual promiscuity and unnatural vice were not discountenanced by the religious authorities, though they personally led lives against which no charge could possibly be made. Possibly at times of festival, especially amongst the more evangelically minded sects of the Tradition, such as the Messalians, this promiscuity rose to the height of a concentrated orgy, though with the Cathars, of whom we have the most evidence, this would seem to be rare. But there was definitely an easy-going attitude about sexual morals, an attitude peculiarly agreeable to the people of Southern France with their troubadours and their Courts of Love. The whole extent of the immorality was certainly exaggerated for purposes of propaganda—for instance, Pierre of Vaux-Cernay was certainly going too far when he declared that the heretics believed that the action of any part of the body lower than the navel could not be considered sinful[1]—but there was enough to give some justification to the attacks of the Orthodox; and we can understand how the name of "Bougre", applied at first to any Dualist heretic, acquired its later sinister significance.

But this question in its turn raises another. Was there some Secret Tradition amongst the Dualists that might support the dark suspicions of the Orthodox? Modern occultists have liked to see themselves as the heirs of Cathar martyrs and to take Montségur to be the Mount Thabor of their magical tradition.[2] It is difficult to support their view. The careful questioning of the Inquisitors, men well trained to unearth any secret, reveal no trace of any occult lore imparted to the Cathar initiates. Except in Psellus's obviously unreliable account of the Messalians there is no sign of any initiation ceremony amongst the Dualist heretics containing more than can be known from the

[1] See above, p. 152. Pierre de Vaux-Cernay, *Hystoria Albigensis*, pp. 17–18, gives a lurid account of Cathar morals.
[2] See below, Appendix IV.

depositions of various initiate heretics and the Consolamentum ceremony itself. Even the work that the heretics called their *Secret Book* merely contained a well-known Gnostic legend. A Gnosis does not necessarily mean the revelation of very secret esoteric occultist doctrine. If that were the case no Gnostic religion could ever have a wide or popular appeal. The earlier Gnostics may have, like the Neoplatonists, displayed a taste for occultism; but ever since the Messalians and the Paulicians made of Gnosticism a popular creed, their creed was secret only in so far as it was banned.

But hints of dark secrets and stories of scandalous morals undoubtedly helped on the decline of Christian Dualism. The Church authorities and the lay authorities in their war against it were fortified by public opinion, which grew in strength when the first friars showed that it was possible to lead pure ascetic lives without countenancing such ill-fitting behaviour. Careful propaganda turned Puritan feeling from the support of the heresy into opposition. But the true cause of its fall was the withdrawal of lay support. When the Balkan Peninsula was swamped by the Turks and Southern France ravaged by conquering knights from the North, the Dualist Tradition was driven underground once more; and this time it has not re-emerged.

In Eastern Europe traces of the Tradition can now only be found in popular legends and fairy tales; and possibly it was the part-inspiration of the fantastic sects that have arisen from time to time in Russia. In Western Europe the traces are even less distinct. Writers who seek to find the heirs of the Cathars in the Protestants of the Reformation or even in the earlier Protestants that we call the Lollards and the Hussites, do Protestantism an injustice. To Wyclif, to Luther and to Calvin, Satan was certainly a great god and the world an evil place, but emphatically God Himself was God the Creator, Jehovah of the Jews. They never rejected the Old Testament nor denounced the Patriarchs. Their anti-clericalism was a movement directed against the morals and luxury of the clergy, not against fundamental Christian doctrine. They wished to reform and simplify the Church, not to introduce a new religion. Christ to them was the Second Person, the God made Man, not an Eon or an eminent member of the Elect. Their spiritual ancestor was Peter Valdes rather than Mani or Marcion or any Dualist prophet. The Tradition undoubtedly helped to inspire St Francis, who moulded it into a legitimate Christian form; but, except in the purest Franciscan teaching, it vanishes from sight. Possibly we can find its symbols in the Trumpcards of the Tarot Pack, where generations of fortune-tellers have handed down the doctrine that the Devil betokens the direction of affairs in this world, and have seen in Pope Joan, the High Priestess, the token of the Gnosis. But other of the Tarot interpretations are clearly begotten of a different tradition. It is more convincing to find Dualist signs in the watermarks used in the manufacture of paper. For the paper-makers of Southern France were of the class most given over to the heresy, and the symbols that they introduced to be the regular watermarks for many centuries to come have a likeness too close to be accidental to the symbols on Gnostic amulets.[1] It may be that the secret practices of the Templars, with their cult of evil and unnatural vice, were partly based on Dualist ideas and usages. But historians must not forget that, first, though the Dualist Tradition had its gnosis, it was not an occultist religion, and, secondly, there were other religions that were occultist contemporary to it. In the Kabbala the Jews preserved an occultist Tradition that had a far greater influence on later Magic than any Dualist Tradition. More popularly, there was the somewhat in-articulate tradition of the Witch Cult,[2] whose devil-worship was not Dualistic but the remnant of an older nature-worship. It is to them that modern occultism should look for its ancestry.

The Christian heresy of Dualism, the Tradition that found its origin in the days of Cerdon and Valentine, died without issue, before the sword of the Turks and the fire of the Dominicans. It was not an ignoble religion. It taught the value of the fundamental virtues; it faced with courage the anxious question of evil. But it was a religion of pessimism. It held out no hope for individual men and their salvation. Mankind should die out, that the imprisoned fragments of Godhead should return to their home. It was a religion without

[1] See Appendix IV.
[2] For which see Miss Margaret Murray, *Witchcraft in Western Europe.*

hope, and such a religion cannot survive unless it be helped artificially. For Hope is a necessary part of religion. Faith and Charity alone are not enough.

Long ago Plotinus, the greatest of the Neoplatonists, cried out against the Gnostics for the tragedy of terrors that they saw in the spheres of the Universe.[1] This tragedy was the tragedy of the Dualist Tradition. Confident of the truth of their cause, but in no expectation of their own salvation, its children went uncomplaining to the stake, and their hopeless faith was burnt with them.

[1] "Τῆς τραγῳδίας τῶν φοβερῶν, ὡς οἴονται, ἐν ταῖς τοῦ κόσμου σφαίραις", Plotinus, *Ennead* II, ix, 13.

APPENDIX I

The Greek Sources for Paulician History

For a long time historians were chary of using the Greek sources for Paulician history with complete confidence, as they were uncertain which of the several similar accounts to consider as the most authentic and reliable. There are four synoptic descriptions of them:

(i) *The History of the Manichaeans*, by Peter of Sicily, who claimed to have visited the Paulician capital of Tephrice as an ambassador. It is given in Migne, *Patrologia Graeca*, vol. CIV.

(ii) A short tract by a certain Peter the Higumen, which was inserted at the head of the other Peter's work.

(iii) A treatise *Against the Manichaeans*, attributed, falsely in part, to Photius. It is published with Photius's works in Migne, *Patrologia Graeca*, vol. CII. The homilies in this treatise are doubtless Photius's own work. The first chapter is a repetition of (ii) and is certainly later.

(iv) A chapter interpolated into the Madrid MS. of Georgius Monachus, which again is a reproduction of (ii). It has been edited by Friedrich in the *Sitzungsberichte der Bayr. Akademie*, 1896, pp. 67 ff.

Georgius Monachus, Theophanes Continuatus, Euthymius Zigabenus and other Byzantine writers base their accounts on these last three.

I shall not go into the various theories that have been held about these sources. It has been left to Prof. Grégoire to sort them out definitively. See his *Les Sources de l'Histoire des Pauliciens*, in the *Bulletin de l'Académie Royale de Belgique, Classe des Lettres*, 1936, pp. 95–114, and his *Autour des Pauliciens*, in *Byzantion*, vol. XI, 1936, pp. 610 ff. He shows conclusively that the account of Peter of Sicily is authentic and genuine and should be treated as the prime source. The trouble has all been caused by the treatise of the Higumen, which is simply a carelessly compiled epitome of the Sicilian Peter's account, but which was sheepishly followed by subsequent writers. This clarification is convincing in itself; and Grégoire supports it with unanswerable arguments.

The only difficulty that remains is the dedication of Peter of Sicily's work to the Archbishop of Bulgaria. Grégoire believes that there may well have been a dangerous number of Paulicians in Bulgaria in 872, the date that he assigns to the work. This is borne out by Peter's own evidence that the Paulicians, settled a century before in Thrace, were still in touch with their Asiatic brothers. The young Bulgarian Church should certainly be warned against these active heretics.

With the establishment of Peter's account as authentic, we may safely conclude that he did in fact go on an embassy to Tephrice.

APPENDIX II

Heretical Movements in the Eighth Century

The Byzantine Empire under the Iconoclastic Emperors was undoubtedly a favourable soil for the spread of Puritanistic heresies. But it would be a mistake to assume that therefore Iconoclasm and the Puritan heresies of the time belonged to the same tradition. There were, I think, five distinct and separate movements.

(i) *Iconoclasm*. This was largely political in origin; it was a movement started within the Church against certain sections of the Church, namely, the monastic vested interests. Theologically it was a Christological heresy. It taught that Christ the God could not be depicted, and therefore pictures of Christ could only show Jesus the man and so were not suitable objects for worship. Similarly, pictures of the Saints could only show their earthly forms and not the Divine spirit that had made them Saints. This theology is somewhat unsound, savouring of Monophysitism; and in the controversy the Iconodule theologians certainly put forward the better case. But Iconoclasm was formidable because of its political background—because of a general jealousy of the monasteries, who championed Image-worship and found it financially profitable, and because of the tendency of the Semitic elements in the Empire to favour a greater simplicity of worship and to take seriously the old Mosaic injunction against graven images. The contemporaneous growth of Islam is another example of this sentiment. But theologically Iconoclasm did not belong to the Gnostic Tradition, and politically it was what we should now call Erastian. It believed in a State Church.

(ii) *Montanism* (see above, pp. 18-20). The Montanists had been almost entirely wiped out in the great persecution of 722. Some of the survivors seem to have joined the Paulicians, but a remnant of Montanists lingered on into the next century. The Montanists were extreme Evangelicals. They belonged to an Early Christian, rather than a specifically Gnostic, Tradition; and they disapproved of an organized Church hierarchy.

(iii) *Paulicianism*. Enough has been said above to show that the Paulicians belonged theologically to an Early Christian Tradition, tinged with Gnostic or perhaps Zoroastrian Dualism, and formed politically a small bellicose theocratic state. They could not have fitted into the Iconoclastic structure.

(iv) *Messalianism* (see above, pp. 21-5). The Messalians were undoubtedly keeping their Gnostic traditions alive throughout this period, and in order to do so they must have had some form of ecclesiastical organization. But it was necessarily a secret organization, and its secrets have been preserved.

(v) *Athinganism*. The strange sect of the Athingani made its first appearance during the eighth century. The Athingani, like the Messalians, clearly preserved a Gnostic Tradition. But they had certain idiosyncrasies. They were considered to be Judaizers and kept the Jewish Sabbath. On the other hand they did not practise circumcision. They revered demons called Sorou, Sochen and Arche (the Gnostic Ἀρχαί?). They were best known as adepts in Magic and in Astrology and provided the most celebrated fortune-tellers of the time. It was for this reason, rather than from any physical connection, that their name was later given to the Gypsies—*Tsigane* is merely *Athinganus*. It should however be remarked that the true Gypsies, the Zátts, appeared in Anatolia in the course of the following century. On emigrating from India, they were settled in Northern Syria and Cilicia by the Califs in the years from 835 onwards, and in 855 they passed into Byzantine territory. (See D. MacRitchie, *Account of the Gypsies of India*, London, 1886.) I do not think that the Athingani had any influence on the history of the Dualist sects.

(The best modern account of the Athingani is given by Joshua Starr in *The Harvard Theological Review*, vol. XXIX, pp. 93 ff. He quotes all the relevant sources. I think, however, that there is still room for a study of the Athingani by some Kabalistic expert.)

It is clear from this analysis that Iconoclasm had no connection with its contemporary heretical sects. On the other hand, the great Iconoclastic Emperor, Constantine V, may have been affected by them. His enemies declared that he rejected the sacrament of infant baptism, and that he would have liked to abolish the name of "saint". He paid no respect to the Holy Martyrs nor even to the Virgin herself. They could not intercede for us, he said.[1] In all this Constantine was probably going beyond the usual doctrines of the Iconoclasts, and was merely expressing his personal opinion; which, being an autocrat firmly seated on his throne, he could do with impunity. His interest in theology was obviously genuine and his attitude sceptical. Probably, like the Emperor Frederick II, he liked to shock his audience. It is perfectly possible that he may have been impressed by Paulician theology, of which he may have been well informed. But it would be most unwise to say that he was therefore a Paulician, and still more to say that Paulicianism was the extreme wing of Iconoclasm[2] (see above, pp. 38, 51).

[1] John Damascene, *Adversus Constantinum Caballinum*, in *M.P.G.* vol. XCV, col. 337: *Vita St Nicetae*, in *Aa. Ss.*, April, vol. I, p. 260.
[2] As Conybeare rashly implies (*Key of Truth*, pp. cxvi–cxvii). He definitely considers Constantine to have been a Paulician (*ibid.* p. clxxiv).

APPENDIX III

Various Names given to the Dualist Heretics in Europe

The names given to the Dualist Bogomil-Cathar heretics varied according to their localities. I therefore give a list of them.

(i) *Bogomils*, Βογόμιλοι, Βογόμυλοι, Богомили. This name, derived from the name of the Bulgarian heresiarch, was invariably used by Bulgarian writers and usually by Byzantine writers. Outside of Bulgaria and Byzantium it seems to have been unknown.

(ii) *Phundaites*, Φουνδαῖται, Φουνδαγιάται. This name, derived from the Φούνδα, or scrip, that the heretics were supposed to carry, is only found in twelfth-century Byzantine writers. See above, p. 72.

(iii) *Kudugers*. The fifteenth-century Byzantine writer, Symeon, Metropolitan of Thessalonica, speaks of Βογόμυλοι, οἱ ὁποῖοι καὶ Κουδούγεροι ὀνομάζονται (see above, p. 97). The name probably comes from the village of Kutugertsi, near Kiustendil, or from the village of Kotugeri, near Vodena (see Ivanov, *Bogomil Books*, p. 36). The latter is perhaps the more likely for geographical reasons.

(iv) *Babuni*, Бабоуны. This seems to have been the name invariably given to the heretics in Serbia and in Bosnia up to the fourteenth century (see above, p. 99).

(v) *Cathars*, Cathari, Kathari, Catari, or in Germany Ketzer, or again, from a mispronunciation of the Greek θ, Cazari or Gazari (Stephen of Bellavilla, p. 90, says "Dicuntur a Lombardis Gazari"). This name is clearly the Greek word Καθαροί and was probably in origin the heretics' own name for their Elect or purified class, and thus gradually came to be applied to the whole church. It is first used by Eckbert in Germany in the mid-twelfth century. It was commonly employed in Italy, for example by both Moneta and Sacchoni. In Germany as Ketzer it became the regular word for any heretic. In France it was less frequently used. I do not think that we need take seriously Mosheim's attempt to derive it from the Chazars, that Judaistic Turkish tribe settled in southern Russia (Mosheim, *Versuch einer Ketzergeschichte*, pp. 357 ff.). The name 'Cathari' had already been used to describe themselves by the Novatian sects of Anatolia in the fourth century. (See Epiphanius, *Adversus Haereses*, p. 505.)

(vi) *Patarenes*, Patareni, Paterini, Patrini, Paterelli, Patalini, and many other slight variations. This name was given in the early eleventh century to the extreme Reform party in the Church of Milan. We neither know the origin of the name in the first instance nor can tell how it came to be transferred to the heretics. It was employed very frequently in Italy, especially after the thirteenth century, and invariably in Dalmatia. The Bosnian heretics also were always called Patarenes by Italian and Dalmatian writers. See above, p. 103.

(vii) *Poplicani*, Publicani, Populicani (Stephen of Bellavilla, *loc. cit.*, "Gallice etiam dicuntur ab aliquis *Popelicant*"). This word is a Latinization of *Paulician*, which from its resemblance to better-known words was soon given a false derivation. It was used especially in Northern France in the late eleventh and twelfth centuries. (See above, p. 122.)

(viii) *Deonarii* occurs once, in the *Chronicle of Vézelay*, and is probably an error for *Telonarii*. *Telonarii* is a natural variant to *Publicani*. See Bouquet, *Recueil des Historiens de la France*, vol. XII, p. 343.

(ix) *Piphles*, Piphiles, Pifli. This was the usual name for the heretics in Flanders—e.g. "Hos...Flandria Piphiles...appellat" (Eckbert, p. 898). This word is probably a corruption of *Poplicani*.

(x) *Bougres*, Bulgari, Bugares. I have discussed this name above, pp. 168–9.

(xi) *Albigeois*, Albigenses. Stephen of Bellavilla says (*loc. cit.*) "Dicti sunt *Albigenses*, propter hoc, quia illam partem Provinciae, quae est versus Tolosam et Agennensem urbem, circa fluvium Albam, primo in Provincia infecerunt." It was occasionally used in the late twelfth century (e.g. in the *Chronicle of Vigeois, ad ann.* 1181, p. 448) to mean the Cathars of the Albigeois. At the time of the Crusade against the heretics it was used to apply to all heretics and even Catholic opponents of the Crusaders. Later it was restricted again to the Cathars. On the other hand, *Toulousain* or *Provençal* usually implies a Cathar.

(xii) *Textores*, Tisserands—Eckbert, *loc. cit.*, "Hos...Gallia *Texerant*, ab usu texendi, appellat". For the origin and significance of this name, see above, p. 169.

(xiii) *Runcarii*, Rungarii, Runkeler. This was a name applied in Germany to a sect of Cathars in the thirteenth century. Frederick II in his law against heresy (Mansi, *Concilia*, vol. XXII, p. 590) calls them *Roncaroli*. This is probably a geographical name.

(xiv) *Bonshommes*. This was the name that the French heretics gave colloquially to their Perfect. Careless Catholic writers occasionally applied it later to the whole sect.

(xv) *Garatenses*. This occurs in the *Liber de Duobus Principiis* (see above, p. 151, n. 4) as the name of the principal school of heretics. It presumably represents the church founded by Bishop Garatus of Concoresso (see above, p. 126).

Frederick II's law also includes *Leonistae* and *Gazari*. The origin of the first of these names is unknown. *Gazari* may be a corruption of *Garatenses* or merely of Cathari.

Such names as *Sperionistae*, *Albanenses*, *Bagnolenses*, etc., represent branches within the Cathar Church. In Bouche's list of heretics (*Histoire de Provence*, vol. II, pp. 213–4), in which he mixes all sects up, there occur names such as *Siccars*, from *sicca*, a purse, a Provencal sect, who may have been Cathars; but we have no theological data to enlighten us.

APPENDIX IV

Dualism, Buddhism and Occultism

There has been so much loose thinking, fostered in particular by the Theosophists and the Neo-Occultists, of the connection of the Dualist Tradition with Eastern religion on the one hand, and with the Occult Tradition on the other, that it is necessary to add a little further clarification.

The resemblance between Cathar-Bogomil asceticism and Indian asceticism has often struck observers. Marco Polo says of Brahmin austerities (bk. III, chap. 20): "In fact they are worse in those whims than so many Patarenes." But, though the practice is similar, the underlying theory is different. To the orthodox Christian, Matter is bad, as a result of the Fall, but can be made good through Christ's sacraments. To the Christian Dualist, Matter is irretrievably bad. To the Brahmin and, still more, to the Buddhist, Matter is an irrelevant thing. The Buddhist initiate is ascetic to show his indifference to material things, or to demonstrate his contempt for them. This difference is so fundamental that there can be no question of the Christian Dualists having felt the influence of Buddhist teaching, except through indirect channels. As we have seen, certain Buddhist stories containing a practical but not a theological moral, like *Barlaam and Josaphat*, were adopted by the Gnostic Dualists. But their religious import must not be ranked too high. Christian Dualist doctrines are far more closely akin to those of the Zoroastrians, on which they were doubtless partially based. Zoroastrianism is a very different religion to Buddhism, and its theory of Matter far cruder. It is also possible to find similar purely Dualist views amongst the heathen tribes of Central Asia (see Ivanov, *Bogomil Books*, pp. 364 ff.), but I cannot think that it is likely that the Bogomils were influenced by them through the channel of the Proto-Bulgars, though it may perhaps have helped in the development of popular Dualist legends.

The tendency of the Christian Dualists to believe in Metempsychosis, and in consequence to place animals' souls on the level of men's, is certainly paralleled in Buddhism. But Metempsychosis was not the exclusive property of these two religions. Centuries earlier, Pythagoras had popularized it in Greece. If it originally came from India, which is quite possible, that happened too long ago for it to bear with it any strictly theological trappings.

Theosophists delight to tell us that St Francis of Assisi was really a Buddhist and that he learnt his doctrines from the Cathars, who were basically Buddhists. It is possible that St Francis was largely affected by the Cathars, though his views on poverty were, perhaps, more Waldensian. But he would have been horrified by the theology of Buddhism, had he anywhere been able to meet it.

Modern Occultists show a marked determination to claim the Cathars as their medieval brothers. There is a tendency amongst them to mix up the Cathar church with the Grail legends, while a society has been recently formed called *Les Amis de Montségur*, which elevates that castle into the Mecca of Occultism and the home of the Grail itself. The Cathars certainly gave Montségur, as their one physical place of refuge, high-sounding titles —as, for example, Mount Tabor—but such names should never be taken literally. The castle had no spiritual significance to them. Its destruction was a great material blow to them, but they were perfectly prepared to seek other refuges elsewhere. As for the Holy Grail, though Grail legends undoubtedly flourished in the Middle Ages, they can have had little connection with Cathar mythology. The Grail story is essentially a story in honour of the Sacrament of the Communion. The Cathar attitude to the Sacraments was wholly alien to its spirit. Its popularity was not improbably due to a taste for legitimate or White Magic on the part of good Catholics. But Catharism had nothing to do with Magic, Black or White. The idea that the treasure smuggled out of Montségur on the eve of its fall was the Grail itself is picturesque but untrue. The treasure may have included sacred books, but was chiefly material treasure, money, a worldly commodity but one very necessary to a church.

It cannot be too often emphasized that the Christian Dualists were not a body with a Secret Doctrine. They only became a secret society when persecution prevented them from performing their ceremonies openly. That is to say, they were a secret society simply in the same way that the Early Christians were, necessarily, a secret society.

The only Occultist product of Christian Dualism may lie, as I have suggested above (p. 179), in the symbolism of the Tarot Pack. These strange cards, which are first found in the fourteenth century, have never been seriously studied by a non-occultist scholar. The results would be interesting. There seems to me to be a trace of Dualism in the pack, but it has since been overlaid with debased Kabalistic lore. It shows in the antithesis of the *Emperor* and the *Empress* on the one hand and the *Pope* and the *Priestess* or *Pope Joan* on the other, in the traditional interpretation of the *Devil* as betokening natural forces—he is represented holding a naked man and woman in chains—and in the card betokening disaster, the *Tower Struck by Lightning*, or *Maison Dieu*, which suggests the heretics' view of a Catholic church. The *Priestess* is also reminiscent of the Gnosis-Goddess of the Gnostics. But the evidence is far too slight to allow of any definite pronouncement. It is perhaps safer to admit of no connection between the Dualist and the Occultist Traditions.

Bibliography

NOTE. The following abbreviations are used in the Bibliography and in the footnotes to the text:

Aa.Ss. *Acta Sanctorum Bollandiana*, see I (i).
B.Z. *Byzantinische Zeitschrift*, Leipzig, 1892– .
C.S.H.B. *Corpus Scriptorum Historiae Byzantinae*, Bonn, 1822–97.
M.G.H. *Monumenta Germaniae Historica*, see I (i).
M.P.G. Migne, *Patrologiae Cursus Completus, Series Graeco-Latina*, see I (i).
M.P.L. Migne, *Patrologiae Cursus Completus, Series Latina*, see I (i).
M.S.H.S.M. *Monumenta Spectantia Historiam Slavorum Meridionalium*, see I (i).
R.H.F. Bouquet, *Recueil des Historiens de la France*, see I (i).
S.R.G. *Scriptores Rerum Germanicarum*, see I (i).

I. ORIGINAL SOURCES

(i) COLLECTIONS OF SOURCES

Acta Sanctorum Bollandiana, Brussels, 1643–70; Venice, 1734–64; Paris-Rome, 1866, 1877; Brussels, 1894– .

L. d'Achéry, *Spicilegium sive Collectio Veterum Aliquot Scriptorum*, Paris, 1655–77.

J. H. Albanès, *Gallia Christiana Novissima*, Montbéliard, 1899.

L. Allatius, *De Ecclesiae Occidentalis et Orientalis Perpetua Consensione*, Cologne, 1648.

du P. d'Argentré, *Collectio Juridica de Novis Erroribus*, Paris, 1725–35.

J. S. Assemani, *Bibliotheca Orientalis*, Rome, 1719–28.

J. Baleus, *Catalogus Scriptorum Majoris Britanniae*, Basle, 1557.

J. C. de Baluze, *Concilia Galliae Narbonensis*, Paris, 1668.

C. Baronius, *Continuatio Annalium*, edited by Raynaldus, Lucca, 1747–56.

M. Bouquet, *Rerum Gallicarum et Francicarum Scriptores* (*Recueil des Historiens de la France*), Paris, 1738–1876, 1894, 1899– .

M. Brosset, *Collection des Historiens Arméniens*, St Petersburg, 1876.

R. H. Charles, *Apocrypha and Pseudepigrapha of the Old Testament*, Oxford, 1913.

F. Combefisius, *Historia Hereticorum Monotheletorum*, Paris, 1648.

F. C. Conybeare, *The Key of Truth*, see II.

Collection Doat, *Les Registres de l'Inquisition*, at the Bibliothèque Nationale, Paris.

I. von Döllinger, *Beiträge zur Sektengeschichte des Mittelalters*, see II.

—— *Dokumente für Geschichte der Valdesier und Katharer*, see II.

C. Douais, *Documents de l'Histoire de l'Inquisition*, Paris, 1900.

D. Farlati, *Illyricum Sacrum*, Venice, 1751–1819.

E. Fermendžin, *Acta Bosnae Potissimum Ecclesiastica*, in *M.S.H.S.M.*, vol. XXIII.

G. Ficker, *Die Phundagiagiten*, see II.

M. Freherus, *Scriptores Rerum Germanicarum*, Hanover, 1600–11.

A. Gorskii and K. Nevostruev, *List of Slavonic MSS. in the Synodical Library of Moscow* (in Russian), Moscow, 1862.

J. Gretser, *Opera Omnia Theologica*, Ratisbon, 1734–41.

C. L. Hugo, *Sacrae Antiquitatis Monumenta*, Etival, 1725.

I. Ivanov, *Bogomil Books and Legends*, see II.

I. von Kukuljević, *Codex Diplomaticus Regni Croatiae, Dalmatiae et Slavoniae*, Zagreb, 1875.

V. Langlois, *Collection des Historiens Anciens et Modernes de l'Arménie*, Paris, 1868–9.

M. Le Quien, *Oriens Christianus*, Paris, 1740.

P. van Limborch, *Historia Inquisitionis*, see II.

J. Lucius, *De Regno Dalmatiae et Croatiae*, Amsterdam, 1666.

J. D. Mansi, *Sacra Conciliorum Collectio*, Florence-Venice, 1759–98: new volumes edited by Petit, Paris, 1901–

E. Martène et V. Durand, *Thesaurus Novus Anecdotum*, Paris, 1717.

—— —— *Veterum Scriptorum Amplissima Collectio*, Paris, 1724–33.

J. P. Migne, *Dictionnaire des Apocryphes*, Paris, 1865.

—— *Patrologiae Cursus Completus, Series Graeco-Latina*, Paris, 1857–66.

—— *Patrologiae Cursus Completus, Series Latina*, Paris, 1844–55.

F. Miklosich, *Monumenta Serbica*, Vienna, 1858.

F. Miklosich and J. Müller, *Acta et Diplomata Graeca Medii Aevi, Sacra et Profana*, Vienna, 1860–90.

—— —— *Chrestomathia Palaeoslovenica*, Vienna, 1861.

A. Molinier, *Catalogue des MSS. de la Bibliothèque de Toulouse*, Paris, 1885.

Monumenta Germaniae Historica, edited by Pertz, Mommsen and others, Hanover, 1826–

Monumenta Spectantia Historiam Slavorum Meridionalium, Zagreb, 1868–

L. A. Muratori, *Annali d' Italia*, Milan, 1744.

—— *Antiquitates Italicae Medii Aevi*, Milan, 1738–42.

—— *Rerum Italicarum Scriptores*, Milan, 1723–51.

J. B. Pitra, *Analecta Sacra Spicilegio Solesmensi Parata*, Paris, 1876–88.

—— *Juris Ecclesiastici Graecorum Historia et Monumenta*, Rome, 1864–8.

A. Popov, *First Supplement to the List of MSS. belonging to A. Y. Khludov*, see II.

M. Pučić, *Spomenici Srbski od g.* 1395–1423, Belgrade, 1858.

A. Pypin, *False and Rejected Books*, see II.

T. Ripoll, *Bullarium Ordinis Fratrum Praedicatorum*, Rome, 1729.

Scriptores Rerum Germanicarum in Usum Scholarum, Hanover, 1839–1920; Berlin, 1922–.

L de Thallóczy, C. Jireček and E. de Sufflay, *Acta et Diplomata Res Albaniae Mediae Aetatis Illustrantia*, Vienna, 1913–

A. Theiner, *Vetera Monumenta Historica Hungariam Sacram Illustrantia*, Rome, 1859–60.

—— *Vetera Monumenta Slavorum Meridionalium Historiam Illustrantia*, Rome, 1863.

N. S. Tikhonravov, *Materials for a Study of Russian Literature*, see II.

C. Tischendorf, *Apocalypses Apocryphae*, see II.

Treasury of Old and New Stories (in Armenian), edited by Sarkisean, Venice, 1897.

A. Vassiliev, *Anecdota Graeco-Byzantina*, Moscow, 1893.

A. N. Veselovsky, *Investigations into the Domain of Russian Religious Verse* (in Russian), St Petersburg, 1883.

N. Vignier, *Recueil de l'Histoire de l'Eglise*, Leyden, 1601.

L. Wadding and others, *Annales Minorum seu Trium Ordinum a Sancto Francisco Institutorum*, Rome, 1740–1886.

(ii) GREEK SOURCES

Anna Comnena, *Alexiad*, Teubner edition, Leipzig, 1884; English translation by Dawes, London, 1928.

Apocalypse of Baruch, in Charles, *Apocrypha and Pseudepigrapha*.

Cedrenus, Georgius, *Synopsis Historiarum*, C.S.H.B. 1838–9.

Chalcocondylas, Laonicus, *Historiae*, C.S.H.B. 1843.

Cinnamus, Ioannes, *Historia Ioannis II et Manuelis I*, C.S.H.B. 1836.

Clement of Alexandria, *Stromata*, in M.P.G. vols. VIII and IX.

Codex Theodosianus, edited by Mommsen and Meyer, Berlin, 1905.

Demetrius Chomatianus, *Epistolae*, in Pitra, *Analecta*, vol. VII.

Eastern Patriarchs, *Epistola ad Theophilum*, in M.P.G. vol. XCV.

Epiphanius, *Adversus Haereses*, edited by Oehler, Berlin, 1859.

Eusebius of Caesarea, *Historia Ecclesiae*, in M.P.G. vol. XX.

Genesius, Joseph, *Regna*, C.S.H.B. 1834.

Georgius Hamartolus Monachus, *Chronicon*, edited by de Boor, Leipzig, 1904: additional chapter edited by Friedrich, in *Sitzungsberichte der Bayrische Akademie*, vol. I, Munich, 1896.

Georgius Monachus, *De Messalianis*, edited by Diecarp, in B.Z. vol. IX, 1900.

Irenaeus, *Adversus Haereticos*, in M.P.G. vol. VII.

Isaac, Catholicus of Armenia, *Verbum adversus Armenios*, in Combefisius, *Historia Hereticorum Monotheletorum*.

John Damascene, *Adversus Constantinum Caballinum*, in M.P.G. vol. xcv.

—— (?), *Barlaam and Josaphat*, edited by Woodward and Mattingly, Loeb classics, London, 1914.

Jubilees, Book of, in Charles, *Apocrypha and Pseudepigrapha*.

Maximus Confessor, *Opera*, in M.P.G. vol. xci.

Origen, *In Johannem*, in M.P.G. vol. xiv.

Petrus Siculus, *Historia Manichaeorum*, in M.P.G. vol. civ.

Philosophumena, in M.P.G. vol. xvi.

Philostorgius, *Epitome Historiarum*, in M.P.G. vol. lxv.

Philotheus of Constantinople, *Opera*, in M.P.G. vol. cli.

Photius, Patriarch of Constantinople, *Opera Omnia*, in M.P.G. vols. ci–civ.

Plotinus, *Enneades*, edited by Volkmann, Leipzig, 1883.

Psellus, Michael, *De Operatione Daemonum*, in M.P.G. vol. cxxii.

Suidas, *Lexicon*, edited by Adler, Leipzig, 1928–38.

Symeon, Archbishop of Thessalonica, *Opera Omnia*, edited by Skatharos, Athens, 1868.

Theodoretus, *Haereticarum Fabularum Compendium*, in M.P.G. vol. lxxxiii.

Theodorus of Mopsuestia, *see* I (iii), Mercator.

Theophanes, *Chronographia*, edited by de Boor, Leipzig, 1883.

Theophanes Continuatus, C.S.H.B. 1838.

Theophylact, Archbishop of Achrida, *Life of Saint Clement*, edited (with Russian translation) by Menshchikov, Moscow, 1855.

Theophylact, Patriarch of Constantinople, *Letter to Tsar Peter of Bulgaria*, text and facsimile in Zlatarsky, *History of Bulgarian Empire*, vol. I, Part II, pp. 840–5.

Timothy of Constantinople, *Opera*, in M.P.G. vol. lxxxvi.

Vita Sancti Nicetae, in *Aa. Ss.*, April, vol. I, Venice, 1737.

Zigabenus, Euthymius, *Panoplia*, in M.P.G. vol. cxxx.

Zonaras, *Epitome Historiarum*, vol. III, C.S.H.B. 1897.

(iii) LATIN AND ROMANCE SOURCES

Acta Bosnae, in *M.S.H.S.M.* vol. xxiii.

Ademar of Chabannes, *Opera*, in *R.H.F.* vol. x.

Alain de Lille, *De Fide Catholica, contra Hereticos*, in *M.P.L.* vol. ccx.

Albericus (de Trois Fontaines), *Chronicon*, in *R.H.F.* vol. ix.

Alcuin, *Contra Felicem*, in *M.P.L.* vol. ci.

Alexander III, Pope, *Epistolae*, in *M.P.L.* vol. cc.

Anonymi Gesta Francorum, ed. Lees, Oxford, 1924.

Augustine, St, of Hippo, *Contra Faustum*, in *M.P.L.* vol. XLII.

Bernard, St, of Clairvaux, *Opera*, in *M.P.L.* vols. CLXXXII–CLXXXIII: also ed. Mabillon, Paris, 1719.

Bonacorsi, *Manifestatio Heresis Catharorum*, in d'Achéry, *Spicilegium*, vol. XIII: also in *Aevum*, vol. XII, Milan, 1938.

Burcé, Salvi, *Suprastella*, in Döllinger, *Beiträge*, vol. II.

Cenomanensium, Gesta Pontificum, in *R.H.F.* vol. XII.

Chanson de la Croisade, ed. Meyer, Paris, 1875.

Eckbert, *Sermones contra Catharos*, in *M.P.L.* vol. CXCV.

Evervin, Provost of Steinfeld, *Epistola*, in *M.P.L.* vol. CLXXXII.

Eymericus, *Directorium Inquisitionis*, ed. Pegna, Rome, 1585.

Gaufredus, *Chronicon*, in *R.H.F.* vol. XII.

Geoffrey of Auxerre, *Sancti Bernardi Miracula*, in *Aa. Ss.*, August, vol. IV: *Epistolae*, in S. Bernard, *Opera*, ed. Mabillon.

Gerbert of Aurillac, *Epistolae (Les Lettres de Gerbert)*, ed. Havet, Paris, 1889.

Gervasius Premonstratensis, *Epistolae*, in Hugo, *Sacrae Antiquitatis Monumenta*.

Godofredus, *Annales*, in Freherus, *Scriptores Rerum Germanicarum*.

Gondola, *Chronicon*, MS. quoted in Jireček, *Geschichte der Serben*.

Gregory of Florence, *Disputatio inter Catholicum et Paterinum*, in Martène et Durand, *Thesaurus*, vol. V.

Gui, Bernard, *Practica Inquisitionis*, ed. Douais, Paris, 1886.

Guibert of Nogent, *Monodiarum sive de Vita Sua*, ed. Bourgin, Paris, 1907.

Guillaume of Puylaurens, *Historia Albigensis*, in *R.H.F.* vol. XIX.

Helmold of Lübeck, *Chronicon*, ed. Bangert, in *M.G.H.* vol. XXI.

Henry of France, Archbishop of Reims, *Epistolae*, in *R.H.F.* vol. XV.

Herbert of Bosham, *Epistolae*, in *M.P.L.* vol. CXC.

Hermannus Contractus, *Chronicon* and *Addenda ad Chronicon Saxicon*, in *R.H.F.* vol. XI.

Herrores quos Communiter Paterini de Bosna Credunt, ed. Rački, in *Starini*, vol. I, Zagreb, 1869.

Hugh of Amiens, Archbishop of Reims, *Opera*, in *M.P.L.* vol. CXCII.

Hugh of Poictiers, *Historia Vizeliacensis*, in d'Achéry, *Spicilegium*, vol. II.

Innocent III, Pope, *Epistolae*, in *M.P.L.* vols. CCXIV–CCXVII.

Jourdain de Saxe, *Vita Sancti Dominici*, ed. Berthier, Paris, 1891.

Landulphus Senior, *Historia Mediolanensis*, in Muratori, *Rerum Italicarum Scriptores*, vol. IV.

Leodensis Ecclesiae Epistola, in Martène et Durand, *Amplissima Collectio*, vol. I.

Ludovici, Sancti, Vita, in *R.H.F.* vol. XX.

Lugio, John de, *Liber de Duobus Principiis*, ed. Dondaine, Rome, 1939.

Matthew Paris, *Chronica Majora*, ed. Luard, Rolls Society, London, 1872–83.

Mercator, Marius, *Excerpta Theodori Mopsuestiae*, in *M.P.L.* vol. XLVIII.

Moneta of Cremona, *Summa contra Kataros et Valdenses*, ed. Ricchini, Rome, 1743.

Monumenta Conventus Tolosani, ed. Percin, Toulouse, 1693.

Nazarius, *Epistola*, in Vignier, *Recueil de l'Histoire de l'Eglise*.

Nicholas I, Pope, *Responsa ad Consulta Bulgarorum*, in M.G.H., *Epistolae*, vol. VI.

Otto of Frisingen, *Chronicon Frederici I*, in *M.G.H.* vol. XX.

Parentii, Sancti, Vita, in *Aa. Ss.*, May, vol. V, Venice, 1741.

Pelhisson, Guillaume, *Chronicon*, ed. Douais, Paris, 1881.

Peter de Vaux-Cernay, *Hystoria Albigensis*, ed. Guébin and Lyon, Paris, 1926.

Peter the Venerable, *Tractatus adversus Petrobrusianos*, in *M.P.L.* vol. CLXXXIX.

Radulf of Coggeshall, *Chronicon Anglicanum*, in *R.H.F.* vol. XVIII.

Radulf Glaber, *Historiarum Sui Temporis Libri V*, in *R.H.F.* vol. X.

Robertus de Monte of Torigny, *Appendix ad Chronicon Sigeberti Gemblacensis*, in *R.H.F.* vol. XIII.

Sacchoni, Rainier, *Summa de Catharis et Leonistis*, in Martène et Durand, *Thesaurus*, vol. V.

Sancti Medardi Chronicon, in d'Achéry, *Spicilegium*, vol. II.

Stephen (de Bourbon) of Bellavilla, *De Septem Donis*, in d'Argentré, *Collectio Juridica*, vol. I.

Summa Auctoritatis (*La Somme des Autorités*), ed. Douais, Paris, 1896.

Tertullian, *Opera*, in *M.P.L.* vol. II.

Thomas, Archidiaconus Spalatensis, *Historia Salonitanorum Pontificum atque Spalatensium*, in *M.S.H.S.M.* vol. XXVI.

Torquemada, *Quinquaginta Errores*, ed. Rački in *Starini*, vol. I, Zagreb, 1869.

Trevensium, Gesta Archiepiscoporum, in Martène et Durand, *Amplissima Collectio*, vol. IV.

Vigeois, Chronicle of, ed. Montégut, Limoges, 1907.

Villehardouin, Geoffroy de, *La Conquête de Constantinople*, ed. Faral, Paris, 1938–9.

William of Newburgh, *Historia Anglicana*, ed. English Historical Society, London, 1856.

(iv) ARMENIAN SOURCES

Aristaces of Lastivert, *History* (in Armenian), Tiflis, 1893.

Eznik of Kolb, *Opera Armenice* (in Armenian), Venice, 1863.

Gregory Magister, *Letters* (in Armenian), edited by Kostanianz, Alexandropol, 1910.

Gregory of Narek, *Letters*: extracts given in Armenian in Sarkisean, *Study of the Manicheo-Paulician Heresy*: in English in Conybeare, *Key of Truth*.

John of Otzun, *Opera* (Latin translation), Venice, 1834.

Key of Truth, the, Armenian text and English translation in Conybeare, *The Key of Truth*, see II.

Kirakos, *Opera Armenice* (in Armenian), Venice, 1873.

Lazar of Pharb, *Letters* (in Armenian), edited by Emin, Tiflis, 1904.

Matthew of Edessa, *Chronique*, French translation by Dulaurier, Paris, 1858.

Mekhitar of Airavanq, *History* (in Armenian), edited by Emin, Moscow, 1860.

Moses Chorensis, *Chronique*, French translation by Le Vaillant de Florival, Paris, 1841.

Moses of Kaghankatuk, *History of the Aghovanians* (in Armenian), Paris-Moscow, 1860.

Nerses Clajensis, *Epistolae*, Latin translation by Cappelletti, Venice, 1833.

Paul of Taron, *Letters* (in Armenian), Constantinople, 1752.

Samuel of Ani, *Tables Chronologiques*, French translation in Brosset, *Collection des Historiens Arméniens*, vol. II.

Thomas Metzob, *Exposé des Guerres de Tamurlane*, French version by F. Nève, Brussels, 1860.

(v) SLAVONIC SOURCES

Apocryphal Books, see I (i), Gorskii and Nevostruev, Ivanov, Pypin, Tikhonravov and Veselovsky.

Athanasius of Jerusalem, *Homilies*, ed. Leonid, in *Moscow Diocesan Reports*, no. 3 (in Russian), Moscow, 1871.

Book of Heaven and Earth (The Palea), ed. Popov, Moscow, 1881.

Callistus, *Life of Theodosius of Tirnovo*, ed. Zlatarsky, in *Sbornik na Narodni Umotvorenie*, vol. XVI, Sofia, 1904.

Cosmas, *Slovo Kozmyi Presbitera*, ed. Popruzhenko, St Petersburg, 1907.

Euthymius of Tirnovo, *Werke*, ed. Kalužniacki, Vienna, 1901.

John the Exarch, *Shestodniev*, ed. Popov, Moscow, 1879.

Nikolski Gospel, ed. Danitchitch, Belgrade, 1864.

Sinodik of Tsar Boril, ed. Popruzhenko, *Blgarski Starini*, vol. VIII, Sofia, 1928.

Stephen Dushan, *Code*, ed. Novakovic, Belgrade, 1895.

St Symeon and St Sava, Lives of, ed. (in Serbian), Belgrade, 1860.

Synodicon for the First Sunday in Lent, ed. Uspenski (in Russian), Odessa, 1893.

(vi) ORIENTAL SOURCES

Enoch, Book of (in Ethiopian), ed. Charles, Oxford, 1912.

Ephraim, St, *Prose Refutations*, see II, Mitchell.

Ibn Tabari, *Chronicle*, extracts in Vassiliev, *Byzantium and the Arabs*.

Masoudi, *Le Livre de l' Avertissement*, translated by Carra de Vaux, Paris, 1896.

—— *Les Prairies d'Or*, translated by Barbier de Meynard, Paris, 1861.

Simeon of Beit Arsam, *Epistola de Bar Sauma*, in Assemani. *Bibliotheca Orientalis*, vol. I.

II. MODERN WORKS

N. Adontz, *Samuel l'Arménien, roi des Bulgares*, in *Mémoires de l'Académie Royale de Belgique, Classe des Lettres*, vol. xxxix, Brussels, 1938.

E. Amann, article 'Messaliens', in Vacant, *Dictionnaire de Théologie Catholique*, vol. x, 1, Paris, 1928.

J. G. C. Anderson, *The Campaign of Basil I against the Paulicians*, in *The Classical Review*, vol. x, London, 1896.

G. Bardy, *Paul de Samosate*, Louvain, 1923.

R. F. Bennett, *The Early Dominicans*, Cambridge, 1937.

J. Benoist, *Histoire des Albigeois et des Vaudois ou Barbets*, Paris, 1691.

N. P. Blagoev, *Legal and Social Aspects of the Bogomils* (in Bulgarian), Sofia, 1912.

—— *The Priest Kosmas' Discourse against the Bogomils* (in Bulgarian), Sofia, 1923.

J. Bonnard, *Traductions de la Bible en Vers Français au Moyen Age*, Paris, 1884.

H. Bouche, *Histoire de Provence*, Aix, 1664.

W. Bousset, *Hauptprobleme der Gnosis*, Göttingen, 1907.

E. Broeckx, *Le Catharisme*, Hoogstraten, 1916.

E. G. Browne, *A Literary History of Persia*, Cambridge, 1929.

G. Buckler, *Anna Comnena*, Oxford, 1929.

F. C. Burkitt, *The Religion of the Manichees*, Cambridge, 1925.

J. B. Bury, *History of the Eastern Roman Empire*, London, 1912.

M. Chamich, *History of Armenia*, trans. Avdall, Calcutta, 1827.

L. Clédat, *Le Nouveau Testament traduit au XIIIe Siècle en Langue Provençale*, Paris, 1887.

F. C. Conybeare, *The Key of Truth*, Oxford, 1898.

—— *Russian Dissenters*, Cambridge, Mass., 1917.

F. Cumont, *Recherches sur le Manichéisme*, Paris, 1908.

I. von Döllinger, *Beiträge zur Sektengeschichte des Mittelalters*, Munich, 1890.

C. Douais, *Les Albigeois: leurs Origines*, Paris, 1879.

—— *L'Inquisition: ses Origines*, Paris, 1906.

M. Drinov, *Historical Survey of the Bulgarian Church* (in Bulgarian), Vienna, 1869.

—— *South Slavs and Byzantium in the Xth Century* (in Russian), Moscow, 1875.

J. Dujčev, *Il Cattolicesimo in Bulgaria nel Secolo XVII*, Rome, 1937.

F. Dvornik, *Les Slaves, Byzance et Rome au IXme Siècle*, Paris, 1926.

E. de Faye, *Gnostiques et Gnosticisme*, Paris, 1925.

G. Ficker, *Die Phundagiagiten*, Leipzig, 1908.

G. Flügel, *Mani*, Leipzig, 1862.

J. Friedrich, *Bericht über die Paulikianer*, Munich, 1896.

M. Gaster, *Ilchester Lectures on Greeko-Slavonic Literature*, London, 1887.

H. Gelzer, *Die Patriarchat von Achrida*, Leipzig, 1902.

S. Georghieff, *Les Bogomiles et Presbyter Kosma*, Lausanne, 1902.

I. C. L. Gieseler, *Über den Dualismus der Slaven*, in *Theologischer Studien und Kritiken*, vol. II, Hamburg, 1837.

E. Golubinski, *A Short History of the Old Slavonic Churches* (in Russian), Moscow, 1871.

H. Grégoire, *La Diète de Jean le Baptiste*, in *Byzantion*, vol. V, Brussels, 1932.

—— *Les Sources de l'Histoire des Pauliciens*, in *Bulletin de l'Académie Royale de Belgique, Classe des Lettres*, vol. XXXVII, Brussels, 1936.

—— *Autour des Pauliciens*, in *Byzantion*, vol. XI, Brussels, 1936.

J. Guiraud, *Histoire de l'Inquisition au Moyen Age*, Paris, 1935–8.

—— *Saint Dominique*, Paris, 1899.

C. V. Hahn, *Geschichte der Ketzer im Mittelalter*, Stuttgart, 1845.

A. Harnack, *Geschichte der Altchristlichen Literatur*, Leipzig, 1893–4.

—— *History of Dogma*, translated into English by Buchanan, Bruce and Gilchrist, London, 1895–7.

—— *Marcion*, Leipzig, 1921.

J. M. Hussey, *Church and Learning in the Byzantine Empire*, Oxford, 1937.

J. A. Ilić, *Die Bogomilen in Ihre Geschichtliche Entwicklung*, Karlovci, 1923.

I. Ivanov, *Bogomil Books and Legends* (in Bulgarian), Sofia, 1925.

M. R. James, *The Apocryphal New Testament*, Oxford, 1924.

K. J. Jireček, *Geschichte der Bulgaren*, Prague, 1876.

—— *Geschichte der Serben*, Gotha, 1911–18.

M. Jugie, *Phoundagiagites et Bogomiles*, in *Echos d'Orient*, vol. XII, Paris, 1909.

V. Klaić, *Geschichte Bosniens*, Leipzig, 1885

—— *Povjest Hrvata*, Zagreb, 1899–1911.

I. G. Klincharov, *Pope Bogomil and his Times* (in Bulgarian), Sofia, 1927.

N. P. Kondakov, *On Manicheism and the Bogomils* (in Russian), in *Seminarium Kondakovianum*, vol. I, Prague, 1927.

G. Lami, *Della Eresia dei Paterini in Firenze*, in *Opera*, Osimo, 1766.

—— *Lezioni di Antichità Toscana*, Florence, 1766.

J. Laurent, *L'Arménie entre Byzance et l'Islam*, Paris, 1919.

H. C. Lea, *History of the Inquisition in the Middle Ages*, New York, 1887.

A. von Le Coq, *Manichaica*, Berlin, 1922.

P. van Limborch, *Historia Inquisitionis*, Amsterdam, 1692.

S. Lindquist, *Manikeismens Religionshistorika Stellning*, Uppsala, 1921.

A. Lombard, *Pauliciens, Bogomiles et Bonshommes*, Geneva–Basle, 1879.

A. Luchaire, *Innocent III: La Croisade des Albigeois*, Paris, 1903.

D. MacRitchie, *An Account of the Gypsies of India*, London, 1886.

T. Merzdorf, *Die Deutschen Historienbibeln des Mittelalters*, Tübingen, 1870.

C. W. Mitchell, *St Ephraim's Prose Refutations*, Cambridge, 1913–21.

V. N. Mochulski, *On the Supposed Dualism in Slav Mythology* (in Russian), Warsaw, 1889.

A. Molinier, *see* Vaissète.

C. Molinier, *L'Endura*, Bordeaux, 1881.

—— *Un Traité Inédit concernant les Sectes Albigeois*, Bordeaux, 1883.

J. L. von Mosheim, *Versuch einer Ketzergeschichte*, Hanover, 1748.

M. A. Murray, *Witchcraft in Western Europe*, Oxford, 1921.

F. Nau, *Bardesane l'Astrologue*, Paris, 1897.

N. A. Nikolski, *Old Russian Christianity* (in Russian), St Petersburg, 1913.

L. Oeconomos, *La Vie Religieuse dans l'Empire Byzantin*, Paris, 1918.

P. Perdrizet, *Negotium Perambulans in Tenebris*, Strassburg, 1922.

N. M. Petrovski, *Letter of Theophylact, Patriarch of Constantinople, to the Bulgarian Tsar Peter* (in Russian), St Petersburg, 1914.

A. Popov, *First Supplement to the List of MSS. belonging to A. Y. Khludov* (in Russian), Moscow, 1875.

M. G. Popruzhenko, *Presbyter Kosma* (in Bulgarian), Sofia, 1936.

A. Pypin, *False and Rejected Books* (in Russian), St Petersburg, 1862.

—— *History of Russian Literature* (in Russian), St Petersburg, 1907.

—— and V. D. Spasowicz, *Histoire des Littératures Slaves*, trans. by Denis, Paris, 1881.

F. Rački, *Bogomili i Paterini*, in *Rad. Jugoslav. Akademije*, vols. VII, VIII and X, Zagreb, 1869–70

—— *Pokret na Slavenskom Jugu*, in *Rad. Jugoslav. Akademije*, vols. II–IV, Zagreb, 1868.

K. Radchenko, *Studies in Bogomilism* (in Russian), Kiev, 1900.

P. Rohde, *Romanische Weltkronik*, in Suchier, *Denkmäler der Provenzalischen Literatur und Sprache*, vol. I, Halle, 1883.

J. de Rothschild, *Le Mystère du Vieil Testament*, Paris, 1878–91.

S. Runciman, *History of the First Bulgarian Empire*, London, 1930.

B. Sarkisean, *A Study of the Manicheo-Paulician Heresy* (in Armenian), Venice, 1893.

C. Sathas and E. Legrand, *Les Exploits de Digénis Akritas*, Paris, 1875.

C. Schmidt, *Histoire des Cathares et Albigeois*, Paris–Geneva, 1849.

A. A. Shakhmatov, *The Explanatory Palea and the Russian Chronicle* (in Russian), St Petersburg, 1900.

V. N. Sharenkoff, *A Study of Manichaeanism in Bulgaria*, New York, 1927.

M. Sokolov, *Materials and Notes on Old Slavonic Literature* (in Russian), Moscow, 1888.

M. N. Speranski, *The Historical Palea* (in Serbian), Belgrade, 1892.

—— *Slav Apocryphal Gospels* (in Russian), Moscow, 1895.

M. Spinka, *A History of Christianity in the Balkans*, Chicago, 1933.

J. Starr, *The Heresy of the Athingani*, in *The Harvard Theological Review*, vol. XXIX, Boston, 1936.

J. Stiglmayr, *Pseudo-Macarius und der Aftermystik der Messalianer*, in *Zeitschrift für Katholische Theologie*, vol. XLIX, Innsbrück, 1925.

E. Tachella, *Les Anciens Pauliciens et les Modernes Bulgares de la Philippopolitaine*, in *Le Muséon*, vol. XVI, Louvain, 1897.

K. Ter Mkrttschian, *Die Paulikianer im Byzantinischen Reiche*, Leipzig, 1893.

L. de Thallóczy, *Beiträge zur Kenntniss der Bogomilenlehre*, Zagreb, 1895.

—— *Geschichte Bosniens und Serbiens im Mittelalter*, Munich, 1914.

—— *Studien zur Geschichte Bosniens und Serbiens im Mittelalter*, Munich, 1914.

N. S. Tikhonravov, *Materials for a Study of Russian Literature* (in Russian), St Petersburg-Moscow, 1863-4.

C. Tischendorf, *Apocalypses Apocryphae*, Leipzig, 1866.

E. Tisserand, *L'Ascension d'Isaïe*, Paris, 1909.

F. Tocco, *L'Eresia nel Medio Evo*, Florence, 1884.

J. Trifonov, *The Discourse of Kosma and its Author*, in *The Proceedings of the Bulgarian National Academy* (in Bulgarian), vol. XXIX, Sofia, 1927.

Dom Vaissète, *Histoire de Languedoc*, edited by A. Molinier, Toulouse, 1874. (Referred to as 'Vaissète-Molinier'.)

A. A. Vasiliev, *Byzantium and the Arabs* (in Russian), St Petersburg, 1900.

—— *Byzance et les Arabes* (French translation of the above, first volume only), edited by Grégoire, Brussels, 1935.

A. Vogt, *Basile Ier, Empereur de Byzance*, Paris, 1908.

A. V. Williams Jackson, *Researches in Manichaeism*, New York, 1932.

Lady Mary Wortley Montagu, *Letters*, edited by Lord Wharncliffe, London, 1837.

I. Zhdanov, *The Palea* (in Russian), Kiev, 1881.

V. N. Zlatarsky, *History of the Bulgarian Empire* (in Bulgarian), Sofia, 1918-39.

WORKS PUBLISHED SINCE 1945

A. Borst, *Die Katharer*, Stuttgart, 1953.

H. Grégoire, *Cathares d'Asie Mineure, d'Italie et de France*, in *Memorial Louis Petit, Mélanges d'Histoire et d'Archéologie*, Archives de l'Orient Chrétien, I, Paris, 1948.

D. Obolensky, *The Bogomils*, Cambridge, 1948.

H. C. Puech and A. Vaillant, *Le Traité contre les Bogomiles de Cosmas le Prêtre*. Travaux publiés par l'Institut d'Etudes Slaves, no. 21, Paris, 1945.

H. Soderberg, *La Religion des Cathares*, Uppsala, 1949.

A. V. Solovjev, *La Doctrine de l'Eglise de Bosnie*, in *Académie Royale de Belgique, Bulletin de la Classe des Lettres*, 5th series, vol. XXXIV, Brussels, 1948.

Index